:‖ Alec Wilder in Spite of Himself

Alec Wilder in Spite of Himself

A Life of the Composer

Desmond Stone

New York : Oxford
Oxford University Press
1996

Oxford University Press

Oxford   New York
Athens   Auckland   Bangkok   Bombay   Calcutta
Cape Town   Dar es Salaam   Delhi   Florence   Hong Kong   Istanbul
Karachi   Kuala Lumpur   Madras   Madrid   Melbourne   Mexico City
Nairobi   Paris   Singapore   Taipei   Tokyo   Toronto

and associated companies in
    Berlin   Ibadan

Library of Congress Cataloging-in-Publication Data
Stone, Desmond.
    Alec Wilder in spite of himself : a life of the composer / Desmond Stone.
        p.   cm.
    Includes bibliographical references and index.
    ISBN 0–19–509600–2
    1. Wilder, Alec.   2. Composers—United States—Biography.   I. Title.
ML410.W6975S76   1996
780'.92—dc20
[B]   95–8968

9 8 7 6 5 4 3 2 1

Printed in the United States of America on acid-free paper

To my wife, Lorraine, and our family,
Howard and Yvonne,
for their love and support

Acknowledgments

Without the friends of Alec Wilder, this book could not have been written, or even contemplated. Their faith and support made the critical difference.

Two of those friends in particular are owed immeasurable thanks—Bill (William) Engvick and Jim (James T.) Maher. In steady correspondence over five or six years, Engvick supplied rich insights into the earlier Wilder years, insights that no one else could have provided. He was endlessly patient, considerate, responsive, and, above all, encouraging, keeping me going when I might have given up. Like Engvick, Maher knew well both the man and the music and was always ready to sort out what was consequential and what was not. His keen, informed judgments over a broad range of both musical and literary matters did much to keep the project on track. He was constantly and courteously accessible. These two men, along with the always helpful Loonis McGlohon and Arnold Sundgaard, use the English language so beautifully that it was a joy to converse and correspond with them. (The book's title comes from Engvick, with an assist from Maher.)

Across the country there were many others who gave generously of their time, their knowledge, and their skills—among them, Manny Albam, Andrew Anspach, Jeff Austin, Whitney Balliett, Sam and Carol Baron, Lorraine Bowen, the late Al Brackman, Judy Bell, Arlene Bouras, Jackie Cain, Sarah Christian, Tony Cichiello, Douglas Colby, Charlie and Terry Davidson, David Demsey for his informed critical analysis, Carl Dengler, Edward DeWitt III, Eileen Farrell, Frederick Fennell, Margaret Foresman, Richard Freed, June Erickson Gardner, Chris Gekker, Steve Hart, Sandy (Ouzer) Hecht, the fine new James Dean biographer Val O. Holley, Milton Kaye, Roy Kral, Barbara Lea, Gladys Leventon, Robert Levy (a tireless advocate), Virginia McConnell, Beverly McGinness, Nan McGlohon, Marian McPartland, Frances Miller, Mike Miller, Mitch Miller, Patti Morrison, Virginia Nanzetta, Janet Pauley, Harvey and Carol Phillips and their family, William Ploss, Howard Richmond, William Roth, the late Lavinia Russ, Martin Russ, Gunther Schuller, Dan Stirrup, Gordon Stout, and Margaret Turner.

It was a great advantage to be able to undertake this work in a city where Wilder had so many friends happy to help out—notably loyal Lou Ouzer, whose superb photos do so much to tell the Wilder story, and his wife, Helen; Director Robert Freeman, Professor Warren Benson, Dr. Ruth Watanabe, and Gerry McDougall, all of the Eastman School of Music; international documentary filmmaker Robert Bilheimer; Sterling and Nancy Watson Dean; David Diamond; Mercy End; and Morris Secon. I am grateful also for the support given by Wilder estate executor Tom Hampson and his wife, Zena; by endlessly helpful Director Mary Wallace Davidson and Rare Books and Archives Assistant Mary Rame of the Eastman School's Sibley Music Library; by Dr. Blake McKelvey through his histories of Rochester; and by the staffs of the Rochester Public Library and the Helen McGraw branch of the Irondequoit library system.

Finally but critically, this biography could not have been published without the patient belief and wise guidance of Sheldon Meyer, Senior Vice President/Editorial, Oxford University Press. Sheldon and Associate Editor Paul Schlotthauer made the task much easier than it might have been.

Contents

:‖ Alec Wilder in Spite of Himself

Prologue

On May 10, 1981, a quiet, overcast spring afternoon, a score or more of the friends and admirers of American composer Alec Wilder gathered in Saint Agnes Cemetery in the small upstate New York village of Avon, not far from Wilder's hometown of Rochester. They had come to honor a man with a song in his heart, a maverick who valued nothing so much as his independence, an old-fashioned knight who lived and died with his lance leveled against the tumultuous modern world.

It happened to be Mother's Day, and Wilder would have seen the irony of that. Although he had found redeeming qualities in his mother, her alcoholism had foreshadowed his own hard struggle, and her failure to put an arm around him as a child had left him with a deep, undermining insecurity. Yet better, he would have agreed, to be buried on Mother's Day than on Father's Day, for this incorruptible composer and fiercely uncompromising individualist had had only contempt for a man he never knew.

Although the moment and the mood seemed gloriously right, Wilder would no doubt have grumped about even this modest tribute. He detested sentimental public fuss. Death to him was always The Big Toboggan Ride. He had wanted, he said, to be forgotten quickly and completely. There was to be no funeral, no religious service, no public notice of his passing. He had not provided money for a gravestone. "I wish none," he had said in a codicil to his will—"no name, dates, and certainly no maudlin verses in the style of Rod McKuen." If a grave marker were legally necessary, then it should be "no more than four inches by four inches and no further above the ground than required."

No one intended to betray the spirit of those last wishes. Yet it would have been wrong, almost indecent, to allow his burial to go unnoticed. Wilder had died of lung cancer the day before Christmas 1980, in Gainesville, Florida. Now, as for some time, the ground in upstate New York was thawed enough for a grave digging.

The interval since Wilder's death had brought a growing feeling among his followers that so remarkable an individual should be honored in some small, appropriate way, no matter what he might have said in his will. Accordingly, Wilder estate executor Thomas M. Hampson had written to friends across the country and told them he was arranging for both a modest gravestone and a short, simple burial ceremony. "I intend," he wrote, "to honor Alec's request that there be no religious service, but a number of his friends have said they wanted to be present, and I certainly think they should be permitted to do so."

Though far from Wilder's sophisticated world, Saint Agnes Cemetery seemed a fitting place for him to end an often tormented journey. Here in this quiet, dewy countryside was peace at last. Trees fringed and hid the small cemetery. The only sounds most spring days are of fiddling insects and songbirds. Along one side of the cemetery runs a railroad track, something that would have delighted the tireless train traveler in Wilder.

Now, beside a venerable oak that harbored cardinals whistling hard, his friends arranged themselves about the open grave. Jazz pianist Marian McPartland and Mitch Miller, oboe virtuoso and music executive, were prominent among the group, but on this day all were equals, for all bore the same indelible marks of Wilder's friendship.

One by one the mourners stepped forward to say a personal goodbye. Hampson spoke first, a man knowledgeable about jazz and about birds. He had been in the Gainesville hospital when Wilder died and told of the egret that had flapped toward the window of Wilder's room the day before. A haunting moment. The big, strikingly white bird might have been a soul about to take flight.

Now Loonis McGlohon, musical partner for many of the later years, spoke directly to Wilder and thanked him for the way he had given of himself: "Letters from strangers never went unanswered, even when they came from, in your own words, people who lived in old soldiers' homes who thought you were Thornton's brother. . . . You were a soft touch, Alec. As long as people believed in *some-thing*, you could not say 'no.' You probably have memberships in every organization from 'Crabgrass is Beautiful Brother' to 'Recycling Wee Bonnie Baker Records for a Better World.'"

Years later, Wilder collaborator Arnold Sundgaard would liken the complex layers of the man to the annular rings of a rugged tree trunk. "Each is of a different grain and texture; to describe one will not fully describe the tree." The mourners had to content themselves with identifying the annular rings they knew best.

Just as his excesses were mostly forgiven in his lifetime, so, at the cemetery, the triumphs of Alec Wilder rose above the tragedies. This was not a day of sadness so much as the celebration of a life lived fully and richly, without apology, without dishonesty. As musician Gunther Schuller would often say, "the quality of incorruptibility permeated his whole life, professional, personal, and otherwise."

So they laughed and rejoiced more than they cried, and they delighted hugely in the Wilder of some years before recalled by his first lyricist, William Engvick:

"There has been a great deal written and reported about Wilder's alleged idiosyncrasies: he is a 'character,' a comic, a penniless poet, an extravagant cynic, the focus of a frivolous cabal; he is Charlie Brown and Daddy Warbucks; he is a Democrat who sleeps in his vest. To this, one can only say, 'I'd like to think so.'"

Surely even the caviling Wilder would not have been entirely displeased by this informal, good-tempered, civilized occasion—no wreaths, just a few small bunches of lilacs, daffodils, and roses placed atop the casket together with some wildflowers Jackie Cain and Roy Kral, that quintessential jazz duo, had picked along the roadside on their way from a gig in Canada; no religious service but reverence all the same; no crowds, just a few old friends speaking briefly about the man they had known and loved.

This was a coming together in another way. In burial, Wilder was joining one of the friends he had loved dearly—the late Father Henry A. Atwell, pastor of Saint Agnes Church in Avon. Their friendship had been an unlikely one—the loyal if questioning Catholic and the agnostic. But there was a breadth to both of them that had dismantled the barriers and made the bond indissoluble in life as in death. They had chosen their burial plots together, and Atwell's simple grave lay only some thirty paces away, beside the same curved path, in the same serene setting.

A soft, sensitive trumpet floated the notes of one of Wilder's songs that became a standard in the 1940s, *It's So Peaceful in the Country*. Sal Sperazza can never have played it more beautifully.

Then boyhood friend Louis Ouzer did something the irrepressible Wilder had often done himself: he stepped forward and blew a string of bubbles. They sailed over the grave and captured for one last shining moment the magic of the man and his music.

The grave diggers looked on in astonishment. They had never before witnessed such goings-on at a burial, never before heard so open an expression of love. They didn't know quite what to make of it all, but then, they had never met Alec Wilder.

Breaking the Mold

Little about his nineteenth-century forebears and nothing about the household and the America he was born into in 1907 could have foretold free-ranging spirit Alec Wilder. As far as history, heredity, and environment were concerned, he might as well have been a changeling.

On the Wilder side of the family, Grandfather Samuel Wilder had traveled in 1840 from Massachusetts to Rochester with his brother Charles to make his fortune. He had been pulled into one of the waves of settlement created by the westward movement. The line of population had by then advanced to the prairies of Indiana and Illinois, but there was still a good deal of growth to be consolidated in such western New York State areas as Rochester. By the time the Wilder brothers arrived, Rochester was already a lively place. The pioneers who had settled near the Genesee River falls in the late 1700s built well. Mills driven by water had made the city for a time the nation's largest flour manufacturer. Later, shoe factories and garment shops made industry more diverse. By midcentury, Rochester could claim two theaters for actors and other entertainers. The opening of telegraph communication with Albany was also bringing news of the world more quickly.

The frontier age left in its wake great independence of spirit and much individual initiative and enterprise. The Wilders seem to have made the most of their opportunities. They started out modestly downtown as dry-goods clerks. Frugal living allowed them to buy an interest in the business when the owner died. They were on their way. Samuel at one point left Rochester to work in New York City for Western Union Telegraph. There he supervised extension of the telegraph line through British possessions to Alaska and thence to Russia. That project collapsed when the Atlantic cable was laid, and Samuel's job came to an end. In 1859 in Rochester, where he had picked up the threads again, he married Emma L. Chaffee, daughter of the Hon. C. C. Chaffee of Springfield, Massachusetts. They were to become the parents of five children: Samuel Jr., Clara, George (the father of Alec), Emma, and

Connie. In the year of his marriage, Samuel made the first of a number of successful real estate deals. Ultimately, he was to put up an eleven-story building at the downtown Four Corners still known today as the Wilder Building. It was the tallest building in town.

The Civil War gave a tremendous push to the economy of the young America, creating many new markets. Samuel Wilder put his wits to work by speculating in wool, and he realized some "handsome profits." Wilder and Rochester began prospering together. Many new trades were setting up. Some bathrooms even had hot and cold running water from a tank in the attic. Opera stars and minstrel groups were coming to town.

Although many Rochester people ignored a war they felt was comfortably far away, a few families followed the example of the city's famous black leader, Frederick Douglass, and sheltered fugitive slaves on their way to Canada. In abolitionist matters, Samuel Wilder showed some mettle. He was a Seward Whig who made plain his strong opposition to slavery, and when the Republican Party was formed to stop the spread of slavery, he joined its ranks. In 1863, the year his son George was born, he ran unsuccessfully as the Republican candidate for mayor of Rochester. The local press found him greatly wanting. "Mr. Wilder is a malignant abolitionist" who stood for "'Liberty to the Slave or Death to the Union.'"

Despite that knockback, Wilder continued his rapid rise in the world of commerce. He was helped by the end of the war. Through the National Banking Acts of 1863 and 1864, Congress had set up a system more favorable to private bankers. Wilder helped found three Rochester banks and became the first president of one of them. Economic growth and change seemed to be everywhere, and Rochester was becoming more sophisticated and cosmopolitan. An art gallery on the premises was the pride of one leading banker. Sarah Bernhardt played Camille in the Opera House in 1881.

Samuel Wilder was now enjoying the fruits of his labors. He was on his way to becoming a millionaire, and in 1894, as was customary in those days for men of wealth, he and a friend made the grand tour of Europe. Most of Wilder's life had been devoted, very successfully, to banking and real estate. He was said to enjoy good books, and he was also hailed as a naturalist who "loved the woods, the fields, the running brooks and all inhabitants thereof." When he died, at age seventy-seven, Samuel Wilder was praised as principled businessman, loyal citizen, and faithful Unitarian. He was remembered, too, as the principal owner of the old Academy of Music, once known as the Corinthian Hall, where Jenny Lind made her first local appearance.

George Wilder, the man who became Alec's father, was Samuel's second son, and he seems to have jumped right into his father's shoes. Little of his life in Rochester is publicly recorded, and there are no private papers. It is known that he followed his father into banking and that he was equally successful. For relaxation, he sang in the chorus in a series of light operas in aid of city charities. He was also a generous patron of the musical arts. His faith was Episcopal.

Alec Wilder's immediate family story began on February 14, 1900, when George Wilder married Lillian Chew, daughter of Alexander Lafayette and Sarah August (Prouty) Chew of Geneva, New York. The Chews were originally a southern family. Lillian's grandfather Chew was collector of the Port of New Orleans in the 1820s. The port collectors in those days received and entertained visiting notables, and some fame accrued to Grandfather Chew as host to the Marquis de Lafayette when the French soldier and statesman returned to the United States to make another triumphal tour. During the time Lafayette was a guest of the Chew family in 1824, a son was born to the port collector and his wife. Lafayette became the godfather of Alexander Lafayette Chew, and the family was presented by the famous Frenchman with an ornate silver teapot inscribed with the infant's name.

Alexander Lafayette Chew, the man who was to become the father of Lillian Chew, traveled north to Geneva, New York, in 1840 to enroll at Hobart College. In 1843 he returned to the South without completing his studies. During his time in Geneva, however, young Alexander's eye had fallen on Sarah A. Prouty, second daughter of Phineas Prouty of Geneva; in 1849 Chew returned to Geneva and married Sarah. Much in the style of the Wilder family, he proceeded to make his fame and fortune as a banker. In 1866 Chew and some of his associates in a private banking venture purchased a majority of the stock of the new First National Bank of Geneva. Chew was elected president and held that office for forty-five years until his death in 1911.

Daughter Lillian married George Wilder relatively late in life. Although nothing is known of their courtship, Alec did once tell Hildegarde Watson, the first wife of his Rochester mentor, physician James Sibley Watson Jr., that according to romantic legend his father saw Lillian on a porch as he was riding through town and came back and married her four years later. Alec recalled:

> In pictures as a young woman, she was very beautiful. She lived in Geneva in a beautiful old colonial house with her very formal father (I was told he was never known to kiss, only shake hands) and mother. Her mother was very mild and gentle and had had a very proper upbringing. . . . My mother was apparently invited everywhere, and all kinds of gentlemen were after her and she waited quite a while before she got married and had absolutely no background for marriage. Nobody had told her about it, and to suddenly find herself living, not only with as rambunctious a man as my father, but with a surrounding family of unpredictable people, couldn't have been very easy for a woman who had been brought up in a very southern atmosphere.

Wilder elaborated on that later for jazz critic Whitney Balliett, whose *New Yorker* essay "The President of the Derrière-garde," is the best piece of published writing about Wilder. His mother, he told Balliett, didn't marry until she was thirty and knew nothing about such household matters as meat bills and coal bills.

> She had been a belle who had been spoiled by her family and by men. She was a Chew, and she had grown up in a colonial house surrounded by English boxwood in the beautiful upstate town of Geneva. It was a conventional, proper, Henry James life—a safe life, where there was safe talk and cheerful people and no arguments.

George Wilder was apparently well regarded by the Rochester community. When he died suddenly in 1909 at age forty-six, he was commended as an ideal citizen and banker. Wilder, it was said, had lived a life that was a blessing to all with whom he came in contact, and an honor to the city in which he had lived since his birth. His generosity, his religious faith, his tastes and ambitions, and his membership in the best clubs in town, were remarked upon. Able and conservative yet progressive in spirit, it was said "he was the ideal banker."

Alec Wilder's ancestry, then, was solid. He was the product of almost uniformly successful, upright, God-fearing citizens of high station, with not a black sheep in sight. And the first decade of the new century seemed destined to keep on favoring the likes of the Wilders and the Chews. Those were years of unbounded optimism, when Europe's troubles were remote, and the Great White Fleet was a symbol of pride and might as sixteen white-painted battleships showed the flag around the world from 1907 to 1909. Growth had no limits. God had made America his chosen nation. Sentiment and patriotism drenched the songs of the day: *A Bird in a Gilded Cage, Hello Central, Give Me Heaven, Sweet Adeline, You're a Grand Old Flag, Shine on, Harvest Moon.*

In Rochester, George Eastman, the man who built the Eastman Kodak Company and later founded the Eastman School of Music, had installed a pipe organ in his East Avenue mansion and begun a program of Sunday musicales. Although unemployed men still broke stone for the city, new manufacturing ventures were driving the economy at a fast pace. Men of means were buying two-cylinder Pope Hartford touring cars for $1,600.

That was the secure setting into which Alec Wilder was born on February 16, 1907; George and Helen were older siblings. Alec's twin brother died soon after birth, and in whimsical moments the adult Alec would sometimes say it was really he, Alec, who had died and that his life was a Great Impersonation. Alec's given names—Alexander Lafayette Chew—would never have survived in the world of popular song, so except in legal matters, he became and remained simply Alec.

Wilder seemed destined to continue the family tradition, but in fact he was to turn all that upside down. He dismissed bankers as a sanctimonious breed and all his life took merciless aim at the establishment in all its forms. The banking tradition that had dominated and distinguished both sides of his family was singled out for special attention. "I wanted no part of it . . . for my family was virtually littered with bankers, nor was I inclined to be friendly with the sons and daughters of the conventional families representative of my family's world." Ironically, Balliett would write that he looked more like a banker than most bankers. Wilder must have been mortified.

Although never personally eager for money, Wilder was well aware of his family's comfortable circumstances. He acknowledged that he came from a privileged family whose position in the community was assured and that was remote from both the working and lower middle classes. "It wasn't rich with country places, yachts and a battery of servants. For the United States, I suppose it was considered aristocratic. I never paid much attention to ancestral matters, though I couldn't help but know that my mother's family were top drawer." From the start, however, Wilder seemed to justify his own unconventional lifestyle by putting down the man who most symbolized the establishment: his father. "From all I've been able to dig up," he was to write, "he must have been the perfect wrong choice for such a pampered woman [as his mother] and possibly for any woman. He was gregarious, noisy, funny in an Irish fashion, a heavy drinker and, my hunch is, an insensitive lover." It was almost as if to say that banking and sensitive loving were mutually exclusive. At any rate, Wilder often talked harshly about his father to his friends.

From the way he spoke, it might be supposed that Wilder grew up an abused child, but he never knew his father, who died when he himself was not yet three years of age. Perhaps he swallowed whole some stories about his father that he heard later. Yet nothing in the record suggests that George Wilder was a man of bad character. His son, so diametrically unlike, was no doubt positioning himself, making the case for his own life as an outsider. He was doing it at the expense of his father's memory, caroming off him as a billiards player might do. He trotted out one story after another to prove his point and never seemed willing to give his father the benefit of the doubt. Hildegarde Watson told him of one story she had heard about George Wilder's behavior as a banker. "Somebody came to him and told him that he'd lost everything: he'd lost his chickens, and he'd lost his cows, his house had been burned down and his wife had died, and he'd like to borrow some money; and it was your father, I believe, who said to him, 'You're too careless. I can't lend you anything.'" Responded Alec: "Oh, that's terrible. I don't doubt it. I didn't know him and I wouldn't defend his name frankly because I have nothing to remember. I think he was a heavy drinker—he died young. Maybe he didn't want to go into the bank, but he did go in and he probably did a lot of nutty things."

Wilder liked to tell how his banker father supposedly turned down Eastman Kodak stock that sold then for one dollar a share and later for vastly more. That fitted the image nicely. As a child and as a youth, Wilder was to come to know his mother all too well. Just as stark in his mind, however, was the father of his concocting.

Even this basically fearful man, who would not have known what to do with untinged happiness, had his moments of childhood pleasure and simple enjoyment. One of the earliest memories was of a stark red cart with steel wheels and springs that he rode around the block. Later he was to love even more than the noise of his red cart the sounds and sights of railroads: the tracks, the switches, the dining cars and sleepers, above all the steam locomotives. He was always to remember vividly his first trip as a child from Rochester to New York to stay at the Algonquin:

We had sat about the living room for a week on chairs with heavy dust covers draped over them, the green shade down, waiting for a cab to take us to the railroad station. We traveled to New York City on the *Empire State Express*. It had an open-end observation car, a dining room, coaches and parlor cars. The parlor cars had large green armchairs which you could swivel around in a complete circle until you were told to stop.

For now, however, the red cart was his transportation and his pride. There were other scattered moments of childhood happiness, such as stopping at the kitchen door of the neighbor's house to chat with the cook. (Wilder was to develop almost as many friendships among the help as he did among his peers.) At home, on Saturday mornings, he sampled with gusto the fresh, hot, crisp crullers, and kissed Sarah, the large black cook who made them. For that, he earned a rebuke from his mother; it was not proper, she said, to kiss dark people. He also remembered stamping around the house endlessly chanting, "Ach! Der Faterland," a phrase that had come down to him from the war; peeping at Santa Claus through the keyhole of the linen-room door; talking to Mr. McFarlin of the neighborhood drugstore and watching his Adam's apple slide up and down. There was innocent fun in running to the grocery store for a tin of biscuits without having to worry about broken glass or traffic, for there was none. He liked having his hair dried by his sister in front of the gas-log fire.

Perhaps Wilder's first awareness of music came from his Aunt Emma's rather sketchy performance on the piano of *The Whistler and His Dog*. He liked it when the record store sent up all the new records to the house for the family to try out—*Esmeralda* was one. The Pooles, two doors down, had two records he said he was nutty about: the six Brown Brothers' (saxophone sextet) *The Darktown Strutters Ball*, and a tune he never heard again called *Siam*. Once, when visiting his aunt and uncle in Geneva, he picked out *Alice Blue Gown* on the piano. Sometimes he put on old piano rolls such as *The Prince of Pilsen* and *Marche Militaire*. The music was like nothing he had heard before, some of it flossy and some of it strong and emotional. He had known only popular music, he was to write later, so it was an unusual, exciting experience. He wondered if he might not one day get mixed up in the world of music.

At least as he spoke and wrote about them, childhood and boyhood were, however, more often a nightmare to Wilder. Shy, insecure, lonely, inward-looking, he shrank from the rough-and-tumble of life. He called it cowardice, a theme he was to return to time and again. No doubt he was a gentle child, and there was apparently endless bullying and harassment in the early years, in Rochester and later in Manhattan:

> In the days when I lived in Rochester on a polite side street, the world outside the house contained only the threat of other small boys. They didn't like me one bit. I wasn't a joiner or a game player or a fighter so I was bound to be a victim whenever they caught me. But they stopped chasing me after a while as it ceased to be fun to beat up a kid who wouldn't fight back.

The young Wilder became so distrustful of other children that he played with only one other boy, who didn't like games any more than he did and who never mixed up in the recess brawling. Even books offered only limited escape. His tastes found no sympathy in his mother, whose reading was confined to the likes of detective-story writer J. S. Fletcher. Wilder says her interest in music did not go much beyond *The Prince of Pilsen*.

Wilder was fond of his sister, Helen. He once said that she was the only person in the family he really liked. He was grateful to her for singing to him the early songs of Jerome Kern. She mysteriously knew the words and melodies of many unlikely songs, at least as he came to think about them later. There was Kern's *Castles in the Air*, his *The Crickets Are Calling* with a "dear" lyric by P. G. Wodehouse, *Won't You Wait Till the Cows Come Home?*, and so on. There was nothing in Rochester, he was to note later, resembling a symphony, chamber music, or concert songs. "In fact after we moved to New York when I was about eleven and went to movies which had orchestras, I assumed that the *Poet and Peasant* and *Sampa* overtures were the really big stuff. And probably this dreadful misapprehension postponed interest in any music beyond the popular for many years."

Those early Kern melodies were important, however. When it came time for him to write *American Popular Song: The Great Innovators, 1900–1950*, Wilder recalled that long before he knew the first thing about music, he knew Kern's melodies. They pleased, even haunted him. Not surprisingly, the Kern song with the most meaning to him in the early days was *And I Am All Alone*. "I learned very early that I was perfectly happy to be left alone. So I suppose I became a threat in my own house—an odd boy who was always reading books and who never fought or even played much with other children but who made people laugh."

Wilder seldom spoke of his sister to friends, and no clear picture emerges. She died very young, in the early 1930s. She had been married first to Edward De Witt Jr. She married again after her first husband died, but that union was soon ended by her own death. Today it is not even known where she is buried. After childhood, contact between Alec and Helen must have been quite limited. Wilder made one other autobiographical reference to her. On a vacation visit to Bay Head, New

Jersey, he danced in a ballroom with his sister, at her insistence. "But as you might know, I fell down, bringing her with me to the great amusement of everyone there."

That was only one in a series of mishaps at Bay Head:

One day I was nearly drowned because of an over-enthusiastic ducking by one of the older boys. I was jeered at by the girls because I was fool enough to sit on the porch railing next to the ballroom exit on Saturday nights. I came in last in a swimming race I was forced into. And when a track-minded friend bullied me into running the length of the board walk, I got a large splinter in my foot.

These were small embarrassments. It was the behavior of his mother, Lillian, alcoholic and often disapproving, that most distressed the young Wilder. He tried hard to be fair in his recollections. Though he remembered her as proud, pampered, and unintellectual, he made some allowances because she had apparently been given no hint of the responsibilities of married life. Wilder did recall one or two moments of tenderness—her making out menus for him when he was sick with scarlet fever; her breaking the word gently that Santa Claus was not the mythical gentleman he seemed to be. After she died, he found in her pocketbook a letter from him alerting her that one of his string quartets might be performed.

Still, his mother's addiction to alcohol threw a shadow over his boyhood years. Later, when the family moved to New York City at the start of the 1920s, her alcoholism often kept him out of the house and was a factor in his return to Rochester before the end of the decade. In his younger years, Wilder was only vaguely aware of the drinking. He would return from school to find the dark-green shades drawn in her room. Her condition was then put down to rheumatism, but gradually he became aware of the real problem. "I'm not asking for sympathy," he was to write:

I can only say that when you're less than a teenager it's very frightening to see a handsome, cheerful lady turn into something out of a horror movie. And as anyone less than a village idiot knows [and, he might have added, as he himself came to know from painful personal experience], the language and hallucinations of a drunken person can be pretty dreadful. To one as young as I was, these 10-day bouts were nightmares.

Loyalty kept the children silent outside the family. Indeed, older brother George would not tolerate any criticism of their mother even within the family. As Alec saw it, his brother was simply not capable of seeing things as they were. George, he said, refused to find anything wrong in his mother's behavior; it had to be rheumatism. Alec's interpretation of George's willed blindness was that acknowledgment of the alcoholism would have shattered George's desperate dream of a lovely, laughing, innocent world in which he and his mother sat about celebrating each other's presence. George might have disagreed with that; his niece Beverly McGinness remembers him telling her that after her husband's death, Lillian Wilder became a closet drinker ("Uncle George's words") and that she would go on a binge that would last for days, staying in her room with the shades drawn.

Whatever the right and wrong of it, Alec and George seemed destined to be forever far apart. Alec saw his brother as a desiccated man even further removed from the real world than he was himself, possessing few graces and having little appetite for life. Ironically, in view of his own rumpled apparel, Alec was often embarrassed by his brother's appearance: "When I meet him it's the most shocking experience in the world because it's not just [that] his clothes are all in shreds but he never gets anything cleaned. His clothes—mine, I know, are bad enough—are spattered, his sleeves are frayed, his neckties, well I've seen them for 40 years."

It was not only his mother's drinking that scarred Alec Wilder. Even more damaging, she never showed any love toward him. He often told friends that he never remembered his mother kissing him or putting an arm about him. "You love your mother enormously," he told boyhood friend Walton. "Well, I'm afraid I don't feel the same way about mine." His mother's lack of sympathy, affection, and warmth stunted Wilder's emotional development and made him permanently insecure. He was always to be immature in his attitudes toward the opposite sex. With some profoundly important exceptions, he was never able to admit women to full partnership in his life, or in society for that matter. Indeed, he often saw women as the enemy. The seeds for that were sown early, and his own bouts with alcoholism were surely influenced by his mother's example.

If childhood had its tribulations, the school years were hardly less difficult. William Engvick, the man who wrote the beautiful lyrics to one of Wilder's popular song hits of the 1940s, *While We're Young,* and who was the author of so many other fine lyrics, once said of his partner: "Child of Edwardian affluence with a longing for something less restricting. Result: Misery. Educated, Lawrenceville—more misery." *Metronome* editor Barry Ulanov wrote that Wilder had gone to three "miserable schools" and had deserted each in turn as it fell below his expectations and he fell below the school's.

The family moved constantly. As the Wilders changed residences during and after World War I, Alec was in and out of private schools in Rochester, Saint Paul's in Garden City on Long Island, Lawrenceville in New Jersey, and, when the Wilders lived in Manhattan, the Collegiate School on West 77th Street in the years 1921 to 1924. There, contrary to the bleak picture he often drew of himself, he was in fact voted the boy most likely to succeed. However, he failed the Regents examination (a New York State higher education test for high school graduates), an event, he said, as catastrophic as contracting a venereal disease. Plans for him to attend Princeton were dropped. They were never his plans but his mother's; Alec had long before set his mind against college.

Throughout his impressionable school years, Alec Wilder saw himself as always the outsider. He did not fit in, and he didn't want to fit in. He refused to measure life by the traditional tests. He once recalled with approval the time when naturalist Sally Carrighar watched some children playing a simple game in an Alaskan community. She was puzzled when all the children dispersed of their own accord before the game was decided. Seeing her expression, an old man mending a net in a nearby doorway smiled at her and said, "Up here, we don't keep score." If he refused to keep score in a society of winners and losers, the bright, inquisitive Wilder was nonetheless learning after his own fashion. He might not be smart at math and maybe he didn't understand Shakespeare or philosophy, but he was reading a great deal.

There were pleasant respites from school. On summer vacation at Bay Head, he found enough courage to hold hands with a pretty girl at a beach party. There were also a few musical moments. Somewhere along the way he had figured out how to read the treble and bass clefs so that he could fumble around on the piano. He heard from a schoolmate that Jerome Kern got many of his melodies from a hymnbook. That had to be the Episcopal hymnal—he didn't know there were others. "I spent days trying to find one melody that might be molded into a tune like, say, *The Crickets Are Calling.* I found nothing even close." Then someone in Bay Head told him about a simple stringing for a five-string banjo. He persuaded his mother to buy one and learned the chords quite quickly. "And why not? This grandly simple method required only three strings. I must have had the ears of an idiot to have listened to those seventh chords or fake ninth dominant chords and not been completely frustrated. On the contrary, I was delighted. I twanged away and started making up tunes to the chords."

In Bay Head, Wilder said he had less trouble with youngsters of his age than he did in his various schools. Even so, there were enough threats to make him gravitate to the young people who treated him with the greatest kindness: the children of the black men and women who worked in the summer hotels. Their common interest was music. Wilder said he got seven dollars a night for playing the banjo at dances, and once he played the piano when the group played for a dance in the ballroom of the very conservative hotel where his family was staying. There was some consternation among the residents over a lone white boy up there on the stage with a group of black boys. Columbia Recording executive Goddard Lieberson, a student at Eastman School of Music in Wilder's time there, would later write:

We cannot, unfortunately, say that the young Wilder's first musical interest amounted to a passionate devotion to Bach and Beethoven, since the instrument which he studied was a banjo. Luckily, his career as a banjoist was short-lived and in its professional aspect consisted only in playing for a few weddings in New Jersey. The banjo was soon deserted in favor of the more legitimate and slightly less percussive piano, an instrument which he now plays with more eclat than technique.

Meantime, most of his school-age experiences continued to be downers, at least as he chose to remember them. Even summer camp on Lake Winnipesaukee in New Hampshire, during a year he was at Saint Paul's School, was a disaster. After looking at sylvan photographs in a camp brochure, Wilder had assumed he would spend his time lazing in canoes, lying in the sun, walking in the woods, looking for birds and flowers. He hadn't reckoned on all the other noisy young campers, and he hated the camp counselors:

> Like an idiot, I wrote my sister that one of the counselors who had once met her and was writing her eye-batting letters, was not a nice person. The idiot part of it was that I wrote her on a postcard. Naturally it was read before it was mailed. The repercussions were, to me, like what I read later of Gestapo grillings. And then it was discovered that my middle initials were L. C. So I was rechristened Elsie with a wet canoe paddle, along with many charming descriptions of my unmanly behavior.

Camp was bad. School was worse. When he was a day student at Saint Paul's, the barber's son and his hoodlum friends chased him home with a hailstorm of stones. Once they caught him and rubbed his nose in the dirt. He never fought back. A happier Saint Paul's memory involved an eccentric schoolmate named Paul Tyler Turner, who was drawn to religion and music both. Wilder remembered once sitting in his room while Turner blew on some sort of pipe and plucked the strings of a zither simultaneously. He also had Wilder imagine that the partially opened drawers of a bureau were the manuals of an organ on which it was his pleasure to have Wilder pretend to play while he conducted with wild wavings of arms: "At the age of six this might pass as happy childish play, but at fourteen I admit it does bear the marks of oddity."

If one good thing came out of Saint Paul's, Lawrenceville in New Jersey was "a total disaster." With first-year boys hazed regularly, life there in Cleve House was a constant torment. No possession was sacrosanct, Wilder recalled. Anything could be taken out of his room by any member of an older class. No drawer, cupboard, or door could be locked. If it was, no punishment was given to the person who chose to break the lock. Once, Wilder was ordered to deliver a student's laundry to a room on the senior corridor, off bounds to freshmen at all times. For that unwitting trespass, Wilder got a thrashing. It was all meant "to make a man of me."

A particularly humiliating incident occurred when the Lawrenceville student body went by special train to New York to cheer the school's football team. Wilder was given permission to stop off at the family apartment in Manhattan. There, he says, he played some gramophone music, including a Paul Whiteman record of *Whispering*, and later rejoined the train at Penn Station for the ride back:

About 15 minutes out, I was told brusquely by an older boy to get two cups of water from the cooler. I knew something was up, but what could I do? Trying to carry the cups down the aisle without spilling them, I was grabbed by some slob, and all my clothes but my shorts were removed and passed down the length of the ten-car train. I was 12 at the time, no sign of muscle, eyes too big to be trusted, and towheaded. Quite a sight I must have been standing in the aisle in my shorts. Frankly, I don't remember if I cried but I do remember walking the length of the train picking up here a sock, there a shoe to the accompaniment, needless to say, of a few hundred jeers.

The final years at Collegiate School in Manhattan were more bearable, for the school was only a few blocks from home at 235 West 71st Street (though the family was apparently at 40 East 62nd Street in 1924). "At least I was no longer a sitting duck twenty-four hours a day. Of course what with the gin and my increasingly unconventional personality, the other [out-of-school] hours weren't all beer and skittles, but they contained fewer nightmares. . . . Thank God I wasn't shipped off to another boarding school." And with the family living on West 71st, Wilder was able to get some new experiences in music. As he told Whitney Balliett:

As I recall, I slept in the same bed with my brother. He insisted I whistle the *Missouri Waltz*, which invariably sent him into a heavy slumber. It does whistle well in thirds. I'd go to a nearby record store to pick up Isham Jones's records, and discovered that the store was near the Sixty-third Street Theater, where Noble Sissle and Eubie Blake's all-black show *Shuffle Along* had just opened. I don't remember how many performances I saw, but it was before the carriage trade found the show. The theater was so empty that I could slip down to the apron to watch Mr. Blake. It was a revelation. It had the same impact that Afternoon of a Faun had on me. I had thought until I heard Debussy's piece that the Poet and Peasant Overture was concert music. I went down to *Shuffle Along* to hear all those friendly songs and all those exciting people on stage the way another boy would have hung out at the candy store.

Wilder was too sensitive, too fearful a boy to acquit himself well in the daily doings of the world. Yet his vulnerability was also a strength. It was always to impress him, for example, that Robert Ardrey, one of his favorite authors, could see all the dark places in the human soul and yet still draw hope from the echo of children's laughter and the innocent sound of a carousel. All his life, Wilder's pores were no less open: "I continue to come close to tears over the beauty of a death's head butterfly, the unawareness of dissolution in a clamorous game of hopscotch . . . the quiet pride of an old lady over a completed patchwork quilt . . . and the patient wizardry of a mountain farmer wood sculptor."

In a vulgar, throwaway world, he tried in vain, he said, to accept plane travel, "the [ballpoint] pen I'm now forced to write with (yes, God damn it, I ran out of ink for my nib pen)", cake mixes, plastic, frozen food, throughways, Muzak, air conditioning, loudspeakers, electronic music, the corruption of words, television, mass production, conformity. "It's useless. I cannot accept them." Here was an example of Wilder looking at life in its worst manifestations rather than as it really was in its fullness. He embodied the theory that holds that a child can decide the shape of the world early and then spend the rest of the days making it conform to that image.

In Wilder's case, it was a world full of woe, and he didn't hesitate to stretch the truth to prove it. A case in point involves those miserable school days, for, as noted earlier, the record at Collegiate reveals Wilder as a student both successful and popular. He was liked well enough by his fellow students to be elected successively class secretary and vice president. He was a member of the debating team, treasurer of the athletic association, and member of the glee club, and was known for his wit as well as his musical accomplishments. Clearly, then, he did not always find life as dark and despairing as he painted it.

Now, as young Wilder ended his schooling in the early 1920s, he would be saved from himself by friends, and he would in turn enrich them by his strong, quickening presence.

Three Saving Friendships

Throughout his life, Wilder was notoriously unpredictable in his day-to-day moods. People moved up and down in his affections like yo-yos. One who knew him well once said of Wilder that the *New York Times* ought to carry a daily box score on the front page so that friends and acquaintances might know how they stood that day in his esteem. There was, however, a small core of friends—perhaps a dozen or so—to whom he remained loyal and constant, and whose love and counsel he depended upon to pull him through. Carroll Dunn, Lavinia Faxon, and Clara Haushalter were three early friends who made a difference in his late teens. Dunn was a young man older by almost ten years whom he had met during one of many Wilder family vacations in Bay Head. Faxon was the girl Dunn was to marry; and Haushalter was a beloved aunt, the only one of his father's sisters he was ever to feel close to.

Although Wilder's ignominious school days were, he was thankful, behind him, he was still adrift in an alien world. His mother continued to drink, and there was no one else in the family he could turn to. Family affluence meant that he would never need to hold down a 9-to-5 job, but how could he express his vaguely felt creative stirrings? In writing, in music, in stage acting, in films? He could run from home, but where would he go? In different but related and equally significant ways, Dunn and Faxon and Haushalter now put out their hands and plucked Wilder from the eddies that were spinning him around.

His brother, George, had apparently bought a catboat from Dunn some time before, but Wilder first met Dunn at a Bay Head drugstore. Wilder had a job that summer taking tickets at the local movie house, his reward being the privilege of seeing all the films. After the show, most of the audience would walk to Chafey's Drug Store for ice cream. There the two young men struck up a friendship. Dunn, who had heard that Wilder knew much about popular song, asked him if he could tell him the publisher and the writers of *Dreamy Melody*. Wilder was never quite sure how his interest in popular song originated—perhaps from listening to George M.

Cohan's *Over There,* or Irving Berlin's *Whose Little Heart Are You Breaking Now?,* or one of the hits of the *Ziegfeld Follies.* Or it may have been that Brown Brothers recording of *The Darktown Strutters Ball* that caught his interest. However it happened, he was undoubtedly fascinated: "I couldn't write music but again, I don't know how, I could read it. So to compensate for not writing, I'd go every week to a wholesale music company and beg (and sometimes steal) copies of whatever song caught my fancy. I had a file I'd made of shirt cardboards stacked on the desk in my bedroom."

Dreamy Melody was not a hit and was only one of hundreds of songs Wilder had acquired in the previous few months, but he was able to identify for Dunn its publisher and writers. That was the beginning of what he was to call a "life-saving friendship." Wilder had finally found someone who cared enough to listen to him. The two were to spend hour after hour talking together.

> Though a prodigious talker, Carroll, in those days, also was a listener. And did I need someone to listen to me! The kind of things I cared about were things no one I knew cared about. Why, for example, lamb and beef tasted differently when sheep and steers both ate grass. Why, why, why. And how, how, how. Animals, birds, boats, flowers, trees, dreams, sunsets, books.

Wilder and Dunn would sit for hours in Chinese restaurants drinking tea and eating almond cookies.

Carroll Dunn, according to Lavinia Faxon, who married him, was a difficult character, "and you had to know a little about him." He was the youngest of eight children of a strong New Jersey Catholic family. The father was a beautiful, calm person who had become wealthy as a house builder. Mrs. Dunn was "an absolute doll. She had no sense of humor that I could ever find but she accepted me who, as far as she could see, had no religion and was kind of a wacky girl." The father apparently lost much of his money overnight in the market crash. "One week they were taking private cars to Bay Head, the next week they were just trying to make do with what they had." The father retained his humor even in adversity, but Carroll Dunn became bitter about the competitive forces in the economy he felt had worked against his father. Partly because of that misfortune, Dunn, a publishing-house reader for a time, was opposed to any kind of conformity, and that attitude may have been the link to Wilder. "At any rate," said Faxon, "he was very kind to Alec and he knew he had genuine talent."

Even in the midst of their troubles, the Dunn family kept up a tradition of producing an original amateur musical show at their New Jersey home every winter. Wilder was to remember that house as a wonderfully ramshackle place surrounded by apartment houses and still lit by gas. Carroll Dunn persuaded him to write some of the music for one of the shows. Although disclaiming any talent, Wilder had already written several tunes for his banjo.

Anxious to please the Dunn family, Wilder had copied a couple of songs from one of the lesser-known Princeton Triangle shows. On his next visit to the Dunn home, he played the stolen songs to great applause. No one had seen the Triangle show, so no one unmasked him, but he was always uncomfortable about what he had done. Thirty years later, when he was being interviewed in Milwaukee about his beginnings in music, he said with his usual devastating honesty that he had stolen his first songs: "The flutist with the New York Woodwind Quintet, Samuel Baron, overheard my confession and walked away—tearing out some of his already sparse hair. After all I was to be their guest the following day on a television program."

Wilder kept up his friendship with Dunn despite his mother's disapproval:

> You might know that she, in her naïve innocence, assumed that a much older man must be a homosexual to be a friend of mine. Of course had she been asked what a homosexual was, she'd have been totally ignorant. She'd probably have said "unnatural love." God knows, she'd have thought pederasty was the dowel on a bannister.

That friendship kept branching out. Through Dunn, Wilder became close to Lavinia Faxon, who had come from Kansas City to New York to study acting. Wilder recalled her as a tall, intense girl who cared deeply about poetry, plays, novels, and who loved to laugh: "She cared nothing for music or politics, thought all birds were neurotic and people endlessly exciting." Faxon, Dunn, and Wilder became inseparable in New York in the mid-1920s, a time of fun, frolic, and flagpole sitting in the United States. For Wilder, the friendship marked a watershed. Now he was seeing life not from the bleachers but from behind first base.

Faxon remembered that the three of them did a thousand things together: "Carroll's family had an old Franklin car shaped like a bath tub and we would take it on weekends and travel up and down the Hudson. . . . Alec tried to teach me to carry a tune. I never could. We were a wonderfully companionable trio." Wilder's relationship with Faxon was to span all the subsequent years—through her second marriage to and divorce from Hugh Russ after Dunn's death, through the rearing of her three children, Sara, Martin, and Margaret—through good times and lean.

Faxon was to be many things in life: novelist, author of children's books, book buyer and reviewer, television commentator, saleswoman, traveler, grandmother. She was a woman of gusto, with a warm embrace of life and a defiant attitude toward death. She noted wryly in her biographical entry in *Contemporary Authors* that her avocational interests were "bad movies and eavesdropping at Schrafft's." Wilder and Faxon, who was older by three years, were kindred souls from the start. Eric, one of the characters in the Faxon novel *April Age* is clearly the young Wilder:

> There he was standing in the hall the next morning when I went downstairs,
> tall and thin, with no hat, in unpressed pants and a sloppy jacket with its

pockets out of shape with papers stuffed in them. He looked like a young
Lionel Barrymore—only messy. He didn't say hello—I found out later he
never says hello. He just asked, "Do you want to walk?"

Faxon also painted an accurate picture of the wary, backpedaling Wilder who would
never be trapped in any kind of domestic arrangement:

A letter came to the pensione for me from Eric this morning. "I had to run,"
it began. "It would be too easy to love you, and loving is too painful—I have
found that out already. I haven't time for pain—or for pleasure, if there can
be pleasure in loving people. We'd use up all our lives demanding. We'd be
trapped in a house, in a room, in a bed, demanding, demanding. . . . To
survive, I've got to possess no one, be possessed by no one."

There was never a romantic link between Lavinia Faxon and Wilder. They were
simply fast friends. Yet important though it was, this Manhattan idyll was often
interrupted. With money in his pocket, wanderlust in his feet, and the world spread
before him, Wilder was forever taking off on brief forays and excursions, a practice
that was to stay with him all his life. No one ever had Wilder in a grasp for very long.
And so, when still fifteen, he left Faxon and Dunn behind for a bit and headed out of
town for a few days to visit his Aunt Clara Haushalter and her husband George at
their Maine summer home in Wiscasset. This was a community as beautiful and
tranquil as an old English village. These were the days before the elm blight, before
the relentless traffic of the throughways, before the stock market frenzy. It
was also the time when a syncopated music called jazz was taking the country by
storm.

In the 1920s the railway sleeping cars went through to Rockland, Maine, drawn
by Wilder's beloved steam engines. This was before air conditioning, "so you could
hear those lovely steam whistles through the half-opened windows." Before the
train reached Wiscasset, it was taken apart at Bath, put on a car ferry, and transported across the Kennebec River. In Wiscasset, the young Wilder found Orchard
House sitting at the edge of a large granite boulder, back in an apple orchard.
Instead of jarring the moment by ringing the doorbell, he wandered around the
lovely little white house, sniffing the applewood smoke as he went. In an old-
fashioned flower garden, he saw a lady with an open wicker basket bending over
delphiniums with garden shears. It was all quite wonderful, and he was to write
later:

I wouldn't be surprised if one of the things I've been trying to say in music all
my life hasn't been to transmute the way I felt walking through Wiscasset
asking wholly friendly and open-faced strangers the whereabouts of Orchard
House. Scarcely heroic music, you may say, and quite so. The heroic never
interested me, nor the passionate aspect of love. The Gothic never impressed

me, so perhaps, as has been said, I *am* a miniaturist, although labels also bore me.

Just as he had found soul mates in Carroll Dunn and Lavinia Faxon, now Wilder was in the same kind of company with Clara Haushalter, a kindly, compassionate woman in her early sixties. He had the feeling that although Clara greatly respected her husband, George, this was not for her a love match. He was a humorless man given, in Wilder's opinion, to decidedly strange behavior. In the back of his house in Rochester, he would emerge into the hallway in the early morning in his long underwear for his daily exercises. The young Wilder would peek at him when he wasn't looking. He would start stretching in his peculiar fashion: "That is to say, he'd hold his hands out at his side and stretch them about three inches to the right to touch the one wall and three inches to the left to touch the other. He considered this very strenuous exercise and he would berate me because I didn't run up and down and jog the way they do now."

Wilder's feelings for Clara were always to be deep and unalloyed, even when she became old and confused. She was so upset after her husband's death, his peculiarities notwithstanding, that she thought it would help to keep his memory alive if nephew Alec were to wear some of his clothes. "She gave me an old fur coat of his that looked like a coachman's coat. And she tried to get me into his shoes, which really would have fitted carrots better than my feet because they were so narrow." Wilder humored his aunt wherever he could, for he owed her much for her earlier support. That support was never more important than during that early-teen visit to Wiscasset. Wilder and his aunt spent long evenings by the fire talking—about the problems he was having coming to terms with a hostile society, about his mother, about his two friends in New York. It may have been during this visit that plans were hatched for Wilder to go with his aunt and uncle on a trip they were planning to Italy. It was Clara Haushalter who persuaded his mother that he should go with them and a cousin on this adventure.

Back in New York with Faxon and Dunn, Wilder enjoyed the happy, heedless tenor of the times. Young people had more money to spend and were no longer accepting parental authority without question. Skirts were shorter, morals were changing. These were the twenties, when the whole country seemed to be on a spree, when the Jazz Age was sweeping everything before it. Speakeasies seemed romantic despite the violence of Prohibition. Broadway was the entertainment capital of the world. Wilder and his two friends loved it all. In the wonderfully casual way of youth, it had been decided earlier that Faxon and Dunn should marry. "I'm not sure whose idea it was," said Faxon, "but Alec didn't resent it. He was the kind of brother you dream about."

Wilder was also now consolidating his friendship with Dunn. Although music had first joined them at Bay Head, it was prose writing they concentrated on in the first months of their relationship in New York. There's no doubt from what Faxon has also said that Wilder did indeed do a great deal of writing: stories, verses, biographical sketches, anything and everything. Wilder also used all that toil to invent one of the tall stories he loved to perpetrate. Every morning, he swore, he would strap himself to the chair he worked in, padlock the strap, and give the key to the man who slept there and left shortly after he arrived. The point of this was to force himself to stay there and write. He even added an extra touch. One day, he said, he forgot to bring his lunch, so he hunched his way down the tenement stairs with the chair attached to him, made his way to a stand-up food counter where he sat down and ordered a sandwich, much to the enjoyment and bewilderment of the onlookers. That story was published in *Seventeen* magazine and in several newspapers, apparently without question. Wilder was later to confess: "I made up that tale about my writing ritual and I told it as gospel for years. The story made lots of people laugh and did no one any harm."

The writing was not leading him anywhere, however, and it was the trip to Italy with the Haushalters that turned him once and for all toward music. The congenial company of his aunt was important to the success of the trip. A year before, he had made a quick summer visit to Europe in the company of "some dreadful people" whose wholesale-grocer sign he had seen for years on the wall of a building as the train pulled out of Newark. On the voyage across, he remembered playing *Tea for Two* seven hundred times or so on a piano in an empty lounge in the stern of the ship. (Some fifty years later, he would devote several paragraphs of analysis to this song in *American Popular Song*.)

Thanks to Clara Haushalter and the people he met in Italy, the second trip was a much happier experience. He felt accepted and understood for the first time in his life, except for the sympathy of special people like Aunt Clara and Carroll Dunn. There was so much about the visit that was to remain vivid: standing in the bow of the ship going into Naples harbor at dawn; walking in a walled orange grove on a back road in Sorrento; eating fresh, hot brioches at roadside bakeries; listening in the night to the steam engines pulling up the long hill out of Florence; hearing barrel organs playing Verdi tunes in Naples.

Italy was also Luciana Aloisi, a tall, older Italian girl who arrived in Florence with her father. Wilder became enamored of her. Although there was no sexual intimacy, Luciana listened to him quite seriously and treated him as an adult. Sometimes he would leave notes under her bedroom door, and when the Haushalters went on to Venice, she wrote to him there. Luciana's open acceptance of him so bewitched Wilder that he risked his aunt's affections by insisting on returning to Florence from Venice instead of going on with the party. The innocent romance was short-lived. Luciana became engaged to a boy her own age. Wilder felt alone and deserted. It was a traumatic moment: "I wouldn't move, and Clara was perfectly marvelous about it because here I was her responsibility to my mother and somehow she handled it. Somehow she worked it out so that I didn't lose face. I didn't feel I'd been destroyed. I don't know how she did it. It was just that incredible easy compassion she had—no tricks, nothing up her sleeve." Thanks to Clara, Wiscasset and Italy were to remain forever places of paradise to Wilder. Toward the end of his life, he ached for those beautiful vanished days. "I want to walk up through those silent evening vineyards on the slopes of Capri. I want more of those dirt roads in the back country of Maine."

During his Italian visit, Wilder had rented pianos in both Florence and Venice, though the piano in Venice had to be taken to the pensione by boat and hoisted with great difficulty and "hundreds of imprecations" to his room. In Florence, he bought piano reductions of half a dozen Wagner operas. That, he always said, was the beginning of his antipathy toward Wagner's music. The music aside, he could never have countenanced a composer who told all who would listen that he was the greatest musician who ever lived. Although Wilder wrote only a piano piece or two on his rented pianos, music began to take on new urgency for him in Italy, especially when he was once introduced as *il compositore*. He told Carroll Dunn that he could not contemplate being a writer of words when everything in Italy was music:

> I know that's not true when I come back from a day moving in and out of the glorious churches of Florence, seeing the breathtaking sculpture and painting, but something keeps shouting at me to look deeper and deeper into music.
> I've heard no concerts, heard no music but that of countless people singing in the streets. Yet I've already started buying stacks of music, in fact I've even rented a piano. I don't know beans about music, don't play worth a damn nor read well, but ever since you took me to that concert at Carnegie Hall and I heard L'Apres-Midi d'un Faune I've got the bug. I've even written a piece of music that's not just a tune. I don't think it's good, but it is *something* which I wrote. And it's the *first one!*"

Back in New York, Wilder began writing tunes, some to the accompaniment of chords on the piano. Then Dunn persuaded him to try something more ambitious. First, there was a tone poem. Then Dunn presented him with the Kipling poem about cargo ships. This he asked him to write for chorus and "God knows what kind of accompaniment." Because Wilder had studied with no one, read nothing about composition, counterpoint, harmony, or orchestration, the whole venture, he felt was ridiculous. This was the composition Wilder would take with him to the Eastman School of Music in Rochester the following year. It may not have been a very good composition, but, as he pointed out, he would never have arrived at even that state of affairs if Carroll had not persuaded him to try his hand at something of a larger canvas than songs or shapeless "tone poems."

Dunn was important to Wilder for several reasons. He entered his life at a critical moment. "He was the first sympathetic and important influence in Alec's life," Lavinia Faxon was to say. "Alec was then sixteen or seventeen, as lonely as a cloud. Carroll, who was older, was very patient. He recognized a genuine talent and he really did encourage him." The young man lonely as a cloud might have blown clear across the sky and out of sight had it not been for Carroll Dunn.

The Eastman Years

In 1926, now nineteen years of age, Wilder returned to hometown Rochester for the first time since the family had left there for Garden City, Long Island, during World War I. With this move, he decided on a career in music, though he was not to immerse himself in music quickly or fully in the Eastman School of Music. Afraid, insecure, diffident, he was by no means sure he could make a success of music. He could also afford to take the time to let his music leanings grow into longings. He had an ample allowance and was soon to pass into a handsome inheritance from that despised father of his.

It's useful also to remember how extrordinary was his range of interests, and how many roles he played. William Engvick has pointed out that "Alec the friend, the benefactor, the witty conversationalist, the critic, the eccentric and the beguiler of kids" was apt to overwhelm the rest, so that the multifaceted man sometimes obscured the work of the multifaceted composer. Wilder insisted that all of life be embraced.

> I love music, and it's the closest I have come to creation. But I'm also con-
> cerned with the miracle of life in all of its incredible forms and I willingly stop
> the act of creating music for any crisis in my small area of the larger creation.
> I can't claim to being like one of those famous composers whose every wak-
> ing moment was given to his art. I'll stop for a spider, a bird, a tree, a
> flower, a child, a book, a storm, a sound, a scent, a smile. I'll play with toys,
> blow bubbles, watch bobble birds, read a dictionary, listen to a sad tale, make
> up a puzzle, row a boat. All these seemingly trifling pastimes are of great im-
> portance to me. They're not just a recess from composing, they're nourishing
> acts of living.

In support of that kind of outlook, Wilder in Rochester immediately set about reclaiming old friends and acquaintances and making new ones. Taking the night train, he arrived in town early on a Sunday morning. He had a compulsion to see

Westminster Road, where he had grown up, so he made his way there along quiet streets. On his way back along Westminster, he noticed on the front porch of a house across the street from where he had spent his childhood a very handsome young woman. It occurred to him that she might be Jane Kelly, the grown-up sister of a boy he had known earlier, one of the less sadistic, less aggressive neighborhood boys he had often fled from. It proved to be so. He rang the bell and found all three Kelly children at home, cheery and welcoming. He spent a happy day with them.

At first, and from time to time later, Wilder stayed in the old Sagamore Hotel on East Avenue but then moved out, perhaps, he speculated, because a piano was frowned on in the hotel. His first rented room was in a side-street two-story apartment building in which "my dear and notably eccentric Aunt Emma" (one of Clara Haushalter's sisters) lived just overhead. Whether it was his faulty sight-reading or her archaic taste, he never knew, but he came to learn that she considered what filtered through the ceiling shockingly "modern" music:

> My musical taste at that time was so sketchy (I had heard so little) that I can't conceive of anything I fumbled at offending the ears of a grandmother. I had heard Bach, whom I had been warned against as being much too dry and intellectual but whom I found to be perfection, which of course he is, and, as far as I'm concerned, the high point of Western civilization. Then there were Ravel and Debussy, who appealed to my sentimental, unaggressive nature. . . . The piano music I bought during this time I could play little of, but I very much enjoyed investigating it.

Wilder put a high value on friendship, and he had the gift of finding it in unlikely places, among unlikely people. Louis Ouzer was a poor young Jew in Rochester with little formal education. His father had been a wine-maker in Minsk until oppression forced him to escape to America. His mother, who had had to wear the Star of David on her dress, bribed border guards to make her own escape from Russia. The two of them met and married in the United States and had five children. After living on a farm near Ithaca, the Ouzer family settled in Rochester on Merimac Street.

The Schiff family lived opposite them and were the only ones on the street with a telephone and a Model T. Son Joe, older than Louis Ouzer, grew up to play the viola in the Eastman Theater movie orchestra but turned to photography to make a living. A fine photographer, Schiff had his studio in a rented room near the Eastman School, and for ten years young Ouzer labored there like a mole in the dark room as a lab technician. That long apprenticeship would one day make him a prize-winning photographer.

It was at the Schiff studio that Ouzer and Wilder, light years apart in social standing, came to know each other and to put down the footings for a lifelong friendship. Wilder was to say of Ouzer that he was a very young, very shy boy who not only stammered whenever he became nervous but had little sophistication or worldly knowledge. Yet he was as absorbent as a sponge. "I sensed," Wilder would say, "that he was as pure and good as eternal truth. I came to know and respect him to a degree that his boss considered almost incomprehensible."

Ouzer, for his part, was eternally grateful to Wilder for throwing open for him the world of literature and learning. They were often together at the studio. Wilder was apt to make dramatic entrances, often wearing a stylish hat, coat, and spats, and carrying a cane and always a book. "He would arrive unannounced and sit there in his coat and hat reading his book, which he would usually leave with me." Ouzer also remembers that Wilder "would create a stir by arriving at Merimac Street [at the Schiff home] in a limousine, and he would have the driver wait an hour or so for him." That was life on a very grand scale. His friends were mightily impressed.

Gradually, Wilder began to spend more time in the company of Eastman students such as Schiff and Frank Baker, a voice student at the school. Ouzer was not a musician, but, interestingly, he would take up composing at Eastman fifty years later, when he was in his seventies; Wilder would have liked to have known about that. Sometimes Wilder, Baker, and Ouzer would go with Schiff by car to Wells College in Aurora on beautiful Cayuga Lake, south and east of Rochester. There Schiff would take photographs for the student yearbook. "It was an age of innocence," says Ouzer. "We traveled over dirt roads and as the spirit moved us to Aurora. . . . The trick was often to see how far you could coast in neutral up and down the hills. Alec loved the meandering dirt roads." Those were bright, cloudless days for Wilder, who was always ready to go anywhere at any time. "I had enough money, but I wasn't interested in what it would buy. So I wasn't burdened with possessions. No automobile, no pets, wife, house, child, garden, nothing to immobilize me."

> When Joe Schiff would suggest going to a village on Lake Cayuga to Wells College, in fact there was nothing to cancel, postpone or change. All my life I've been suspicious and fearful of plans. So on a fleecy autumn morning we would set out, not on some impersonal, unrelated-to-the-landscape throughway but on roads that twisted and turned and passed by farms and through villages until we arrived at a very small community, Aurora, the lifeblood of which is Wells college. We'd leave our bags at the inn which backed up against the unpolluted lake and which was quiet, safe and almost English in atmosphere. In the village, there was one hardware store, one drug store, a tea room, a railroad depot, an inn and a college. The innocence of it.

Month by month, Wilder was becoming more familiar with Eastman. It had been hard at first. He was loath to plunge in, and shy about speaking to most of the girls. He always insisted there had been no sexual intimacies in those years. He would always do a lot of sidestepping. He once told a friend that he never completely accepted sex because "it's too personal." When Wilder finally became comfortable in the corridors, he found the student world even more exciting than he had expected: "No banks, no dull talk, no keeping everything you say within the limits of propriety and prissiness. No, it's the wild, free, searching, roaring world of young people who know what they want . . . and my God, how they love music!" Some of those young people remembered Wilder bursting on the scene like Halley's comet, trailing clouds of mystery and romanticism, chain smoking the cigarettes that would kill him one day. He was the wealthy, well-born stranger who had lived in the Big City. His intensity, his flamboyant dress, his dark handsomeness, his exotic air set him apart from all the rest. Frances Alexander was a sixteen-year-old pianoforte student from the Midwest when Wilder was in his early twenties: "He seemed as old as God, and a lot like John Barrymore as he stalked around the corridors with cape and cane."

It was the students he came to know and love and hang out with who confirmed for Wilder that music was his destiny: French horn players John Barrows, Jimmy Buffington, and Sam Richlin; oboist Mitchell (Mitch) Miller; violist Joe Schiff; clarinetist Jimmy Caruana; tenor student Frank Baker; composition student Goddard Lieberson; Frances Alexander (who later married Miller). Many would go on to become important figures in American music and the entertainment world, and each, though some more than others, would become a major force in Wilder's life. As he acknowledged later, he also had a freedom that made a difference:

> Music, its sounds, rhythms, patterns and unverbal implications, directions and secret affirmations had always fascinated me. The more I heard, the more I learned, the more dedicated I became to trying to speak its language. Of course the fact that I had enough money to experiment without the need to make a living from it was probably the principal reason I went on with it. Those who knew that it was to be their means of survival, now that I look back, I should have held in higher esteem than I did. For had I had to suffer the drudgery of teaching what I loved, I'd have stopped loving it. This was true, of course, of many who took it up simply as a way of making a living. Indeed, it is that type of education in music today that is its single worst influence.

Though now so thoroughly part of the Eastman School community, Wilder did not enroll as a student. He was never a joiner to begin with. Crowds, even large groups, scared him, even made him panicky. He was older than most of the others, and that would have made him uncomfortable in the classroom. Moreover, he would have tired quickly of a formal, structured academic framework. He did, however, decide to study privately at Eastman, and he began taking lessons from two faculty members. Wilder had said once that he had a hunch he would go on pretty much on his own, taking forever to learn orchestration by listening instead of studying, "and stumbling around like someone in a dark room looking for the light switch in my effort to find *my* way to compose." As a composer, he would always be his own man.

Here he was, however, making at least some acknowledgment of the need to get some disciplined education. So he started learning counterpoint from Herbert Inch and composition from Edward Royce, son of the famous Harvard logician Josiah Royce.

Retrospectively at least, he played down his skills and aptitudes, maintaining that he was not very good material. That should be doubted strongly. His teachers had the choice of the best students in the country. They would not have bothered with a young man of no talent. Both faculty members had good credentials. Inch, teacher and composer, was a graduate of the University of Montana, with a Master of Music degree from Eastman. In 1931 he would win the Prix de Rome. Royce was a Harvard graduate who began in the theory department at Eastman in 1923. He also studied at Stern University in Berlin and taught in several American colleges, including Middlebury. He, too, did some composing.

The same wealth that now gave Wilder a special status as a private student at Eastman in the later 1920s also allowed him to indulge in what seemed at times to be a frenzy of spending. This was hedonistic America. The dollar was everything, the gross national product was soaring, and no one seemed to be worrying much about the Negro sharecropper. A carnival atmosphere masked a sense of futility in the nation. In Rochester the times were still solid. Manufacturing was giving the city a firm foundation. George Eastman in his retirement was spearheading the development of the Chamber of Commerce and other institutions. The University of Rochester was busy with a new campus on the Genesee River.

An inheritance estimated at $70,000 (perhaps the equivalent of a million dollars today) allowed Wilder to be endlessly generous. He was an easy touch, but he seemed not to care. Though he disliked being without it, if only because he could not then give it away, Wilder never considered money to be the beginning or the end of anything. More important to him were the taproots of friendship put down in those carefree Eastman days. Despite lectures from his friends on the virtue of prudence, Wilder continued to be incredibly casual with his money. Says Mitch Miller: "He was always sitting around the [Eastman] hall writing. He used to have negotiable bonds in his pocket. When he needed some money, he would just go cash one of them." Wilder himself said he never bothered to take his money to a bank:

> I kept it all in my pocket. I didn't have a bank account for years. The money
> was drifting in. Taxes weren't so bad in those days, so you didn't have to
> keep track of what you spent. So I just kept the money in my pockets. I was
> crazy. To walk around with three or four thousand dollars and not be able to
> pay any bills by check. Just crazy. I carried thousand-dollar bonds in my
> pocket, and when I would run out of money I'd cash one.

Sometimes he gave away his money blindly. In lonely moments, he seemed almost to be buying the conversation of the person on the next bar stool. Composer

David Diamond often saw Wilder at the old Town Tavern, which had an upstairs speakeasy, and was at times appalled at Wilder's improvidence: "I went to the tavern one day for lunch and saw him giving away one hundred dollar bills. 'But, Alec,' I remonstrated, 'who are these people?' And Alec would say, 'It's all right. They'll pay it back.' But they often didn't."

Many students benefited from his generosity. Allen McHose, then an Eastman School administrator, was often witness to his open-handedness: "Alec did a lot for the students. He often paid their tuition. That's why he was always going broke" (in between checks). Sagamore bellhop Bill Champaigne remembers: "Every morning Alec would sit in the corner coffee shop. The students from Eastman would come over, have breakfast and walk out, and at the end of the morning he would have about 10 checks, and he would pay them all gladly." Frances Alexander has given the same kind of witness: "Alec's generosity was legendary. One story has it that he bought up the entire contents of a grocery store and sent them to the apartment of a poor student who had just married. If not the whole store, then 90 percent of it." Mitch Miller says Wilder was well known "for giving away his money if the kids needed rent money or something. I don't know if he ever got any of it back." There was almost nothing he would not do for needy students.

Wilder and his friends spent a great deal of time hanging out in restaurants and speakeasies. On those occasions life was an overflowing bowl of cherries. But behind the playboy Wilder was a budding musician, a young man of purpose. Miller seemed to sense that early. He has pointed out that the students were for real: "These were first-class, serious musicians. Where work was involved, nothing stood in our way. Then late at night we'd go over to Michael's speakeasy on Stone Street where they had the home brew. Alec introduced me to great booze and great food there. We didn't have any money, so Alec always picked up the tab."

Miller in turn introduced Wilder to some superb oboe playing and helped light the fire of creativity. At any rate, it was the serious musician who presented himself to Eastman professor Herbert Inch, taking with him the Kipling cantata that Carroll Dunn had persuaded him to write earlier. Although the piece wound up in the trash basket according to Wilder, Inch, "a marvelous, twinkling" man, said he would be glad to teach him beginner's counterpoint in private lessons. Inch deeply impressed Wilder with the importance and indeed the "glory" of contrapuntal writing—the writing of music in parts in such a way that separate lines can be traced as distinctive strands of sound.

Wilder told Inch that although he knew very little about counterpoint, he was already convinced that it represented the bones of music. "Without the strength of interdependent lines, the musical building may collapse. Such a statement from a beginner may sound sententious but I want you to be certain that it is no casual impulse that brought me to study with you. And though I hear less and less counterpoint in contemporary music, I wish always to keep it an integral part of any music I write."

Inch's legacy to Wilder was an invincible belief in counterpoint. Wilder even tried writing a fugue based on the second theme of Gershwin's *Rhapsody in Blue*. "It was a bust." But even if Inch's instruction did not move him closer to composition, it did make him feel like a sculptor who had learned the muscles and skeletal structure of the human body. His experience with Edward Royce was apparently less rewarding. He did appreciate the pianoforte lessons, though he found himself unable to share his teacher's enthusiasm for the Beethoven piano sonatas. He acknowledged Beethoven as a master but found himself drawn more to Moussorgsky and Debussy and Ravel, particularly the Debussy string quartet and Ravel's *Daphnis and Chloe*. Johann Sebastian Bach remained for him the greatest composer, and if he didn't listen to him more often, it was only because he feared that Bach would drive all his own music out of his head.

Wilder appreciated Royce's patience in trying to give him the tools of musical composition but ran into a problem of approach and outlook that was to set him on a collision course with the Eastman music establishment presided over by Howard Hanson. Wilder would write: "The man with whom I had tried to study composition, though concerned and friendly, was of such a hyperlogical caste of mind that I couldn't find a way to grow under his tutelage." Wilder had no liking for anarchy in music or anything else, nor did he want to be hamstrung by order and logic.

Royce's tightly structured teaching faithfully reflected Hanson's philosophy of music, so inimical to Wilder's views of what music should be all about. Wilder and Hanson were destined for disagreement by the very nature of their characters and backgrounds. Wilder was always to follow his intuitions and convictions wherever they took him, even if it was sometimes far afield. He was always to put originality before everything else. With that outlook, with his inborn dislike of authority in all its forms, it was inevitable that he would collide with the man who held the school so tightly in his grip.

As musicians and composers, Hanson and Wilder were both to put their mark on American music. Yet two more dissimilar men would be hard to find. As pointed out by Ruth Watanabe, formerly the head of the Sibley Music Library at the Eastman School and later the school's historian, it was simply not in their basic natures for them ever to be close. Their chemistry was as wildly incompatible as their music. Hanson was to devote himself to composing music on the big scale, in a conservative, lush, religious, nineteenth-century romantic idiom. Wilder for the most part eschewed large works, making music in a much more personal, often highly idiosyncratic style, and across a great range of idioms. There was little common ground. To Wilder, Bach was the classical composer beyond compeer. Hanson admired Beethoven more than Bach, and he enjoyed Handel, Scriabin, and Liadov—"every note is in the right place at the right time."

Hanson was to become a major figure in twentieth-century music. Through the Eastman School, undeniably his creation, he brought music education in the United

States to the highest level it had ever reached. He was an unflagging champion of American music. He established the American Composers Concert series at the school after his first year; ten years later they were replaced with the Symposium of American Music each spring and fall. The forty-year-long series Festival of American Music begun in 1931 was his doing, as was the legitimizing of the serious study of musical performance at American universities. He helped found the National Association of Schools of Music.

This, then, was the man Alec Wilder loved to hate: an authoritarian figure who headed up a school that taught music in an authoritarian style. Hanson, says current director Robert Freeman, was a distinguished musician with a very strong, clear idea of what lay within the canons of music and what lay outside: "If you didn't agree with him, that was just too bad. He either tried to force you into his way of looking at the music world or you could go off somewhere else. Sometimes a student decided on his own that this was a very inhospitable climate. Sometimes Howard decided for him." Some able young musicians who disagreed with the party line left and became considerable figures in the composition world. More patient students stayed through graduation and went on to become their own persons anyway.

The notion of placing music in a kind of straitjacket was alien to Wilder. Fundamentally, music in those days may not have been taught much differently at Eastman than at other institutions. By virtue, however, of its more isolated social and cultural environment, the Rochester community may have laid extra restraints on the music school. This was a proud provincial city with a history of economic success. Light industry was inventive, productive, and locally owned. The business leaders were highly competent, hardworking men who were also the city's movers and shakers. They sought no help from the outside in solving their problems. The day would come several decades later when that self-sufficiency would smack of parochialism and complacency and would blind the city to its growing racial problems. Even in the years when Wilder was walking the corridors of Eastman, there was an unspoken resistance to external artistic influences, a resistance that would lose the school and the community important chances to create fresh cultural ferment and loosen music's straitjacket. Freeman puts it plainly:

> One of the things people had against Eastman School in the 1930s goes to the time when Hitler was stirring things up in Europe. This country was overwhelmed with European immigrants, most of them Jewish, but not entirely. Some of them were composers of major international reputation. None of them came here to Eastman . . . not Bartok, Stravinsky, Hindemith, Schoenberg, or any of the others. This was not a place in which such people were welcome. They could have been appointed to the school and they could have been a major start here.

Hanson's actions and attitudes, then, were shaped in part by the setting he worked in. Even though he may have dimly divined this, Wilder was bound to struggle against the status quo, and there was always that extra measure of personal resentment. One of his early attempts at composition was a so-called tone poem (*Symphonic Piece,* 1929). The Eastman rehearsal went badly, in Wilder's opinion. He confessed to being so chagrined that he refused to attend the official performance at the school. Instead, he was to recall, "I got drunk in a speakeasy up a filthy flight of stairs above an organization called Jesus Lighthouse. I guess that was the night I lost Dr. Hanson. For when, at the end of the piece, he turned summarily (I imagine) to the audience for me to take a bow, I was stoned many blocks away."

Wilder did acknowledge in regard to the presentation of his orchestral tone poem that Hanson had had the decency to rescore a section in which he had messed up the four French horns and the three trumpets.

> Until the piece for orchestra I had attempted nothing more ambitious than concert songs. I had no background for such a piece, for all I had done was study a little counterpoint and composition. No orchestration or theory. Nor did I know more than a pinch of the vast body of music I should have known. But I'd managed to turn out a ten-minute piece, orchestration and all. But oh, that French horn section!

Hanson once said about Wilder that he attended his classes as a visitor and that he was able to help Wilder with a few things when he was just starting in composition. Wilder attended all the symposia of student compositions and absorbed everything he could. His music, "intimate, appealing and very well done," said Hanson generously, had great charm. Wilder, he noted, never tried to storm the heights.

It's too bad the two men were not destined to be closer, for there was a private, unautocratic Howard Hanson of whom even Wilder would have approved and enjoyed. John C. Brzustowicz, whose family lived next door to the Hansons for twenty-seven years in Rochester, once recalled that as a child he was always welcome at the Hansons: "Musicologists will some day wonder why soda stains, greasy little hand prints and an occasional badly scrawled note appeared on his musical scores. They appeared gratis of one small child who pestered this man after school. And this child never received a single reprimand for one of them."

The private Hanson was to be found every summer on his Bold Island off the Maine coast, seventy-nine acres of pines and granite beaches. There, Hanson, his wife, Peggy, the young Brzustowicz, and two dogs, Tamara and Peter Bolshoi, created a world of their own far from the telephone. Hanson would carry in water from the well, search in his boat for driftwood, and later saw it into fireplace lengths. In July 1981, some four months after the composer's death, Brzustowicz remembers, "Howard and I made the trip one last time across Penobscot Bay to Bold

Island. I scattered his ashes on the beach where he loved to swim. Peter Bolshoi is buried close by. Together, I imagine, they discuss the virtues of an unwritten piece and listen for the dissonant objection of some crow."

Wilder loved the quiet places no less, often seeking and finding refuge in the country, in Maine, in Key West, on Grand Cayman Island. He could not, however, abide a man he considered authoritarian and reactionary. Wilder the mocking outsider also found it hard to stomach a man so wholesomely dedicated and consecrated to God, humanity, and the arts. Inevitably, he became part of a student protest that in memory has grown in magnitude through the years but that amounted to just a small ripple compared with student protests of the 1960s. It was, however, real enough at the time, for any kind of student dissent was rare in those tightly disciplined times. The mutterings apparently began among the French horn players, one of whom, John Barrows, was to become a lifetime friend. "John," Wilder recounted, "was part of that little revolt at Eastman. It could have been a beauty, but it got started too late in the year. He was deliberately rude to Howard Hanson, and God knows, Hanson deserved it." Barrows would leave Eastman and get his degree at Yale. The horn players were evidently angry because they had received what they felt to be an inadequate cross-section of orchestral literature during their years in the Eastman School Symphony Orchestra. Said Wilder:

> One of the fomenters trusted me enough to let me see the broadside he'd written to be printed and distributed in every mail box. It was much too vilifying, too far out of control to achieve any result, in my opinion. I had money in those days and offered to pay for the printing if the horn players would permit me to rewrite the diatribe. The permission was granted. I rewrote it; the sheet, it was decided, was to be called *The Bird,* which in those days meant a nose-thumb, and caustic little remarks were invented to fill the opposite side of the printed sheet. I found a courageous printer whom I warned that there might be repercussions, but he was willing to risk them.

The sheets were printed and placed in all the faculty mailboxes. However, before more than a few were picked up, the front office got wind of them and removed the remainder. That only made the sheets already picked up by the box owners that much more valuable. Soon everyone was making copies. "Well, I tell you! It was as if someone in Berlin had put on a screening of Chaplin's *The Great Dictator.* Hanson's Gestapo went steaming about town cross-examining every print shop, dozens of people were hailed into Hanson's office, speeches of treason were trumpeted and the peapatch was truly torn up." By today's standards, much of the content of the two issues of *The Bird* was basically mild, although Wilder did take anonymous aim at both the director and the faculty for failing "to elevate the school until it rises above the dull horizon of American pedagogy." There would be no point in criticism, he wrote, if the Eastman School were content to hitch its wagon to a star no farther than the Milky War of "pastoral, bovine pedagogy (which brings small salaries to the lives of dull uninspired teachers and not even that to their pupils)."

Although Wilder did not claim authorship, his hand can also be seen in another *Bird* essay, this one on the student orchestra. After criticizing the official conductor, the piece went on to pan the conducting style of Hanson, saying that "once or twice a year there descends upon the orchestra a man who is grimly determined to demonstrate his ability to make soldiers out of musicians. His is the hand of iron." He was accused of prolonging rehearsals beyond the breaking point and of holding the pieces together "as if the glue of his discipline could mend the shattered morale of the bewildered company." A more substantive criticism had to do with repertoire:

> The classics still form the backbone of major orchestra programs, and it is essential that a student orchestra should have a thorough understanding of traditional literature. Music about which there is any doubt has no place in the rehearsal time of a student group. The encouragement of modern American music is (no doubt) a fine thing; but its growing pains should be borne by a professional orchestra. Something must be radically wrong when a group rehearses approximately a hundred times a year, and is given at the most ten standard works in that time.

The so-called revolt at Eastman fizzled with time, and apparently there were no lasting penalties for the students. Though he certainly had his suspicions about Wilder's role, Hanson seemed not to carry a grudge through the years. Indeed, he included *An Entertainment* in 1961 in the Festival of American Music series, and excerpts from the same work the following year. There were to be other ironies. Wilder was younger by ten years, but both men died within two months of each other. And both were remembered and saluted in the same 1981 issue of *Eastman Notes*, the bulletin of the school. Wilder would have snorted at that, for he was always to remember his first encounter with the music establishment in the shape of a school inflexibly run by Hanson in those early years.

Wilder was not so preoccupied by his experiences at Eastman that he stopped riding the trains. Indeed, he was constantly traveling, constantly escaping, glorying in the steam locomotives, reveling in the luxury of distance and silence, of birdsong and new mornings, and of new beginnings. Familiar to many was the sight of this man, with his long, creased face looking as if he had slept in it, clutching a fat dog-eared volume of railroad timetables as he waited for a train. He was a master of scheduling, stringing together cities and villages by rail as if he were working on a piece of tapestry. He knew all the branch lines, all the spurs. Louis Ouzer remembers from the Eastman days that "Alec was often absent on train rides in the U.S. and Canada. He knew all the timetables. I went with him once to Interlochen, the trip being timed to take a look at another steam engine. . . . Trains gave him privacy."

When the first telephone was installed on the *Empire State Express,* a drunken Wilder called Ouzer to say he was clocking the telephone poles as they flashed by: "One-and-two-and-POLE, two-and-three-and-POLE." Ouzer was familiar, too, with Wilder's custom of always taking a train at Christmas so that he would not be alone in his hotel room. "He would take a train—it didn't matter where it was going—so he could be among people (and yet apart from them) and watch the scenes go by. He liked the motion of the train and the feeling of hugging the earth." Although Wilder by this time knew that it was the world of music to which he most belonged, the trains were never far away:

> Music was the constant factor, the dominating compulsion but never to the exclusion of my love of railroads, of reading, of spending time in strange communities. I say "strange" because, in spite of my love for a few people, I still preferred to spend most of my time alone and I was happier in towns where I knew nobody, had no fear of the phone ringing, no threat of appointments or dinner dates.

Fittingly, it was during one of his train rides to New York that Wilder tried to come to grips with some of the things he had been learning as a music student. Yes, he had found Professor Royce stultifying and the school climate uncongenial, but he had stayed around. He had studied no orchestration, though he had read a book about it by Cecil Forsythe. He recalled the author's reminder that the orchestra has no pedal, "obviously a warning to those who composed at the piano." His first efforts at orchestration, he told himself, hadn't sounded too bad to him all the same. He was to say later about his Eastman studies:

> I am reminded of a lovely spring afternoon in 1930 when I took the Empire State Express to New York. In those days it had an open end observation car, and a stylish dining car filled with cheerful waiters. I had taken along my first musical notebook. . . . That afternoon I looked over what I had written. As I recall, they were pieces ranging from 16 to 32 measures. And that afternoon, as I looked at them, I was ecstatic, not because they were good, but because I had written them. I was a composer. There was the proof. Of course I wasn't a composer at all. I was an unschooled young man who wanted to create something and I certainly hadn't learned how to. But, darn it! There were the notes and the bar lines. It must be something.

No record remains of those first exercises, or of a few pieces he says he wrote for piano, for flute, and for cello. Sibley Music Library, however, has eight songs he wrote in 1928 for voice and orchestra from the poems of James Stephens, including *The Ancient Elf* ("I am the maker"); *And It Was Windy Weather* ("Now the winds are riding by"); *And on That Mind-Blinding Hue* ("And on that mind-blinding hue to gaze an instant"); *Besides That* ("If I could get to heaven"); *Chill of the Eve* ("A long green swell slopes soft to the sea"). He also wrote the song *Annabelle Lee* from a text by Edgar Allan Poe ("It was many and many a year ago"). In 1929 he wrote *Symphonic Piece,* with its troubled French horn section, which had its premiere in Eastman's Kilbourn Hall in June of that year.

In addition to the so-called serious music, Wilder was also going back and forth with popular song. His music bridgings began early. On the night that Hanson was conducting the performance of his *Symphonic Piece,* Wilder in the speakeasy heard over the radio something that made him jump out of his chair: "It was a voice the like of which I'd never heard and seldom have since. It was true as a springtime bird, young, innocent, ingenious in its phrasing and free of cliche. It was marvelous Mildred Bailey singing with Paul Whiteman." He could not know then that she would one day become a close friend and a singer of his songs. Until *Symphonic Piece* for orchestra, he had attempted nothing more ambitious than concert songs:

> I think I have a natural flair for melody, and tunes have always come easy. But much as I love to write them, they don't provide an adequate emotional reward. And that's why I was trying to learn how to handle the larger, more complex forms. And [the performance of *Symphonic Piece*] tonight was to be the proof that I could do it (less the horn parts). Yet here I was in a speak-easy listening to Mildred Bailey and loving it. And it's been like that ever since, loving both.

In the student days, Wilder wrote a number of tunes with specific singers in mind—Mildred Bailey, Ethel Waters, and Bing Crosby: "Mildred wound up singing some, Ethel Waters none, and, at the end of his career, Crosby a few." Although it did not appear until 1941, *Soft as Spring* was written during the Eastman years. The occasion was a springtime excursion by auto into the country with a friend: "We stopped on an unpaved country road and just sat there. Lilacs were in full bloom beside a deserted farm, and a joyous chorus of birds were celebrating life and love. My friend and I almost thumbed our noses at old age and all such dreary impossibilities." Back at Eastman, Wilder rushed down to the basement and wrote the tune in an empty practice room.

However, it was not the serious music or the individual songs that Wilder was most known and remembered for at Eastman, but a highly successful musical revue, *Haywire,* that played twice in Kilbourn Hall in 1933 (April 3 and 4) and more or less wound up his days at the school. There are several accounts of how the show originated. Fellow student Mitch Miller has said, "He was a very complicated man. I forced him to face his own talent, however. I got him to write *Haywire.*" Wilder recalled that "some tacky fraternity kids [Phi Mu Alpha Sinfonia] approached me to write a show. They had, I think, $400. I frankly don't remember consulting them about any aspect of the show. I wrote all of it, skits, lyrics, music."

No money was made from the revue, which Wilder said cost much more than the $400. Although some lyrics were provided by Frank Baker and Leighou Little, and there were one or two interpolated musical numbers, this was basically a Wilder show and full of his wit. He gave one of his songs about a marriage proposal the title *Howd'ya Like My Name on Your Tombstone?* A mocking tone poem, *By Bicycle Through the Mohawk Valley,* had three movements: *Syracuse ma non Utica; Utica ma non Albany; Albany and That Dream Girl O'Mine.* A series of asterisks was attached to the tone poem's title: *First Performance in Rochester; **First Performance in United States; ***First Performance in Entire World; ****Last Performance. Wilder was positive that he had stolen *Howd'ya Like My Name on Your Tombstone?* from P. G. Wodehouse's *Leave It to Psmith.* He reread the book without finding any reference to it but did, in any case, write to Wodehouse to tell him of the filching. Wodehouse didn't write back on that occasion, although he later responded generously when Wilder, in the course of writing *American Popular Song,* asked him about his collaboration with Jerome Kern.

Shortly before the *Haywire* opening, Wilder hid for a time in a movie theater showing *The Sign of the Cross.* Surreptitiously returning before the curtain went up, he watched it turn into a "howling success." Cast, chorus, and orchestra were very talented, and the local reviews would be highly complimentary. Rochester band-leader and composer Carl Dengler tells of what followed the last curtain call. Wilder and others had arranged for a bootlegger to make a preshow delivery to the basement of Kilbourn Hall for a party after the show. But either the chosen locker had been carelessly filled or its door was incautiously opened by the partiers, for the bottles crashed onto the floor and the sweet sickly smell of bathtub gin permeated the "halls of academe." Several students were subsequently dismissed.

Even so, nothing could dent the positive reception given to the witty, melodious *Haywire.* It had been a good showcase for Wilder's talents, and it had also exposed him to contemporaries his money and his timidity had separated him from before:

> It was a revelation for me to find boys from truly poor families coping with their poverty, laughing at it, doing extra jobs while studying music. These students opened up a giant slice of life for me, and without them I probably would have remained a rabbity stick-in-the-mud. Frank Baker, Sam Richlin, Nate Emanuel, Huntington Burdick, John Barrows, George Finckel, Rosemary Finckel, John Celentano, Emanuel Balaban, Bernard Rogers, Herbert Inch and many others turned me into a slightly less frightened person and gave me a more realistic approach to the business of functioning in an alien world.

Haywire almost sent Wilder on his way musically. One man who saw the show was Leopold Mannes, coinventor of Kodachrome, the color film that had so much to do with Eastman Kodak's success. He liked the score so well that he used one of his many connections in New York and made an appointment for Wilder with a Broadway producer. In high hopes, Wilder traveled to New York on the *Empire State Express* with Frank Baker, who had sung tenor in *Haywire*. Standing on the open observation platform of the last car on a lovely June evening, Wilder listened as Baker sang *Stormy Weather*: "I'll never forget the effect it had on me. God bless Harold Arlen!" On arriving to keep the appointment with producer Dwight Deere Wiman, they were told he was in Moline.

Much later Wilder learned that the receptionist had mistakenly sent them away; Wiman's assistant was to have seen them in his absence. Said Wilder later:

> We never went back. I suppose that goof changed the course of my life. For even had that assistant not liked the score, my hunch is that he would have wanted to hear the next one, and, lacking in assurance as I am, I think there would have been acceptance of my talent within a short time, which would have turned me into a show writer, successful possibly. A ghastly speculation.

No one could better rationalize a missed chance than Alec Wilder. Opportunity and success would often go by him like a fast train in the night, leaving him waving from the other side of the platform.

4

His Mentor

It was also during the Eastman years that Wilder found a substitute for the father he never had, James Sibley Watson Jr., and through him would gain his first exposure to filmmaking and film scoring. Watson was a true renaissance figure: physician, major influence in American literature in the 1920s, translator of French poetry, pioneer in radiology and in amateur filmmaking, artist, flyer, expert marksman, inventor, millionaire philanthropist. This man of many brilliances would become mentor, father confessor, and financial backer to Wilder.

Watson and his first wife, Hildegarde Lasell Watson, highly talented in her own right, were both impressed by Wilder when they met him. "The first time I saw Alec Wilder," she was to recall, "he was standing with his friend, the black porter, at the door of the Sagamore Hotel on East Avenue. He was striking looking enough to make me turn as we whirled by in a car, wondering who that young man could be." She was no less struck when Wilder made his first visit to their home soon after:

> When he entered the living room, Sibley and I were standing by the fireplace. There was a fragrance from burning logs of apple wood, a pleasant atmosphere. I was impressed then, and as always, seeing Sibley and Alec together. Almost immediately, Alec began to converse—these meetings continued all the years. . . . So unlike anyone we ever met: composer, poet, wit, a conversationalist—his words flaring at a touch, as of a match to a rocket, often charming, in fact almost always so, even when, at times, lewd (my only procurable word) but wonderfully to bring others into that mesmeric circle with him as a mimic, never allowing his talent to offend, the center wherever he appears (I never saw it otherwise) in a whirlpool of his admirers—any one of these acts of his possible on a Broadway stage.

It was in connection with filmmaking that Watson and Wilder first became aware of each other. A story of Watson's work in that field appears in the University of

Rochester's winter 1975 *Library Bulletin.* Watson, with Melville Webber, produced two films that became landmarks in American cinematography: *The Fall of the House of Usher* (1929) and *Lot in Sodom* (1932), both still regarded as minor classics. In the words of film archivist James Card, "Watson produced avant-garde films long before there were avant-garde films." In 1941 Watson was named a Fellow of the Amateur Cinema League for his contributions to the development of motion pictures as an art form.

Wilder has told how he came to be involved in Watson's life. Sitting one day in 1930 in Eastman's main hall, he became aware of the presence of a solemn-looking stranger. "I wouldn't have been surprised to learn he was a dairy farmer dressed up for a day in the city." The man smiled rather lopsidedly and asked if Wilder would like to act in a movie. "All the most nourishing rewards of my life have resulted from fortuities. And this meeting with Remsen Wood, a painter (and never of cattle), was one of the greatest of these." Had he not been there just at that precise time on that very day, he said, he might have missed a unique experience and a friendship that would survive the wear and tear of almost half a century. Bizarrely enough, Wood said he was scouting the town for a "sex-besotted butler," and Wilder had that look. "Irony of ironies!" reacted Wilder. "I was a virgin, terrified and deeply suspicious of all females except little girls and elderly women! But when I learned the person who was planning to make the film was the Watson who was part owner of *The Dial* magazine, I contained my fears and agreed to go up to the filming place for a screen test."

Wood had begun to work with Watson on a film about a butler who becomes sexually obsessed with a maid hired to serve at a large dinner party—the film would be called *The Dinner Party.* Wilder had heard about the earlier experimental film production in Rochester based on Poe's story, *The Fall of the House of Usher.* The other guiding hand in the filmmaking was Meville Webber, scenarist, idea man, scene painter, costume designer, makeup man, and director.

Watson was an extremely tall, thin, craggy man, desperately shy, given to the most minimal speech. "But," said Wilder, "I soon learned that he loved to laugh and was particularly tickled by outrageous puns. I knew I would be a dud were I to attempt to speak knowledgeably of literary matters, so I stuck to buffoonery as a way to his affection." Watson was to say of Wilder: "He helped us no end in the recruiting of actors. He knew how to coax exactly the right expression from performers of both sexes. Hence he was in constant demand to direct any of our scenes that depended on facial expression. Not only that: When on the set, he could put the whole crew in a good humor. It was a gift."

Watson had become seriously interested in motion-picture photography after *The Dial* stopped publication. He began referring to himself as an "independent film producer," though he frankly confessed that no one in the group, least of all himself, had had any experience with professional film production. The "studio" where the films were being made was the old carriage house behind Watson's father's home on Prince Street. Part of the building was being used as a garage for automobiles, including an "electric," the fashionable vehicle of the 1920s powered by batteries recharged nightly. Outside was a spacious area that served as a kind of village green for the bordering houses, all but one occupied by members of the Watson and Sibley families. Undoubtedly, recalled Wilder, it symbolized wealth, but it was beautiful as well and made him feel safer than he had in years: "Oh, my, my, what happy, laughing gemutlich days those were. No threats, no deadlines, no competition, no cigar-chewing 'backers,' no venom. Of course I'm sure there were moments of irritation and tension and differences of opinion, but they couldn't have been of any magnitude for I'm sure I'd remember."

The film about the butler, *The Dinner Party,* was apparently the brainchild of Hildegarde Watson, but it was never finished. The day Wilder arrived to learn if he would be a suitably lascivious butler, the cubist sets used in *The Fall of the House of Usher* were still standing. Later he was given a showing of the Usher film in which Hildegarde Watson played the role of the doomed sister. "The film," said Wilder, "is not only an extraordinary cinematic achievement and one of almost unbearable suspense, but it has continued to this day to create the illusion that it is at least 45 minutes long. When I was told it ran only 13 minutes, I refused to believe it."

Soon after the showing, Wilder was asked by Watson to do a background score for *The Fall of the House of Usher.* Wilder agreed, reluctantly. Though he felt honored, he was uncertain that he was up to the task: "I had, after all, only recently learned enough about music to write even a short piece of any merit. . . . To compose a score to span 13 long minutes—long, that is, to a person who had managed to turn out only pieces lasting a few minutes at most—seemed an awesome task." However, he set to work ambitiously on a score for an eighteen-piece orchestra, no less. It was not a success. "Ah, the innocence of youth! For had even a superior conductor ever attempted to record the score, with its many synchronization points, he would have broken his baton into slivers." When the time came for Wilder to play a pianoforte reduction of his score to the showing of the film, things did not go well—the consequence, he said, of "my extreme nervousness, my monstrously bad piano playing, my inability to watch the music and the screen simultaneously (for the purpose of synchronizing the music with picture), the inadequate light for reading the music, and the presence of an audience." The score was shelved.

Years later, after the film had become famous in cinematic circles and had been given a sound track of recorded music, Hildegarde Watson asked Wilder if he would try again to score it. This time he did so more modestly, for six players, and limited the synchronizations. Then he obtained the services of what he considered to be the best woodwind quintet in the world in those days, and one he was to become closely associated with in later years: the New York Woodwind Quintet. He also found a fine conductor: "This glorious man, Leon Barzin, is one of the most extraordinary talents I have ever encountered in my long life among musicians. And I am honored that he has respected me and agreed to conduct not only the score to this film but others as well."

The Rochester filmmakers chose for their next experiment the Genesis account of Sodom and Gomorrah. They called it *Lot in Sodom;* Hildegarde Watson played Lot's wife. During the production, Wilder seemed to be everywhere. He took a hand at direction, once with dramatic results. In the scene where Lot tries desperately to stop the Sodomites from breaking into his home, Wilder suddenly shouted out a four-letter word and thereby achieved the effect he felt the film needed: a look of consternation on Lot's face. Wilder displayed other talents. According to Hildegarde Watson, he "imitated to perfection the most flagrantly homosexual types in the film." He also did the casting and coaxing of the effeminate, lavishly costumed Sodomites.

Although his role was a limited one, Wilder always took great pride in the fact that *The Fall of the House of Usher* and *Lot in Sodom* became minor classics. Artistically and technically, both broke important ground. Later in his career, Wilder would compose the scores for a number of short films, and he would also do a stint in Hollywood with lyricist William Engvick. His work with Watson on these pioneering amateur films served as his introduction to this exciting new medium. That early association between Wilder and Watson was also the beginning of a friendship that was to last fifty years and was to be one of the great joys of Wilder's life. In 1975 he wrote to Watson from the Algonquin Hotel. "Forgive me, my most patient and loving and constant friend for subjecting my tribulations upon you. But you are, and always have been, my mentor, my spiritual and creative stanchion."

In Watson, Wilder seemed to find the qualities he might have wished for in his own father. His autobiographical *Letters I Never Mailed* was dedicated to Watson, who was older by twelve years, but whose bearing made the difference seem greater. The generous-hearted millionaire who dressed in almost-shabby clothes was a man of the keenest intellect who stayed remote and anonymous even in a world growing ever more personal. Both men came from privileged families, and both possessed sharp, searching minds. Watson was the son of the head of two Rochester banks and the grandson of a cofounder of Western Union Telegraph. As Wilder was also able to do, he lived his life exactly as he chose, but with vastly more money behind him.

Popular Rochester author and columnist Henry Clune has written of Watson:

As the only living son of a family that possessed an ocean-going steam yacht, Sibley Watson was indulged. He was able to travel at will. He played polo. He won ribbons with saddle horses at the Rochester Horse Show. He flew an airplane of his own, and frightened the wits out of Alec Wilder, the witty, distinguished and prolific Rochester composer, when he flew from Rochester to Portland, Maine, in an era when Wilder (with poetic license) averred there was no landing field between the two cities. "I really shouldn't have worried," Wilder said admiringly. "Sibley put that plane up perfectly, flew it perfectly, and put it down perfectly, with the kind of genius he has."

The intellect Wilder so admired in Watson had its most public expression in the 1920s when *The Dial* magazine was flourishing. Watson, the scholar who translated Rimbaud from the French and Catullus from the Latin, had wanted most of all to be a writer. When he found he could not write to his own satisfaction, he provided a forum for others by buying *The Dial* in 1919. It was then a languishing leftish Chicago review. Another wealthy Harvard graduate, Scofield Thayer, was his partner in the venture. When they moved *The Dial* to Manhattan, it began publishing what Watson and Thayer considered the best art and literature of the time—work by James Joyce, Ezra Pound, William Carlos Williams, Marianne Moore, e.e. cummings. *The Dial* was critical to the careers of many artists. T. S. Eliot's *The Wasteland* appeared in its pages when the poet was struggling. It gave a year's income to Joyce when *Ulysses* was being censored.

This was all part of the formidable reputation of the man Alec Wilder came to respect above all others. Wilder was also to come to know well the woman Watson married, Hildegarde Lasell, heiress to a Massachusetts manufacturing fortune. No less indulged than Watson, she belonged to a gilded, highborn world now long past. It was a world Wilder enjoyed hearing about and sometimes glimpsing. In her memoir, *The Edge of the Woods,* Hildegarde Watson recalled the days when she and her sister took dancing lessons from a Frenchman: "Like little ships with their sails up, our sashes in wide bows behind, stiff hair ribbons as spinakers on top of our head, we would hurry breezily into the ballroom, there bowing, hand on midriff, to our partners." There was skating after school on a small pond; a bonfire was kept blazing on the edge of a pine grove. "Sometimes my sparkling Aunt Mary Lasell would be there, making graceful figure eights, dressed in a dark trim suit and a long, swirling skirt and looking like a heroine out of a Tolstoy novel." Hildegarde Watson had something of Wilder's wonder about the world. She once asked sensitively:

Where are they gone, those few places, fewer and fewer, to sit in, on the outskirts of time? . . . I came, one soft night, on a very young couple sitting hand in hand against a Fifth Avenue store, feet outstretched on the sidewalk, looking up and talking to a small patch of sky, the dim stars barely flickering over blazing New York, indifferent there to passing pedestrians—not even, for them, a waiting bench.

A many-talented woman, Hildegarde Watson was an accomplished soprano who made several concert tours in the United States, Canada, and Europe in the 1930s.

Prominent musicians and writers were often guests in the Watson home. She has recalled that the opera *Four Saints in Three Acts* was given for the first time in their Rochester home, with composer Virgil Thomson playing and singing all the leading parts in a "high pretty tenor." This, in itself, she said, was a tour de force, though not fully appreciated by several sleeping dignitaries.

The friendship between Watson and Wilder was in some respects an unlikely one, for each often had trouble understanding the other's genius. Wilder was to say that he learned from Watson "many mysterious things the meaning of which I'm not certain of to this day, but which I think I have revealed a somewhat foggy notion of in the hundreds of (dare I call them) poems I've written." Long before their first meeting, Watson's *Dial* had exposed Wilder to the higher reaches of the human mind. However, he admitted he did not always grasp what he was reading. He bought the magazine "as might have a Roman Christian the new chapters of the New Testament, but I found most of its pages tough sledding and some incomprehensible."

If Watson's mind was always to be difficult for Wilder, Watson for his part had little feeling for Wilder's music or for any music. Though he had many of Wilder's records, it is not known that he ever listened to them. Nancy Watson Dean, Watson's second wife, has said that her husband simply did not care for music. She remembers when his mother's piano in the Sibley Place home had become too dry to tune; time had shrunk the pegs. Nancy wanted to know if she could get them fixed. Said Watson: "If you do that, someone will play the piano." "Then you don't want it fixed?" "No."

Watson's indifference to music notwithstanding, Wilder's friendship with him was almost worshipful. Wilder wrote from Michigan in 1961: "Dear Doctor Watson. Had I any degree of stature, dignity, intellect, maturity, my respect for you would be worthy, but for a maze-addled mouse to salaam the wisest creature in the kingdom is both pathetic and ludicrous." Wilder was irreverent toward most people but never lost his awe of Watson—his mind, his formidable bearing, his puzzling reticence. The care with which both men observed the proprieties strengthened the relationship. Until the later years, they remained to each other "Dr. Watson" and "Mr. Wilder." One witness to this formality was Wilder's other lifelong Rochester friend, Louis Ouzer. In the early 1930s Wilder rented a summer cottage on Canandaigua Lake just south of Rochester. Word came of an impending flying visit by Watson. Recalls Ouzer:

> There were the early brave days of the aeroplane. I remember I walked with
> Alec to a farm field. There we waited and watched as a small cub plane
> owned and piloted by Dr. Watson made its landing. Dr. Watson stepped out.
> He and Alec looked at each other and smiled and greeted each other and
> bowed. Then shortly after, Dr. Watson flew off again, wings flapping in sa-

lute. Both were tall men, Watson especially, and the solemn bow they exchanged beside the plane seemed strangely ritualistic.

Among Watson's unusual qualities was an almost soundless presence. Everyone remarked on it. Wilder said "he moved like an Indian in a forest." Poet Marianne Moore, a friend of the family and a recipient of Watson's philanthropy, said of him: "He stimulates part of the landscape as if he weren't implicated in it and yet he's all alert in there and responsible—so wary you hardly dare breathe, for fear you might be threatening his technique." A memorable portrait was provided by another friend, the English novelist and essayist Llewelyn Powys (1884–1939). In the spring of 1924, Powys was invited by Watson to join him on an expedition into the Rocky Mountains. Powys had known Watson in New York City and had observed him closely:

> It used to amuse me to watch him drifting through life with the unresisting adaptability of a long, drooping straw caught in the current of a lively trout stream. He was enormously rich, and yet liked to appear poor. He was extremely wise, yet preferred to be thought foolish. With a small black bag, held in the long, sensitive fingers of an artist, he was to be encountered on a perpetual drooping peregrination through the sidestreets of Greenwich Village.

Watson, Powys also noted, was a very able physician who never practiced, a good writer who never wrote, a man possessed of a strong, subtle mind that he sought to conceal. His extraordinary presence was well caught by Powys: "He made me think of those silent, evasive eels one hears about, eels that find their way to the ocean from remote ponds, sliding their sinuous bodies through night-dusky, dew-drenched pastures." Silent and soundless and disembodied though Watson may have been, he and Hildegarde always made Wilder welcome, whether the family was in town or country. There were many idyllic days on Hildegarde's family farm near Northbridge Center in Massachusetts. "The country undulated around us," she remembered, "into fields, woods and pale blue distant hills. There were flowers among the pines and the scarlet cardinals and wild orchids against a moss-covered mill race." The house was always full of people. Once, a stage of logs was constructed on one of the ponds for the presentation of Gilbert and Sullivan's *Pinafore*. Wilder was often part of the scene.

Those were watershed days for Wilder. He once described them as "lovely springtime years which were perhaps the happiest of my life. I came to know Dr. Watson very well. Indeed so well that he has been my mentor and confidant ever since. I have written him hundreds of letters, hundreds of pieces of verse and have received sometimes highly cryptic, often very profound letters in return. It has been the great friendship of my life."

Filmmaker Jerome Hill, for whom Wilder would write a number of scores, once said that everyone who became a friend of Alec Wilder's was turned into a mail drop. To no one, however, did he unburden himself more completely than to Watson. Letters, poetry, and short stories were to flood into Sibley Place for the next half century. Wilder would have been crushed had he known that Watson paid them scant attention. According to Nancy Watson Dean, he made little comment on them. He did not, however, throw them away, for he deeply respected creativity and would do nothing to discourage Wilder. Perhaps it was enough that he was willing to serve as a repository. Wilder had a place to put his thoughts and musings while he pursued his career in music.

5

Bridging the Tributaries

Although he always maintained that he never made a plan in his life, Wilder's return to New York in the mid-1930s to try his luck at popular song and lyric writing and arranging was both sought and inevitable. With his inheritance now spent, he had a need to make some money. Visits through the years had made the Algonquin a home base, and there he could press his nose against the window and watch the famous come and go. Musically, his collision with Howard Hanson and the departure of close colleagues John Barrows and Mitch Miller had diminished Rochester's appeal. His ties to the school and to mentor Sibley Watson would always be secure, but he could advance his career only in New York.

There had been plenty of stirrings. For years he had been writing unpublished songs for singers such as Ethel Waters, and very early he had been pulled toward popular music by the writings of Jerome Kern, Vincent Youmans, and Harold Arlen, whose 1930 song *Sweet and Hot* had electrified Wilder. In the late 1920s, during one of the many jaunts he made from Rochester to New York, he had met a "smiling fellow" named Eddie Brandt and written "frightful" lyrics to some of his tunes. One was called *Yes, Today? No! Yesterday.* They were not all as bad as that one, and the better ones they hawked to the song-publishing houses on Tin Pan Alley. "Did I sing them? I doubt it, as Eddie was a singer-piano player." They made a tin record and left it at the stage door of the first *Little Show* for Marian Harris, one of the first good pop singers.

In 1930 Wilder had formally entered the world of popular song with *All the King's Horses,* a song he had written with Brandt; Howard Dietz provided the lyrics. It was included in the 1930 Broadway revue *Three's a Crowd,* starring Libby Holman, Fred Allen, and Clifton Webb. It was a good, lively tune on its way to becoming a hit, but any hope that it might have a life beyond the show was ruined when an English song came out about the same time with an almost identical title, *The King's Horses:* "And that was the end of our song, except that it was kept in the show." Wilder did wryly note that the loss was not total "insofar as one of my stuffed shirt uncles had heard the English song and presumed it was mine. I did nothing to disabuse him of his error. As a result, he became less hostile to the shocking fact of my being a musician."

Wilder was not having much luck in getting his work noticed. His song *Time and Tide* in the 1934 *Thumbs Up!* revue apparently drew favorable notices during the out-of-town tryouts but was dropped for some untold reason before the show got to Broadway. Wilder learned later that composer Vernon Duke had argued to keep the tune in the revue. Bill Engvick considers *Time and Tide* one of Wilder's most effective melodies, but it remains unpublished today. Wilder had had a taste of the popular-song world, however, and the local success in Rochester of his 1933 show *Haywire* convinced him he had a talent worth developing. Clearly a city as off the beaten track as Rochester could not provide a launch pad, yet success kept eluding him in New York.

Part of the problem was the stiff competition. "As great as Alec was," Mitch Miller has pointed out, "among those writing at that time were Irving Berlin, Richard Rodgers, Arthur Schwartz, Harold Arlen. . . . These were his heroes and these are the guys Alec wrote his book about. . . . Publishers weren't interested in taking chances on somebody new." Nor was Wilder capable of writing the robust kind of songs that might have sent him over the top. Instead, he was turning out the slender, sensitive, elusive melodies that were to be his hallmark. He might as well have been singing Schubert lieder to a baseball crowd, and he knew it.

> I couldn't turn out the ordinary song. My sights were too high and I couldn't, no matter how I tried, write straightforward, unsophisticated tunes. I would have been proud to have written a song as spare and direct as *Sing Something Simple* or *Jeepers Creepers*. It wasn't that I was overtrained musically; I think I was potentially a theater writer, even if I never managed to sell a score.

Wilder would go backstage one night to see Count Basie, for he loved his band. Basie told Wilder he would like him to write some music for the band, "but you've got to go to college to play your kind of music." But more than the nature of his writing was involved. Constitutionally, Wilder was incapable of pushing and plugging his songs in the manner of the day. He could not and would not shill for himself, and was indeed often appalled by the world of popular song he found himself in. He didn't like the tawdry people he met. He recalled once having to see a "dreadful" publisher because he wanted him to sign a contract for a song. The man was typical of that breed: "illiterate, cheap, greedy, corrupt and as sensitive as a stone." The publisher took Wilder to task for having the reputation of being a nut, a screwball, and implied that he would have to pull himself together if he wanted to get anywhere. "He took me to one of the windows overlooking 50th Street and 6th Avenue. He pointed at a billboard on a low building across the street. It was an ad for liquor. The man said to me: 'That's what you are: a product. You shouldn't sell your music, you should sell yourself.'"

The disenchanted Wilder could always retreat from Tin Pan Alley to the clubs and cabarets and stages frequented by such famous artists and personages as Mildred Bailey and Libby Holman. Here he could brush shoulders with and occasionally meet some of the people he deeply admired, such as that superb lyricist Lorenz Hart. In the theater, too, Wilder was able to find some guiding lights. There was a memorable introduction to Libby Holman, an inimitable torch singer whose personal life was to become tragically haunted; Wilder would one day know her well. The first occasion was a performance of *The Little Show,* a revue. According to biographer Jon Bradshaw:

> When Libby appeared on stage in a dark cerise gown to sing 'Can't We Be Friends?' the audience rose to its feet. The young composer Alec Wilder was in the audience that night. He watched as Libby stood in a slit in the curtain singing 'Can't We Be Friends?' She sang very slowly and stood perfectly stationary. 'A freak,' Wilder later said, 'but so dramatic. Such daring, the balls of it.' It was one of the most theatrical moments he had ever seen.

It was not in songwriting but in arranging for radio, then sweeping the country, that Wilder first got off the ground. Today, when radio no longer is the sole measurer of the pulse of the nation, it is hard to realize the great impact it had in the 1920s and 1930s—on music, on drama, on comedy, on news. During the fifteen minutes that *Amos and Andy* was on the air each night, the whole nation came to a stop. Vaudevillians Ed Wynn, Eddie Cantor, Jack Benny, Red Skelton, Will Rogers, and George Burns and Gracie Allen in their new venue were household names. Bing Crosby, Kate Smith, Nat King Cole, Al Jolson, Rudy Vallee, Frank Sinatra, and Dinah Shore were among the many who became popular vocalists. The audience buildup was big for individual vocalists, for the *Bell Telephone Hour,* the *Ford Hour,* the *Prudential Family Hour,* and for the dance music of Tommy and Jimmy Dorsey, Paul Whiteman, Guy Lombardo, Percy Faith, Benny Goodman, and many more. Radio now did the song-plugging that vaudeville used to do. Music arrangers became more and more in demand for broadcast music.

Wilder always said he owed much of his successful entry into the growing body of arrangers to his Eastman colleague Jimmy Carroll. During his student days, Carroll often played saxophone, clarinet, and trumpet with his brothers Leonard (guitar) and Frank (bass) in the old Eggleston Hotel in Rochester. Wilder said he first met Carroll when he burst into a practice cubicle where Wilder was working on the *Haywire* revue at Eastman. He told Wilder that he played both clarinet and trumpet and could orchestrate. Wilder recalled:

> He was then Jimmy Caruana, who changed his name later to Carroll because of the inevitable rhyme and became one of my best friends. Indeed, he is to

this day a saintly man and one of the very best clarinetists I've ever heard. He has made a fortune out of the Sing Along television show but is unhappy, living in Los Angeles in the arms of a Moog synthesizer and doing little creative work. Rock music has made many talented musicians cynical, sad and broke.

Wilder said that Carroll taught him most of what he knew about arranging, helping him to adjust his style and, God forbid, become a little more commercial. Rochester composer and bandleader Carl Dengler recalls that music totally absorbed Carroll. "Some times he would never get out of his apartment in the Woodward Hotel at the corner of 6th [Avenue] and 57th Street for three or four days, just writing. He smoked those little Cuban cigars, and you had to cut your way through the smoke." At one point in the 1940s, Carroll had the Lucky Strike, Chock Full o' Nuts, and other big radio accounts. He would write and arrange commercial jingles for a time slot of a minute or two. When he had written a score, Dengler recalls, Carroll would take it to his brother Leonard, who lived in a downstairs apartment of the hotel. Leonard, regarded by Wilder as one of the very best copyists in New York, would then take the score and make out the individual instrumental parts.

If Carroll helped give Wilder the requisite skills, it was Mitch Miller who provided the opening by securing for him the job of staff arranger for the 1936 CBS Friday night radio show *Ford Hour.* As this chapter makes clear, Miller time and again did his best to push his foot-dragging friend up the ladder to success. Wilder did his Ford arranging for a fine thirty-six-piece band in which Miller played oboe and English horn and that included such other great players as Mannie Klein (trumpet), Charlie Spivak (trumpet), Charlie Margulies (trumpet), Will Bradley (trombone), and Toots Mondello (alto sax). Not everything went smoothly. Apparently thoroughly disliking the static harmony of Cole Porter's *De-Lovely,* Alec introduced his own changes: "Even the Bach-oriented organist conductor could sense the ineptness of my alterations and spoke rather harshly to me from the podium. Though only ten o'clock in the morning, I removed myself quickly to Hurley's Bar where I got crocked." He was able to make amends with several fine numbers: a swinging arrangement of Bach's *Fugue in G-minor* in which he kept every note but had everyone play dance style; "a truly swinging" arrangement of Debussy's *Golliwog's Cakewalk;* and also the first popular music orchestration of Ravel's lovely *Pavane. Golliwog's Cakewalk,* orchestrated by Carroll and Wilder, was played by Rex Chandler's orchestra in a broadcast on March 19, 1937.

The position of staff arranger with the *Ford Hour* was apparently well paid, but Wilder could not tolerate what he felt was its tyranny and left. But Miller was not about to give up on Wilder, and he would be mainly responsible for Wilder's writing of the famous woodwind octets recorded as The Alec Wilder Octet. The relationship between the two men was not an easy one. Wilder was often ambivalent and not always completely fair in his attitude toward Miller, his colleague from the Eastman School. Their backgrounds were very different. Wilder was the wealthy, elegant young man descended from an impeccably WASP family, he told Whitney Balliett, that "lived that whole ambience of voting Republican and hating the Jews. They didn't really *hate* of course. They just maintained the proper prejudices." Miller was the son of a poor wrought-iron worker and a woman who had been a seamstress in the Russian czar's summer palace outside Warsaw. Both parents were Jews who had emigrated to the United States in 1904. "We never lacked for food," Miller has said, "but we never had anything else."

Music was the bond between these two talented men whose careers were to diverge so sharply. Miller became the popular entertainer who taught the world to sing along with a bouncing ball on a television screen. And when *Sing Along with Mitch* went off the air in 1967, millions continued to follow him through his record albums. Not all the buyers appreciated that back of the showman was a superb musician. Miller, who took up the oboe at eleven, was playing first oboe with the Syracuse Symphony at sixteen. The next year he won a full scholarship to Eastman, where he met Wilder. Miller remembers that soon after their meeting in the late 1920s, Wilder fell ill with the flu. "So what's the best thing for flu? I was living home so I got my mother to make chicken soup for him. I took over the soup to this bare apartment he was then living in on or near East Avenue. He got better and we became friends."

After graduating from Eastman, Miller went on tour with an orchestra organized by George Gershwin, and played in the pit for the original Broadway production of Gershwin's *Porgy and Bess*. Later, he became a house musician with the Columbia Broadcasting System. He played in various combinations, including the Andre Kostelanetz orchestra, and so impressed the maestro that his playing can be heard in all the Kostelanetz recordings. Miller was also the oboist on Charlie Parker's legendary *Charlie Parker With Strings* 1949–50 recording sessions.

It was the musician with a reputation as one of the world's foremost oboists and English horn players that Wilder so loved and admired. Miller, however, had other ambitions that sat less well with the uncompromising Wilder. With that strong entrepreneurial flair of his, Miller turned out a remarkable range of hit records by various artists for both the Mercury and the Columbia record labels. He had a genius for invention and improvisation. That enormus popular success was often seen by Wilder as a repudiation, certainly a neglect, by Miller of his talent as an incomparable oboist.

When Wilder was being completely honest, he fully acknowledged his long-standing debt to Miller:

> Mitchell Miller did a great deal for me not only by way of encouragement but
> by introducing me to people of power in musical circles in New York. I wrote

a lot of music for him, including a concerto which, ironically, he performed the same day that he became head of pop music at Columbia Recording Company. He's younger than I, but during those early years I turned to him, I'm sure, as a father figure. His approach to the rough world of business, with all its violence and corruption, was much more realistic than mine and naturally was of great help to me. He was my sponsor and spokesman.

Though his patience was often tried, Miller remained a steadfast admirer of Wilder the composer and the man. Late in 1938 he began playing a pivotal role in the Wilder woodwind octets. "Subtract Mitch," says James T. Maher, "and you subtract the octets, and subtract those and much is lost from Alec's career." Wilder has said that it was not until he wrote some of those octets for the old Brunswick Recording Company that he started to move ahead at all. The venture began curiously. Miller had been playing baroque music with an accomplished harpsichordist with the unlikely name of Yella Pessl. He had often thought about combining harpsichord and woodwinds. According to Wilder, Pessl had been asked by Paramount Pictures to make a short film. In addition to her regular repertoire of baroque works, they wanted her to play a "jazz" version of a concert piece. No doubt through Miller, Pessl knew Wilder was familiar with the jazz idiom, and she asked him to write something she could use in the film. Wilder was able to find a Couperin piece for harpsichord that suggested jazz rhythms, but before putting an arrangement on paper, he asked if he could try out Pessl's harpsichord. Miller took him to her apartment, and in the course of experimenting with the German-built instrument, Wilder fell in love with its sound.

The film venture went nowhere, but Miller prevailed on Joe Higgins, an official of the Brunswick Recording Company, to listen to some Wilder songs. On the morning of the audition, Wilder had a monumental hangover.

> I somehow managed to get dressed, into a cab and up to the office where I was to perform. By the time I got to the audition room, I was scarcely able to sit upright on the stool. I'd had no breakfast, no restorative, my mouth was dry as ashes and my head was throbbing. God knows what I sang for poor Joe. All I remember is that it seemed to put him into a state of shock. Mitchell was muttering and fidgeting; little wonder. For I had messed up whatever good fortune might have resulted from the audition. . . . I presume in desperation, Joe ignored the songs and asked me if I could write instrumental pieces and what instruments would I use for recording.

Thus the day was saved for the sodden Wilder. Yes, he told Higgins, he did indeed write instrumental music. Then, could he write some pieces in the style of Raymond Scott, who not long before had written and recorded a number of successful instrumentals for Brunswick?

Hung over as I was, my head splitting, my lips parched, I managed somehow to speak convincingly of my ability to write as well as Scott. When asked what instruments I would use, naturally I thought first of the oboe, Mitchell's instrument. Then I added flute, bassoon, clarinet, bass clarinet—all woodwinds—and, suddenly, I recalled the marvelous sounds the harpsichord made. So I added that. Later, I added bass and drums for rhythm. Thus, haphazardly, I arrived at an Octet."

A strikingly new ensemble sound was far from the mind of Brunswick's Higgins, more businessman than musician. However, his generous instincts had provided the opening. "I managed to get out of the office and into a bar without collapsing," said Wilder. "Mitchell, my sponsor and friend, was far from pleased with my dreadful behavior. But he did see that such a combination of woodwinds, and harpsichord, might make an interesting musical sound." Wilder wrote a sample piece, Miller gathered together some first-class players from the staff at CBS, and a rehearsal was held for the "bigwigs." The two who showed up were, said Wilder, the musically ignorant president of the company and "a young man with a cheery air and a bright look about him. But for him, nothing further would have come of the audition." His name was Morty Palitz, "a great musician and later a great friend and collaborator."

When Wilder found himself committed to writing some instrumental pieces, it was not the sophisticated novelty jazz of the Raymond Scott quintet that he drew upon. Much more in his mind, he told James Maher, were the strikingly different earlier compositions by Reginald Forsythe and Red Norvo. The ground they broke became his own point of departure.

Forsythe, well known in the jazz world in both New York and London, where he had been born, was the son of a black West African barrister and a German woman. He was an excellent pianist. In a famous recording session at Columbia in the early 1930s, a rare group of good studio musicians (Benny Goodman was on bass clarinet) played four small original compositions by Forsythe: *Dodging a Divorcee, Serenade to a Wealthy Widow, The Greener the Grass,* and *Melancholy Clown.* Cutting across the musical grain of the day, these little pieces with a chamber music quality were played constantly on the radio in 1933 and 1934. Eminent jazz critic and composer Leonard Feather has noted that Forsythe pioneered the use of woodwinds in a jazz ensemble, as Wilder would do in the octets.

Red Norvo, Wilder's other important creative influence, had by the end of the 1920s established the xylophone as a fixture in jazz. He was always the innovator. About 1931, shortly before Forsythe started catching the fancy of radio listeners with his pseudofugues, Norvo had composed a number of small, very different jazz "chamber music" pieces. He had a contract in 1933 with Brunswick Records and several of his lighter, more traditional numbers were recorded. However, he could never get a studio date for his more serious pieces. The then head of Bruns-

wick believed they had no commercial potential at all, so the compositions lan-
guished.

Fortunately, Norvo had a believer in Brunswick producer Palitz, the young man
who helped to get the Wilder octets recorded and who would later compose with
him two important popular songs, *While We're Young* and *Moon and Sand*. Palitz, a
fine musician with a fabulous ear, recognized the unusual merit of Norvo's more
daring compositions, just as surely as he knew the studio frowned upon them. So he
made special plans and ushered Norvo and several other players into the studio one
evening (most official recording was done during the day) for a tryout of several
numbers, notably Norvo's *Dance of the Octopus*.

It was an interesting linking of players—Benny Goodman, who had not then
broken into fame, was there with a borrowed bass clarinet, Artie Bernstein played
bass, and Dick McDonough was on guitar, its sound, at Norvo's suggestion, given a
soft Debussy quality through a felt pick rather than a plastic one. Norvo presided
over a five-octave marimba, wielding with flair the four hammers whose use he had
mastered not long before in Chicago. It was a difficult orchestral combination and
the players had had no rehearsal. Only a superb musician such as Palitz could have
managed the accoustics of the recording successfully. "A shot in the dark" was how
Palitz described the little conspiracy. The shot was not heard around the world but it
did eventually find a mark in England.

But first repercussions were swift and unpleasant. Norvo says that when the
test pressing came to the Brunswick boss, he called Norvo into his office, excoriated him for using his musicians and his valuable studio time to fool around with junk,
and then and there tore up his contract and tossed it into the wastebasket. Norvo
was so shattered by the experience that he destroyed about twenty more such
compositions. They could never be reconstructed. Fortunately for music and for the
octets, the story does not end there. The matrix (master mold) of the recording
somehow arrived in London with other matrices sent to English Brunswick. The
record was issued in London and became a critical hit, if not a popular one. The
English jazz critics knew they were hearing something extraordinary. As a result,
the recording had to be put out in the United States, where it became a milestone in
jazz recordings. "When Alec heard such wildflower inventions as *Dance of the
Octopus*," says Maher, "it absolutely turned him around." It was, then, the new
music of Norvo and Forsythe that he heard when he sat down to write the octets.

Wilder composed more than twenty pieces for the group gathered together by
Miller. They were billed on the Brunswick label as The Alec Wilder Octet. At a time
when no one used woodwinds in pop music and when only Artie Shaw used the
harpsichord, the impact of these charming, literate, impossible-to-categorize pieces
was sharp, on professional musicians particularly. The Wilder group did most of its
work in front of the microphone and must have set a benchmark for good human
chemistry. Those inspired players were Jimmy Carroll, clarinet; Eddie Powell,

flute; Mitch Miller, oboe; Frank Carroll (Jimmy's brother), bass; Harold Goltzer, bassoon; Toots Mondello and later Reggie Merrill, bass clarinet; Walter Gross, harpsichord; and Gary Gillis, drums.

The impact of the pieces was heightened by the fanciful titles Wilder bestowed on them. With perhaps one exception, the titles were not descriptive; this was not program music. The names were intended to be only whimsical and entertaining: *Sea Fugue Mama* (a play upon the phrase "I want some sea food, Mama," from the song *Hold Tight,* recorded by the Andrews Sisters); *It's Silk, Feel It* (suggested by an old friend from Rochester days, Sam Richlin); *Jack, This Is My Husband; The House Detective Registers; The Amorous Poltergeist; Neurotic Goldfish; A Debutante's Diary; Bull Fiddles in a China Shop; His First Long Pants; Her Old Man Was Suspicious; The Children Met the Train* (suggested by singer-arranger and author Kay Thompson), and so on. All the octet compositions were recorded, but the pressings were small. Though they gave Wilder a permanent niche in jazz, they conferred no wide fame. As critic Gene Lees was later to point out, the octet tracks were so new, so unfashionable, that only a few musicians understood what Wilder was doing.

That was to be true in great measure of most of Wilder's music, for he stubbornly declined to popularize it, maintaining that those who turned to music in order to make money and achieve fame were as contemptible as "old ladies' purse snatchers and about as much a part of creation." Wilder in later years found another reason to dismiss the octets: they were too far back in the past. He got tired of hearing people talk about them and ignore all his later work. Wilder by then had amassed a considerable body of most diverse work: popular and concert songs, chamber music, television scores, movie scores, musical comedies, short operas, and much else. Yet it was the happy, inventive, irreverent octets that first put Wilder on the music map. With their unique blend of jazz and popular and classical elements, they were daringly different enough to be historic.

When the octets first appeared with their curious mix of jazz rhythms and Bachlike melodies, the music world was both beguiled and puzzled. Wilder's highly personal idiom and his original approach kept the music fresh and free, and nearly all of it was notable for what was called a "sunny lack of banality." Indeed, so fruitfully inventive and unorthodox were their instrumentation and harmonization that it is hard to believe they were written as long ago as the late 1930s. Discerning musicians recognized their worth. Wilder himself said at one point that they had been well received by all manner of musicians from Dave Brubeck to Igor Stravinsky. Musicologist Charles W. Fox was to say later that the style of these little pieces "is so individual that they cannot be pigeon-holed. While they are based fundamentally upon jazz rhythms, they show many other features—traces of the impressionism of Debussy and Delius, melodies with the modal coloring of medieval music or folksong, irregular phrasing, contrapuntal devices such as fugato or ostinato."

In the broader spectrum of music, it was that same lack of a pigeonhole that condemned the octets to comparative obscurity. They were neither one tributary of music nor another. Like so much of Wilder's music, they fell between stools. As Wilder told Whitney Balliett, when the records came out they were gunned down by the jazz boys because they had a classical flavor, "and they were gunned down by the classical boys because they had a jazz flavor."

It was an undeserved passing over. Composer Warren Benson notes that many years after the octets, in the 1960s, the French vocal pop group known as the Swingle Singers achieved at least a measure of fame by doing much the same thing Wilder had done twenty-five years before. These were eight academically trained singers who, under the leadership of Ward Lemar Swingle and Christiane Legrande, developed a distinctive style with scat-singing arrangements of baroque and classical instrumental music. They toured both Europe and the United States and made several recordings. "They did what Alec had already done with the octets," says Benson. "No one ever said that. Nobody paid attention. Alec didn't play Bach, he played like Bach. These delightful non-pop tunes with pop idioms were also very much what LeRoy Anderson wrote, with *Sleigh Ride, Typewriter Concerto,* and so on."

Mitch Miller, excellent musician as well as stouthearted friend, has asserted that the octets are "the wellspring that all of the jazz chamber music came from." And just two or three years later, he gave Wilder's career another push, again on behalf of music that fitted into no category snugly. This time, however, Wilder had a famous name to help the effort along: Frank Sinatra. In an extraordinary move, Sinatra, then the idol of swooning bobbysoxers, astonished the music world by conducting some of Wilder's orchestral pieces under the album title *Frank Sinatra Conducts the Music of Alec Wilder* (Columbia 1945). Sinatra had not conducted before nor has he since, and indeed could not read an orchestral score, so his gesture was the talk of the town. In fact, the recording was an aspect of a friendship between the two men that began early and lasted even through periods of neglect until Wilder's death.

When Sinatra was in New York appearing at the Paramount Theater in the early 1940s, Wilder spent a great deal of time with him in his dressing room. The hysteria created among his fans by the skinny little kid from Hoboken far exceeded any excitement stirred up by popular singers before him. Unrestrained, the bobbysoxers would have devoured Sinatra like piranhas. Girls even plucked hairs from his head. Wilder was also to tell of the time when Sinatra was advised to get his teeth capped before going into movies. That involved making an appointment with a New York dentist, a procedure just about as complicated and secretive as the planning of the Allied invasion of Normandy. The appointment was made, and supposedly only Sinatra, the dentist, his nurse, and Wilder knew about it. When rain began falling heavily during the capping procedure, Sinatra asked Wilder to get him a cab. Outside, Wilder ran into a score of determined young women laying siege at the door to the building. According to Wilder, they were most disconsolate and near tears over Sinatra's dental work. "They hadn't gathered around so much to see him as to get possession of the tooth they had heard he was having pulled." By whatever means, Wilder was able to get Sinatra safely to the cab and thereby earned his gratitude.

Wilder and Sinatra were also associated during the musicians'-union ban on recording activity from the fall of 1942 to the fall of 1944. Only vocalists could be used by the studios during this time, and Wilder was called on to make some arrangements for Sinatra—*People Will Say We're in Love* and *Sunday, Monday or Always* were two of the songs. According to Wilder,

> There was one fellow, Andy Love, who could put his mouth right up to the microphone and make a sound like a string bass, quite extraordinary. Bobby Tucker had a marvelous choir and I tried to make arrangements sound as close to instruments as I could without sounding like the Ink Spots. One of the songs I made I never liked very much, but I loved Frank, and I loved the challenge. The money was non-existent, but that was all right.

Around this time, CBS had a wartime music exchange program with the BBC, and Miller suggested to Wilder that he write some pieces. "So he wrote a piece for oboe, for all my friends—an air for flute, air for English horn, air for bassoon. . . . And we did this on CBS and they were sent over to England." In return—and this was a high honor—the BBC sent across music by Benjamin Britten. Wilder took the air-check acetates of two of the pieces he had written for the BBC to Sinatra at the Paramount Theater. Sinatra passed the time between his shows by listening to records, and he had stacks of both classical and popular platters. That same night after he heard Wilder's record, Wilder received an urgent telephone message from Sinatra. He had liked the pieces enormously, and he thought the world should hear them. When Sinatra proposed that the numbers be recorded, Columbia, not so surprisingly, at first demurred. Miller remembers: "When Frank relayed the message from the head of Columbia that they didn't have the shellack to press a record, I said to him, 'Why don't you tell him that you'll conduct it?' After all, he couldn't refuse Sinatra. That's how he became the conductor." As Barry Ulanov wrote about it,

> Frank turned to the musicians at the record date. The string men looked particularly unbelieving, traditional skeptics as fiddlers, violists, cellists and bassists are. "Look, fellows," Frank said, "I don't know anything about music. I can't read music. I love this music! Will you help me?" The looks of disbelief disappeared, and the help was quietly and enthusiastically forthcoming. Frank looked down at his score, which had no notes but simply noted the entry of soloists and sections, and the Sinatra-Wilder album was off to a great start.

The album was a suite of six numbers. Two were earlier pieces scored for octet and strings—*Theme and Variations,* and *Slow Dance*—and the other four were for solo woodwinds and strings: *Air for Bassoon* with Harold Goltzer as soloist; *Air for Flute* with Julius Baker; *Air for English Horn* with Mitch Miller; and *Air for Oboe,* also with Miller. Wilder said incidentally about *Theme and Variations,* "It's a kind of passacaglia, but, good lord, what a word to use." He felt that people should listen to music without wondering what it was; just enjoy it for itself.

Sinatra was not only willing to lend his name and fame to the work of a relatively new and little-known composer but also concerned that Wilder should figure prominently on the cover. Wilder was in Sinatra's office in Hollywood when the album cover proofs, or layout, were delivered. As Wilder told friends about the incident, Sinatra became angry when he found a great disparity in the type sizes of the Sinatra and Wilder names. He straightaway called Columbia in New York, raised hell, and got a bigger album billing for his friend.

The Sinatra album of Wilder pieces was significant in Wilder's musical development. Bill Engvick says in TRO's *Songs by Alec Wilder Were Made to Sing* that Sinatra's dedicated efforts were "a turning-point; Wilder escaped the popular mills of the Brill Building [where many of the music publishing concerns had their offices], and turned his attention more and more to classical forms."

Once again of course, the album pieces fitted no one category, for they mixed classical music, jazz, and pop. Like the octets, their subtle melodies moved back and forth between one style and another and thus confounded and confused the experts. "This problem," noted Gene Lees, "has dogged Wilder's career, though part of the reason he has been given insufficient recognition is that, because of whatever devils in his soul, for whatever reason he loves the darkness, he has scrupulously avoided fame. Who knows how much beautiful music lies unperformed in the drawers of Wilder's desk." Indeed, unperformed Wilder pieces are still turning up today.

Sinatra himself was well aware that Wilder's music did not run in conventional channels and often overflowed the banks, and he liked it the more for that reason. In 1954 Wilder wrote some music for Mundell Lowe, a top jazz guitarist, and his orchestra, and Sinatra provided the liner notes for the Riverside Records album. From the titles he gave to these pieces, Wilder once again seemed to be defying the world to put him in a pigeonhole or indeed to take him seriously: *Suggestion for Bored Dancers; She Never Wore Makeup; Mama Never Dug This Scene; Around the World in 2.34; Tacet for Neurotics.* Sinatra, who said he had liked Wilder's music from the time he first heard it, welcomed these new compositions as important and fascinating. He acknowledged a musical debt to Wilder: he "helped my own musical conceptions to reach a higher plane than would have been possible without him." He also emphasized the point made by Goddard Lieberson, head of music at CBS, that Wilder music needed to be played by a special brand of musicians. The ten-man orchestra chosen by Wilder and Lowe for this Riverside recording session included former Eastman colleagues Jimmy Buffington, John Barrows, and Jimmy Carroll, and the results were happy. "The lineup," noted Sinatra, "turned out to be what must be a unique mixture of jazz and concert musicians: men able to meet the considerable technical demands of these scores and also able to play them with the necessary swing."

Two things emerge clearly from Wilder's adventures with the octets, the airs, and like compositions. One is that Mitch Miller and Frank Sinatra were there for him from the beginning, just as they would be there for him at the end. The other is that his music simply would not fit into any convenient niche, so that many people did not know what to do with it. Classification was a problem early, and it remains a problem today. The experience of David Demsey, an associate professor of music and the coordinator of Jazz Studies at William Paterson College of New Jersey, is relevant and illuminating. Demsey, the author with Ronald Prather of *Alec Wilder: A Bio-Bibliography* (1993), one of the Greenwood Press series, is an accomplished saxophone player. In 1985 he recorded an album under the Golden Crest label titled *Demsey Plays Wilder.* The pieces included *Air for Saxophone, Sonata for Alto Saxophone and Piano, Suite No. 1 for Tenor Saxophone and Piano,* and the songs *I'll Be Around, If Someday Comes Ever Again, Summer Is A-Comin' In, It's so Peaceful in the Country,* and *A Long Night.* He says about the problem of classification:

> My Golden Crest Wilder album is a perfect example: Most retail record chains literally did not know what to do with it. They didn't feel comfortable putting it in the jazz bins with Sonny Rollins, Duke Ellington, etc., and they didn't feel right about putting it in the classical bins next to all of the Yo Yo Ma Deutsche Grammophon discs; it often ended up in the dreaded "instrumental" bin along with Lawrence Welk, Percy Faith and The 101 Strings. This happens with many artists, but Alec's music is a classic example of a music marketing impossibility.

6

Song Takes Center Stage

In the decade of the 1940s, in a time span overlapping the octets and the airs, Wilder would give most of his creative attention to writing popular songs; among the best were *Give Me Time* (1940), *Who Can I Turn To?* (1941), *It's So Peaceful in the Country* (1941), *I'll Be Around* (1942), *Is It Always Like This?* (1943), *While We're Young* (1943), *Tain't a Fit Night Out* (1943), *Trouble Is a Man* (1944), *Did You Ever Cross Over to Sneden's?* (1947), *Where Is the One?* (1948), and *Goodbye, John* (1949). And once again he would cross up the establishment with songs that were difficult to classify and not at all in the style of the four-square, middle-of-the-road, harddriving, or handholding songs that were the order of the day. Wilder's melodies were leaping and lovely, sinuous and sequestered, elusive and wistful. All the top vocalists would record and praise them, but not many people would sing along. They were not cut from common cloth.

First, however, Wilder had to establish his own distinctive presence in New York and elsewhere, for his lifestyle was as much a shout of defiance as his music. As Barry Ulanov wrote in 1947, his name was a synonym for eccentricity from 1935 on. "His music sounded different, he dressed differently, he acted differently. Different from anything in classical music or jazz. . . . Alec didn't try to make friends or influence people. He just wrote what he wanted and the devil take recording supervisors, radio executives and bandleaders." The man could not be labeled any more easily than the musician. He seemed to be absenting himself even from his own life:

> After I began to sell songs and have them recorded and, in the concert world, get obscure performances and have pieces recorded by obscure record companies, I never or seldom bought the records, read reviews or had a scrapbook or subscribed to a clipping bureau. All that seemed beside the point to me. I had no desire to keep a record of my life. I hated to be photographed. I very early on shied away from possessions. I bought nothing bigger or

heavier than could be carried in a suitcase. I read a great deal and gave all my books away. (I suppose there are ten well stocked private libraries containing mostly my books.) I would never rent an apartment or a house very simply because the encumbrance of a lease was like something too heavy to carry. Perhaps that's why I never married. I always feared the worst so constantly that I couldn't consider houses, children, pets simply because of my fears for their survival.

He sought to be as untethered as a cloud, and he was certainly as changeable: high cirrus one day, dark nimbus the next. Nowhere was he less encumbered than at the Algonquin Hotel, where he could come and go as he pleased. He was also drawn by the hotel's storied past, by its elegance, and by the presence of a maitre d' who, he once said in an outrageous bit of punning, could be depended upon to separate the chic from the gauche. The Algonquin also called to him from the past. As a youngster staying there with his mother, sometimes with an uncle, he had been indelibly impressed by the romance of the hotel, the spotless napery, the serving dishes with large beaten-silver covers, the passing of hot popovers in huge silver tureens with hinged lids, the presence of famous people.

There were times when Wilder did try to adjust his standard of living to his circumstances. Writing to Sibley Watson in Rochester in May 1939, he told his friend and benefactor that the Algonquin was not where he was staying, that he was doing his best to live on a lower level and succeeding to an extent: "I stay in a six-dollar a week room and try to limit needs to low-priced restaurants." Wilder, however, was not conditioned for privation, and he usually went back to the Algonquin like a homing pigeon. And when his quarterly income from a family trust fund was not enough to cover the bills, he could usually turn to Watson for help. In letter after letter in 1939, Wilder poured out his gratitude to his friend for his philanthropy: "You are kind. I will repay you. I am ashamed."

In or out of funds, Wilder would use the Algonquin as his base of operations for most of his life. It was, he felt, what a home should be: "a refuge, made secure by solicitude and tolerance." He felt he belonged there, as perhaps no one else has done before or since.

I have been, if such a phrase doesn't sound too old-fashioned, a son of the house, and I'm sure I have taken advantage of the fact. Also I have been around long enough to have assumed the protective coloration of the lobby furniture, a condition that pleases me, for many of the pieces have about them an air of dignity. And the bellmen humor me by paging me with a code name of their own creation.

They did much more than that. Time and again in the thirties and forties, and the fifties, too, they rescued Wilder when he emerged besotted from the Algonquin's

Blue Bar or some other drinking establishment nearby. The whole staff was often involved. During the war, when his drinking was at its worst, the restaurant waiters would sometimes set a tall screen around Wilder's table to save him from making a public spectacle of himself. Like family, bellmen and waiters shielded him, never breaking ranks publicly. Privately, they agreed that Wilder was delightful when sober but ugly and baleful when drunk.

That transformation was not only complete but took place apparently in an instant. Martin Russ, the son of Lavinia Faxon Russ, remembers that the "Big Switch" always happened abruptly. "His face became like a study in evil, as though he had suddenly been possessed by a demon. He did have a Shakespearean actor's face, and his projection of malevolence was scary as hell." When that occurred, nothing was sacred or safe from violation.

Russ remembers having dinner with Wilder in a French restaurant on the East Side "when he went into his Mr. Hyde routine and began talking in a loud voice about a man seated with friends at a nearby table. Alec was acquainted with him and proceeded to expand on the man's shortcomings as a moral being. The poor fellow remained dignified and mildly amused throughout the whole tirade while his friends looked confused and distressed. Me, I was in agony."

Below the level of drunkenness, alcohol often served as a stimulant to some wonderfully witty talk among a whole range of friends and acquaintances. During World War II, actor Jim Backus and his wife lived across the street from the Algonquin in the Royalton Hotel. "In those days Jim liked to drink as much as I did," Wilder recalled. "He was without doubt one of the funniest men I've ever known." Wilder and Backus were seeing the same psychoanalyst, Sonia Stirt, and there was a day when Backus, as he got quickly into a cab outside the Algonquin, yelled to Wilder: "I'm late. If I don't hurry, Sonia will start without me."

Deep in his cups, however, Wilder was someone to be feared and avoided. He would one day confess to Sibley Watson that he had often behaved abominably, leveling a thousand insults at people. Yet his drunkenness never seemed to submerge him for long. Such was his extraordinary constitution that he threw off his black bouts as a shaggy-coated dog shakes off water after a swim. And never, he always maintained, did he allow his excesses to deflect him from his music. He held onto that as if it were a silver chalice, which indeed it was.

Nothing would be more significant for Wilder than his meeting in 1939 with the talented lyricist William Engvick, who had come from California to follow his star in New York. Earlier that year, Engvick had written a show, "a sort of biographical revue," called *Ladies and Gents*. It depicted comic scenes in the life of a man from birth to death. Not knowing anyone who wrote lyrics or music, Engvick decided to try the lyrics himself. By early 1939, the book and lyrics were finished and the manuscript wound up with Marc Daniels, then at the William Morris Agency and later a well-known director, chiefly of television sitcoms. After reading the manuscript, Daniels arranged a meeting between Wilder and Engvick. It was to be the start of a long and productive association. Recalls Engvick:

> Alec said he had a couple of pieces just out on a record and if I'd accompany him to a nearby record store, we could hear it in the listening booth. He explained that I'd have to ask the clerk for it, as he'd rather worn out his welcome. He owned neither the record nor an instrument to play it on. So I got *A Debutante's Diary* and *Neurotic Goldfish* [two of the octets], and was absolutely stunned and delighted. I bought a copy right there, and almost wore it out in the next weeks.

Wilder no less appreciated Engvick's skills. When he finally returned with the manuscript to Daniels's office, he slammed it down on the table and said, *"That* is fresh air." Engvick, Wilder was to recall, was delighted with all the songs he had composed. Walter Gross, the superb pianist who played the harpsichord in the octets, was agreeable about playing auditions with a group of singers. And Audrey Wood, who later became the agent for Tennessee Williams and William Inge, arranged an audition in which a group of actors ran through the script and very good singers sang the songs. "It's hard to believe," said Wilder, "but the people for whom this audition was given were those zany comics of the period, Olsen and Johnson. And they were completely bored and/or bewildered by this sophisticated and tender piece of work. Nothing came of it then or ever after." Walter Gross did play an audition of a later version of the show, and the singers, to the delight of Engvick and Wilder, were Mabel Mercer and Kay Thompson. The show was revised several times and given different titles, but never produced. In the summer of 1941, Engvick and Wilder were asked to revise *Ladies and Gents* for production at a summer resort. They called it *Peter and the Wolves,* and it bombed. There was no further interest in it, but TRO later published three songs from the show: *A Month in the Country, A Season or Two Ago,* and *City Night. Ladies and Gents* was important for bringing Wilder and Engvick together in their first collaboration.

Morty (Mortimer) Palitz, who had helped Wilder with the octets and who was himself a fine conductor and musician, also played a key role at this time in opening up the world to the young composer.

> It was Morty Palitz who introduced me to Frank Sinatra when he was recording with Harry James, Peggy Lee after he had found her and taken Benny Goodman to hear and hire her, Lena Horne, Dick Haymes, Jack Jenney, Kay Thompson, Percy Faith, Andre Kostelanetz, Mabel Mercer, Cy Walter—God knows how many people I met during these years, but please note: they still represented the pulse of the popular song world.

Jack Jenney was a phenomenal trombone player who played on the old Chesterfield radio show in which Kay Thompson, his wife, "had the great chorus." They both loved swinging music and were talented musicians. And they both liked

Wilder's songs one of which (*City Night,* lyrics by Engvick, from *Ladies and Gents*) wound up as the theme song for the Jack Jenney Orchestra. When he was around Jenney, Wilder said he always felt completely relaxed. Jenney was what he had always assumed a jazz musician should be: "laughing, not too bright, intense about his horn, easily irritated by conductors and inferior players and arrangements, and with child-like mixed with street-arab characteristics. In Jack's case there was an extra elegance. He could wear full formal evening wear without looking like an Italian wedding."

Wilder noted about Jenney's wife, Kay Thompson, that she used to say *Give Me Time* was her favorite of all his songs. "But I suppose if you're not far over thirty, you won't know what a marvelous person she was and is." Sadly, Thompson has left few footprints, but she was a prominent figure in the entertainment world in the 1930s, '40s, and '50s, and she had a remarkable range of talents. Among other things, she was voice coach to Judy Garland at MGM. Although he spoke warmly about her in The TRO Song Book, Wilder felt that Thompson became changed by her success in Hollywood. She now seemed to him tougher, harsher, more cynical.

Wilder demanded that his artist friends remain true to their essential character and not assume foreign airs and graces. Fame should not twist them out of shape. He was not always fair or reasonable in his judgments, for success on a large scale is always hard to handle. Yet Wilder did have an uncanny ability to spot fraud and cant and pretension, just as he knew at once when a piece of music sounded false. His hammer of disapproval often rang loud. That would never be the case, however, for Judy Holliday or Mabel Mercer or Mildred Bailey. These were artists who were not changed by success, whose essence, he felt, remained the same. Wilder made clear distinctions even among the Goodman brothers. He once said that he would have stopped writing songs if it had not been for Harry Goodman, who had played bass in his brother Benny's band but then decided to quit and go into music publishing. Wilder said he could not remember when or where he met him, but he was the only publisher at that time who would publish his tunes. The first one he took was *Out on a Limb,* with Wilder's lyric. It was never printed, but was used as a theme by a group on NBC and recorded by Chick Bullock and his orchestra. Wilder also said he loved Benny Goodman's trumpet-playing brother Irving.

Wilder had much less liking for the "King of Swing" himself, Benny Goodman. That became noticeable when Mildred Bailey was singing on the *Camel Radio Show* with Goodman's band. She asked Wilder to make an arrangement of *Sleepy Time Down South.* In rehearsal, Goodman was apparently critical of the harmony. Wilder wrote:

Your complaint about the unexpected harmony, not only embarrassed the men in the band, Mildred, and myself but just maybe reveals one of your better-known weaknesses: a bad ear. I'm not saying that the harmony was the best;

I'm simply saying that you would be the last musician to know if it were the worst! The fact that I studied music for much longer than you did does not make me a better musician than you. But it does imply that I would be less likely to write down a bunch of unmusical harmonic sequences than someone who had studied nothing.

Subsequently, an angry, brooding Wilder drank himself senseless in the Algonquin Blue Bar. Before blacking out, he said, he remembered looking in the mirror at the back of the bar and seeing Goodman's face. The next day, on his arrival at the rehearsal hall, Wilder said he was saluted by the piano player Jess Stacy:

> Stacy was noodling at the piano and gave me a big grin when I tottered in. "You get the Crux di Gurr," he shouted. In my hangover haze I had trouble translating this into "Croix de Guerre," but I managed to do it. Naturally I was interested to know why I was so deserving of such a high honor. He told me that the band manager, Leonard Vannerson, had called all the members of the band to tell them that at last it had happened. "It" was simply that I, Alec Wilder, the President of the Mouse Society, who had been running away from fights since childhood, had asked Goodman to take off his glasses and step outside the Blue Bar.

The only thing wrong with this story that Wilder told with such glee was that it simply wasn't true. He later admitted it: "In the first place, I hardly know how to make a fist. Second, I get physically ill at the sight or sound of violence. Third, the only fight I was ever in when I fumblingly struck back was when I was a child in St. Paul's School. And that hadn't lasted more than a few moments." James Maher had doubted the story from the beginning: "I never believed the Take Your Glasses Off story. . . . The last thing Benny would do would be to come within an inch of someone taking a swing. The two of them were the great walk-away artists. Alec was always extremely brave as an anecdotalist."

Interestingly, the same detested Benny Goodman in 1941 was one of the first to play one of the early successful compositions by Wilder and his new collaborator, William Engvick, the song *Moon and Sand*. Xavier Cugat and his orchestra had introduced the song, but Goodman and his orchestra played it in the Hotel New Yorker on October 21, 1941, in a program broadcast by CBS. Wilder in this instance was helped with the music by Palitz. The song was written, he said, on one of the many occasions when he and Palitz were noodling around having fun, "he on violin, I with my clumsy ten thumbs on piano. I'm sure we found many good melodies which I was too unenterprising to put on paper. But *Moon and Sand* I did jot down. I'm glad I did because I think it's good. As always, when he participated, Bill Engvick wrote a splendid lyric. I wish this song were better known." Since then Eileen Farrell and Jackie Cain and Roy Kral have helped to lift it out of obscurity. *Moon and Sand* has been recorded by Roland Hanna, Chet Baker, Kenny Burrell, Fred Hersch, Ellis Larkins, and others.

In that same year, 1941, Wilder and Engvick produced an even finer song, *Who Can I Turn To?* The title was tossed to Wilder one day by Mildred Bailey: "I liked it in spite of the fact that grammatically the first word should have been 'whom.' But who could love a 'whom'?" One who did in fact love and insist on a "whom" at a recording session was John H. Hammond Jr., the jazz record producer who gave many career chances to talented young black artists. The story of his grammatical insistence ran quickly through the small world of popular music. Wilder waited a couple of days and then put through a telephone call to Hammond, a man of laughter who had not much sense of humor. "By the way, John," Wilder said to him, "have you seen that marvelous new film *Better Foot Forward?*" It sailed over Hammond's head.

Wilder has recalled that after he gave him the tune, Engvick telephoned to ask if he considered one of his lines too far out: "Ghosts in a lonely parade." Wilder felt it was perfect. In his analysis, Ronald E. Prather has called the lyric haunting, and so it is. The song concludes:

> But now the enchantment is over
> The echo and I remain
> People are strangers who walk through the town
> Ghosts in a lonely parade
> Oh, where are the dreams that we made?
> Who can I turn to now?©

Prather notes that the matching of words with music has "a magical effect, as in so many of the later songs of this collaboration."

Although Wilder and Engvick had clearly shown what they were capable of as a song-writing team, it was Wilder's own lyrics and melodies that gave him his first two hits, *It's So Peaceful in the Country* and *I'll Be Around.* According to Wilder, *It's So Peaceful in the Country* became a success almost in spite of itself: "That it was published and very nearly became a big hit came as a total surprise to me. For when I submitted it to the first, second and third publishers, they all wound up bewildered, saying the equivalent of 'where's the broad?' You see, the countryside is the real love affair and the absence of the other kind nearly kept the song from being published." Like the music, the words spoke directly to pastoral peace:

> It's so peaceful in the country.
> It's so simple and quiet.
> You really ought to try it.
> In rain or shine
> You're feeling fine
> And life is sweet and slow.©

Critics have praised this song for its tender pastoral evocations. Musicologist and noted Ellington scholar Mark Tucker has said about it: *"It's So Peaceful in the Country,* like Wilder's *Just an Old Stone House* and *A Month in the Country,* hearkens back to a nostalgic, pastoral songwriting tradition rooted in the nineteenth century and carried on most faithfully in this century by Hoagy Carmichael, Johnny Mercer, Willard Robison, and Wilder himself." The song was beautifully crafted. Tucker observed that the chorus begins with two big downward leaps remarkable for the pop-song genre, yet perfect for conveying the sighing relief of the text. "Like his hero, Harold Arlen, Wilder took care in composing (not just filling in) accompaniments and the lazily swooping vocal line is answered by minor-second suspensions that lend warmth and intimacy."

Just as he had written *Give Me Time* for Mildred Bailey back in Eastman School days, Wilder said he also had her in mind when he wrote *It's So Peaceful in the Country.* "Mildred Bailey, due to a singing engagement one summer," he wrote, "was unable to get to her country place. So I, with no thought of more than giving a friend, a present, a kind of vicarious weekend out of town, wrote *It's So Peaceful in the Country."* There are various versions of how the song came to be. Loonis McGlohon says many people have said that Wilder wrote the song at their home: "I know one woman who claimed that, and Alec dumped a pitcher of water on her head. In fact, he wrote it on a beatup piano at the Algonquin Hotel."

Wilder's love of Bailey was equally for the singer and the person. As a great jazz stylist, she was often compared with Ella Fitzgerald and Billie Holiday. She became known as the "Rocking Chair Lady" for her rendition of the Hoagy Carmichael song. Her interpretation was so completely satisfying to Wilder that he found it hard to get her voice out of his mind when it came time for him to stand back and take a critical look at the song for *American Popular Song.* Wilder first met Bailey and Red Norvo, to whom she was married, when he was writing his octets. "She sang with his band. They were marvelous, exciting, terribly witty people as well as superb musicians." Wilder had written all his pop songs in terms of the great singers he had heard, and to meet one of them was "simply astounding." Bailey was the sister of Al Rinker, who, along with Bing Crosby and Harry Barris, constituted the singing group known as the Rhythm Boys. Crosby would later credit Bailey with getting them their first job in Los Angeles in 1926. He said she had a heart as big as Yankee Stadium.

When Bailey signed with Paul Whiteman's band in the late 1920s, she was on her way. It had been a long, bruising climb, and she would later tell Wilder about some incredible hardships she had gone through as a teenager. Wilder deeply admired Bailey for surviving: "She lived the life she sang about; it's all there in her music. . . . She was a very shy kind of a gal, with such a naïve quality to her on stage. No matter how she would rock, there was something in her eyes that would say there was a little girl quality about her." In 1934, Bailey married musician

Red Norvo, and the two of them—they were known as Mr. and Mrs. Swing—subsequently formed a twelve-piece band that featured Bailey as vocalist. Later she went out on her own. Wilder had no less admiration for Norvo. He considered him an unsung giant among older jazz musicians and devotees.

Bailey and Norvo were married for ten tempestuous years (the two remained friends even when the marriage broke up), and in a National Public Radio tribute to Bailey in 1978 Wilder said that the two of them were crazy about each other but used to get in some awful fights: "They had quick tempers both of them, especially Mildred. Red is really kind of a dear. He's very patient, but Mildred did have a quick temper. Everything she did was fast except her singing." Wilder had Norvo tell about the memorable occasion when their wrangling reached the point where each began throwing the other's possessions in the fireplace—until in the end the fire engine had to be called.

In a 1981 NPR tribute to Wilder, Norvo said that he and Bailey first became aware of Wilder when the two of them were in the habit of lunching at an open-air restaurant on Seventh Avenue between 51st and 52nd Streets.

> This fellow would walk by, and I was sure he knew who Mildred was, because he kept looking at her. Finally, Mildred said, 'Who is that?' Someone said he was a composer, and she said, 'My goodness. If he goes by tomorrow, or the next time I'm here and he goes by with that egg on his coat I'm going to get a glass of water and walk right out on the sidewalk and clean it."

Wilder had a habit of wearing his meals on his clothes.

After Wilder finally met Bailey and Norvo through Morty Palitz, he soon became part of the crowd they mixed with. He was often at their Forest Hills home, a place of pilgrimage for many people in the music world. Wilder maintained his friendly relationship with both of them even after they had split up. Norvo lived at the Century Hotel for a time after the failure of the marriage.

> Alec was at the Algonquin. We'd meet late, maybe for dinner, and go hear something, maybe Cy Walter, or something on the East side. Then we'd walk back and forth between the two hotels. It seemed like every time he would get me to the Century he'd be into another subject, and he would not want to stop until he got through. And he'd say, "Come on, walk me back." So I would walk him back to the Algonquin, and by that time we would be into something else, and he would walk me back, and this usually went on until daylight.

What was notable about Wilder's attitude toward Bailey was that for her he suspended his customary insistence on complete fidelity to the song as written. Bailey was one exception to the rule that there must be no deviation from the original composition—such was his awe of her artistry. In a radio tribute to Bailey after her death, Wilder told his audience that from the middle 1940s on, her diabetes was complicated by other complaints and she was often in poor health. She made a few more recording dates, but her voice sounded strained. Finally, she was admitted to Saint Francis Hospital in Poughkeepsie. When Wilder got word of this, he went to the hospital with Palitz and another friend. His willingness to make such a visit was in itself a measure of his affection because usually he ran from sickness as a panicked creature does from a burning forest. For Mildred Bailey, he conquered his fear:

> There she was in a ward with these depressing old ladies. "Get me outa here," she said, "it's going to kill me." She couldn't stand it, but she had no money for a private room. Nor could I or Morty afford to pay for the move. Word must have reached Sinatra, who had never even met Mildred but had such an enormous respect for her that within two hours she was out of that ward in a private room with everything she wanted. This was one of those extraordinary things that Sinatra would do and still does. He's so maligned in the newspapers, and deservedly so in some areas, but they never mention all the fine and humane things he does.

The next year Wilder followed his 1941 success with *It's So Peaceful in the Country* with the second of his standards, *I'll Be Around,* the song with which he is probably most identified. It's Manny Albam's fine arrangement of this ballad that concludes the annual birthday concert tribute that has been paid to the composer in New York every year since his death. Wilder did not give *I'll Be Around* a romantic origin, explaining simply that he was crossing Baltimore in a cab one day to take an interurban trolley to Annapolis when the title of the song came ("literally popped out of nowhere") into his head. He scribbled it on the back of an envelope. "Quite by accident I spotted it as I was crumpling up the envelope some days later. Since I was near a piano, I wrote a tune, using the title as the first phrase of the melody. I remember it only took about twenty minutes. The lyric took much longer to write. God bless Frank Sinatra for singing the definitive version of this song."

Here again, in *I'll Be Around* the melodic line is smooth and strong, and the leaping intervals have no trace of awkwardness. The song also shows Wilder's penchant for working always a little off center, always a step or two away from the trodden path. Mark Tucker has commented that the text about a jilted lover might well have invited a self-pitying or bitter musical treatment

> but Wilder's setting assures us that the lover has not lost for long, and certainly not forever. While popular songs commonly depict agitated states— people pining for love, pained by loss, or eager to share happiness with others—*I'll Be Around* shows another side of experience: the philosophic calm that may follow emotional turmoil. In tone and mood, it is close to Harold Arlen's *My Shining Hour*, which Wilder once praised for its "spare,

hymn-like translucence," and achieving the objective of "sexless innocence and distilled simplicity."

James R. Morris, in his analysis for the Smithsonian American Popular Song collection, also wrote: "The symmetry and order of *I'll Be Around* make it a model of compositional virtue. . . . *I'll Be Around* is a masterful piece of song writing by a superior composer who knew the value of understatement." Most of the best singers recorded it. Ironically, although the artistic applause was strong, the only recording of *I'll Be Around* that made any real money for Wilder was the one he thoroughly disliked: that of the Mills Brothers on the reverse side of their huge hit *Paper Doll*. Even as *I'll Be Around* was being thus piggybacked to commercial success. Wilder was complaining bitterly.

The late Milford Fargo of the Eastman School of Music faculty would say: "At a record shop in New York, he listened to the record, broke it over his knees, threw it out on to the floor, paid for it and walked out, because, he said, those awful men changed his chord progressions and changed the melody, and he just hated the record." Wilder himself has said that when he wrote that tune, it was listed as the A side of a Mills Brothers record. But the public preferred the other side: "a 'thing' they called Paper Doll . . . not something to listen to unless you're twenty, a sailor or a drunk." Fortunately, the jukeboxes of those days could play only one side of a record, and so not to waste the other side, the operators turned the record over when *Paper Doll* was worn out.

If Wilder in this instance got a quick and rare financial return from his composing, that would not be true for the third and perhaps the best of the standards, the 1943 *While We're Young*, praised by Prather as "an absolute gem." The music was written by Wilder and Palitz together, and the craftsmanship was superb. Morris says that

> the ABAB melody, cast in sixteen-bar phrases, is so well-balanced that occa-
> sional departures from step-wise writing, as on the words "sing," "spring,"
> and "blue," create a well-calculated tension that is arresting, never jarring.
> The harmonic flavor is particularly distinguished by Wilder's use of a super-
> tonic minor seventh chord to set "sing" and "spring." . . . The tender lyric
> by William Engvick is one of the best in contemporary song.

Indeed, Wilder would say that James Thurber told him he considered this lyric to be the finest piece of English writing that he knew. And starting with the opening phrase, "We must fulfull this golden time, when hearts awake," the lyric moves and builds beautifully:

> Songs were made to sing
> while we're young.
> Ev'ry day is spring
> while we're young.

None can refuse,
times flies so fast,
too dear to lose
and too sweet to last.

Though it may be
just for today
share our love we must
while we may.

So blue the skies,
all sweet surprise
shines before our eyes
while we're young.©

Engvick says that Palitz should be given a full share of the credit for the music. "His part in this song was most important—he wrote the melody." In a fascinating case history of the evolution of a song, Engvick recalls that the three of them had repaired to a vacant studio at Columbia Records (a musicians' strike was going on). Wilder and Palitz sat themselves at two grand pianos, where they noodled and invented ditties and duets. They were enjoying having the place to themselves.

At length Alec said, pointing at me, "Do you know what this man does? He invents tunes to make the words fit the thirty-two bars." Then, referring to a song we had recently written, "What was your dummy tune to 'Everywhere I Look?'"

With one finger I picked out eight notes that comprised the (essence of the) first eight bars, and they both said, "That's enough! That's it." And they immediately began to develop the idea. Morty started with the first five notes, and took off from there, Alec giving bass support. I remember being delighted with Morty's wonderful taste, and at the same time being uneasy at some of the daring phrases. I couldn't imagine a publisher of that day accepting anything so unusual.

There were no moments of trial and error: Morty's melodic line came forth naturally and easily, and that was it. In a very short time Alec had written a lead sheet, which he handed to me, saying, "Go home right now and write it!" "But I don't know what to call it." Without hesitation Alec said, "Call it 'While We're Young.'"

The next morning I spent a couple of worried hours, not about the words, which came readily, but because they were so "uncommercial." And there was a kind of wartime sadness that I felt kept coming through. Fortunately, I wrote them as I saw them, and felt Alec and Morty would agree. They did. Years later, Alec explained that his contribution was the bass line, and he had a firm hand in the shape and direction of the piece. He also wrote the verse.

While We're Young was originally written in $\frac{4}{4}$ time, and an important footnote to its evolution was when a perceptive music man, on hearing it, said, "now play it as a waltz." My reaction, was, "Not only do we have an un-commercial tune with rather sad words, but now it's a waltz in the era of war-time swing!" I was half right. It was uncommercial. But it has been durable, and it's still a nice song.

Not at all surprisingly to Engvick, *While We're Young* was slow to make its way to the public. James Maher has told how hard it was to get the ear of hard-boiled publishers uncomfortable with the gentle and the sensitive. Wilder, he says, took the song to the Brill Building, "Attila's last outpost," and played it for one of the most powerful sheet-music publishers of the day. Recalls Maher:

The man complained about the long held-note cadences. "For Christ's sake," he said, "that's not the way to write a song. Fill up those goddam empty bars. Get some notes in there!" (Just the man to plug those concertina figura-tions that make so many French songs sound like they're dying of elm blight!). Later, another publisher took a chance on those "goddam empty bars." Still, five years passed before the public took up the song. Recordings by those most musical of singers, Mabel Mercer and Peggy Lee, alerted other musicians to its lean beauty. And, just as they have always done, and continue to do with Alec Wilder's music, the musicians welcomed the song into the family. They feasted on its secrets, to use a word that Wilder himself reserves for the essence players so deeply enjoy searching out in his work.

Although Mercer introduced *While We're Young*, it was Lee who took it out of the doldrums. As had been true for Mildred Bailey, Lee also came to occupy a special, if more variable place in Wilder's affections. This immensely talented artist—she has been called the greatest white female jazz singer since Mildred Bailey—worked day and night to get herself out of North Dakota into music's mainstream. Eventually, she joined Benny Goodman's band as a vocalist in place of Helen Forrest. She went from that to a soaring career as a solo artist and also wrote a number of hit songs.

Wilder fell quickly in love with the artist and the woman, and Ronald Prather has said in *The Popular Songs of Alec Wilder* that none of his relationships was deeper or more complex than that with Lee, from the time she was with the Goodman band through her career as an independent vocal stylist. "With each of Wilder's songs that she performed, she made them her own, and she was immensely effective in communicating them to the public, helping to ensure their acceptance." This was certainly true for *While We're Young*, although Wilder seemed to have trouble forgiving her for changing the tune of the song. According to the story that was retailed throughout the popular-music world, Wilder wound up saying, "The next time she gets to the bridge [the transitional middle passage], she ought to jump off." The two of them did seem to be at cross-purposes at times. Lee complained to one radio interviewer that although she introduced *While We're Young*, "I've noticed that in anything I've read about Alec that he has written he never mentions my singing it and I know why, because I sang one note incorrectly. He was so fussy, because it wasn't a bad note that I sang. Just different than [what] he had written, and he wanted it the way he had written it." Lee said she didn't blame him for that but she did think it "sort of funny" that he should never mention that her recording of *While We're Young* was, so far as she knew, the biggest hit that the song had.

For Lee and Wilder, the early memories were particularly warm. Lee told the radio interviewer that Wilder had "struck up a friendship when I was very shy. He would get me to do what he called curb sitting and we would discuss life in general. He knew that I was sort of a strange child. He was a lobby sitter also. But he really liked curbs the best." Lee in her autobiography has also told of a later time in New York when she was saved from loneliness at Christmas by the arrival of her young daughter Nicki and nurse and housekeeper Alice Larson, and then Wilder.

> Alec Wilder, that superb composer and friend—Mabel Mercer was now singing all his songs—pitched right in to the Christmas spirit and came over dragging a huge tree into the apartment as though he had just cut it down in the forest. We had heard of making snow for the tree, but unfortunately had the wrong method. We whipped up boxes of Ivory Snow with the Mixmaster, and, as we covered the tree, its poor limbs bent lower and lower. Finally, though, we managed to finish it and turned on the lights!

Wilder, in what had to be a rare departure from his usual shunning of the holiday, joined them for Christmas Eve and Christmas Day.

In spite of the magic moments, there were reservations. Lee felt she never really understood Wilder. For his part, Wilder felt that the essence of the young girl he knew when she was singing with Goodman somehow became lost in the elaborate stage presence she began to create. There were no such reservations when Peggy Lee was first singing *While We're Young*, the standard that owed so much to her and to Engvick's lyric.

It's too bad that Lee could not also have rescued some of the other songs that the new young partnership of Wilder and Engvick came up with in the first half of the 1940s. Two in particular should be noted: *Tain't a Fit Night Out* (1943) and *Everywhere I Look* (1945). Neither has had much exposure, and indeed *Tain't a Fit Night Out* has never been recorded. But Barbara Lea, one of the most admired performers of the classic American popular song, who has the same streak of independence as Wilder, likes it and sometimes sings it.

Everywhere I Look is another good song that has not had much success. Fran Warren introduced it. Wilder himself has said about this song:

> Cy Walter was a marvelous pianist and a dear friend. His first wife, before she became Society conscious, was a lively, engaging girl. One day she offered me the title of the song. I, in turn, gave it to Bill Engvick. This is the song to which Bill had sung me the first line of his "dummy" tune and which was so provocative that Morty Palitz and I developed it into what became *While We're Young. Everywhere I Look* was once recorded by Eileen Farrell. And that more than compensated for the fact that it today remains virtually unknown.

The song is no better known now than it was when Wilder made that comment in 1976, and more's the pity, for lyric and melody are a sensitive match.

All these songs were written against the background of World War II, but none was colored by that conflict, which Wilder did his best to ignore. He was genuinely terrified of physical violence, whether a street mugging, a shoving in a queue, or a clash of nations. He could never have survived life in the army with its rough, unwashed masses. Says Martin Russ: "He once told me that he had endured a period of terror that he would be drafted into the Army. The terror-image he had was of having to go naked into a communal shower and having the other draftees laugh at the size of his dork. He wasn't being funny when he told me this—it was something that had really scared hell out of him."

Wilder's civilian status did often discomfit him: "I was very embarrassed to be a civilian during those years even though I had made all kinds of unpatriotic gestures in order to remain one. Most of my good friends were in outlandish islands (what else could an island be but outlandish?) or in England, Africa, Germany, and here was I, trying to make a living in New York City writing songs."

His discomfiture was not so great, however, that he was willing to embrace military service. When induction loomed on his horizon, he started preparing his defenses by putting himself on record with New York City psychoanalyst Sonia Stirt. "I did a lot of rationalizing about why I needed to see a psychoanalyst at that time, but the reason was very simple. I was scared to death of being drafted." When he realized that not even consultations with an analyst might save him from being pressed into service, Wilder turned for help to Sibley Watson in Rochester. That obliging father confessor obtained the services of a lawyer who got Wilder excused, though not before some panicky moments: "I remember my total terror when I was told early on to remove all my clothes and was given a cardboard label which had a clumsy number marked on it in red crayon and a hole through which a frayed loop of store string had been passed." He said it was not the fear of dying that bothered him so much as the enormous embarrassment of communal living.

Surprisingly, Wilder was persuaded to take part in one of the "Victory disks" during the war. "We want you to greet the soldiers and introduce Frank Sinatra," he was told. He did so reluctantly, but he did it, telling the troops, "Hi fellers, my name is Alec Wilder. Believe it or not, Frank Sinatra can do a lot more than sing. In fact, he conducted some music of mine which you're about to hear." Wilder was also to say: "Can you believe that I wrote, during the war, a piece of music for an antiaircraft battery on Okinawa called *Ready, Willing and Able?* I'm told it wasn't easy to sing but it WAS SUNG by those boys while I was in the Algonquin reading about the Civil War." Nephew Edward DeWitt III remembers sitting with Wilder in a movie theater watching a newsreel: "It showed an American bomber leaving England to bomb Germany in World War II. It was named *I'll Be Around,* and the quotation marks were musical notes instead of punctuation marks. Alec never blew his own horn, but he was almost noticeably taller after he saw that."

It may be, as Ronald Prather has suggested, that the Wilder standards, with their tender, quiet, wistful air, appealed to war-weary Americans. "Who would not prefer the peace and quiet of the country?" he asked about *It's So Peaceful in the Country.* "Perhaps because we were then a nation at war, this theme was all the more seductive, and the song enjoyed a considerable popularity."

Wilder could not have written or abided an unabashedly patriotic song. For him, the act of creation was something quite apart from the world he lived in. War or peace, storm or calm, it made no difference. He detested program music—that is, music that seeks to tell a story or reflect a mood or imitate extramusical sound such as a train passing by. The issue is more relevant to orchestral music than to popular song, for words provide a picture frame. It should be noted, however, that sometimes the words followed the composition of the music. In Engvick's experience, Wilder was always happy to have words to work to, and in the case of topical or plot-related or comic songs, usually the words were written first. But with the so-called pretty tunes, the melody was often composed first. *While We're Young, Moon and Sand, Remember, My Child, I Like It Here,* and *Listen to Your Heart,* for example, all had the melodies first. *The April Age, Crazy in the Heart, A Season or Two Ago,* and *A Month in the Country* had the words first. Across the broad spectrum of music, however, Wilder was concerned that the music should tell its own story. He sought no inspiration himself:

> I completely isolate music. I don't think music is a reflection of the times you live in. It's a reflection of you. I keep something inviolate, something intact. It has nothing to do with life, nothing to do with the way I live daily. There's an area in every creature which is absolutely sacrosanct. Inspiration? None. Just a need to create. I would write exactly the same in a garbage can that I would on a Hawaiian beach.

The fact that Wilder could and did compose anywhere—in the Algonquin lobby, on a train, in a motel room, beside a pond full of peepers, in a supper club—does suggest that attitudes toward war or peace or any other state of the world had little influence on his composing. And yet that inviolate, sacrosanct center he speaks of was surely in harmony with, if not nourished by, life in the country. After all, he did say he wrote *Soft as Spring* after stopping on an unpaved country road beside a deserted farm with lilacs in bloom. So it may have been relevant that he spent part of several summers in the 1940s in a house owned by musician Eddie Finckel and his wife Helen near Kutztown in Berks County, Pennsylvania.

The Finckels were Manhattan friends who had an apartment over a garage on East 22d Street. Finckel was a fine self-taught jazz pianist. He had married a girl whose family's home, Wilder remembered, "had been chock-a-block with smarmy Jesus pictures and whose father kept a notebook in which he listed every expenditure down to pennies." Helen, however, had survived. Wilder visited the Finckels often and also came to know Eddie's family in Washington. They were, Wilder said, as barmy, as talented, as wild as any group of people he had ever known. Sanger's Circus in Margaret Kennedy's *The Constant Nymph* was, he said, "as close to the Finckels as I've ever read."

In that East 22d Street apartment, Finckel and Wilder smoked their share of pot, which, he reckoned, seemed in those days more for the purpose of laughter "than the solemn ceremony of today's knot-hole starers." The two of them wrote "some very tasty songs" together, using Wilder's lyrics. Finckel's melody for *Where Is the One?* (1948) so captured Wilder that he agreed to try write to words worthy of it. "I hope they are. I only know that when Sinatra recorded it, he made me believe they were. But he was always making miracles." Another of their songs was recorded by Nat "King" Cole but never released, though, said Wilder, it was a very good song. The two of them also played a game in which Finckel would write a top piano line and Wilder would add a contrapuntal bass line, and they would play the finished piece on the piano. Wilder was so much a member of the family that he would sometimes make the Finckels a special cheesecake of his. Once, he painted a picture under Helen Finckel's persuasion.

One spring weekend Wilder rode with the Finckels to their old-fashioned fieldstone-schoolhouse home. It stood in a protected little valley and could be reached only by a rutted track over adjoining farmland. The outside was as littered as a town dump, and Wilder set about transforming things. First he built a dry wall to enclose the garden. Then he dammed a nearby brook to have water for dry spells and subsequently hauled pailsful by the hundreds for the perennials, flowering trees, vines, and seventy rose plants that soon flourished. Muskrats kept deconstructing the dam, but Wilder just as persistently rebuilt it. Later he and Finckel set out well upward of a thousand tree seedlings on a hillside.

The day came when the Finckels sold the property. In a desperate bid, Wilder called the new owner and offered him in cash what he had paid for it, $10,000: "Of course, I didn't have half that, but for once I'd have crawled to a rich friend for the loan. But the man cheerily informed me he didn't wish to sell."

The Kutztown garden is representative of how wholeheartedly Wilder threw himself into a multitude of pursuits and avocations. He always wanted to write music but given the chance to create, say, a beautiful garden, he switched off the main line to a siding far from the smoky, shadow world of nightclubs.

I remember one afternoon lying flat on my stomach on one of the crushed limestone paths. The Finckels had gone in to Kutztown, the nearest community, the garden had responded miraculously to my obsessive care and I was, as probably never before or since, content. As I lay there on the hot gravel, invisible to any possible passerby because of the dry wall, I had what, from all I've read of such experiences, must have been a revelation. I don't know precisely what occurred unless it was a very powerful realization that I was totally aware of my being, that it was functioning better than it ever had before, that it was in perfect balance and, best of all, that life was complete.

All his life Wilder would remember Kutztown as an oasis that he kept green, where he was safe for a time from the fears that ever bedeviled him, where he made temporary peace with himself before returning to his jousting as an out-of-fashion composer.

7

Homage in a Supper Club

More than Peggy Lee, more even than Mildred Bailey, Wilder worshipped Mabel Mercer and her exquisite artistry. She was, for him, "the guardian of the tenuous dreams created by the writers of songs." It was a mutual love affair, and two Wilder songs from the second half of the 1940s would become particularly associated with her: *Did You Ever Cross Over to Sneden's?* with lyrics by Wilder, and *Goodbye, John,* lyrics by Edward Eager. As a supper-club or cabaret singer, Mercer had no peer, and many were the artists who sat at her feet and learned from her style, her taste, her phrasing. Frank Sinatra once described her as the best music teacher in the world: "Everyone who has ever raised his voice in song has learned from you, but I am the luckiest one of all because I learned the most of all." Tony Bennett, Lena Horne, Nat "King" Cole, and Johnny Mathis were also influenced by her singing.

In many ways, Mercer and Wilder were made for each other. Mercer never had a hit record, seldom ventured into big arenas, and inspired a following almost cult-like in its loyalty and intensity. That no less described Wilder. Both were acquired tastes, and both artists also exceled in small, intimate settings and in songs that lay outside the mainstream.

This singer who so excited Wilder and Sinatra and so many others was born in England in 1900 to a black American jazz musician and a white English vaudeville singer. It was not until she went to school that she found out what it meant to be black. "She was so frightened," Wilder has said, "that she cut off all her hair and masqueraded as a boy." At fourteen, she, her mother, and stepfather began touring as a song-and-dance act in Britain and on the Continent. Ten years later she met the American-born singer and hostess Bricktop (Ada Smith), who was then operating a stylish Parisian cabaret on the Rue Pigalle (Ernest Hemingway, F. Scott Fitzgerald, and Gertrude Stein were among its patrons). Mercer sang at Bricktop's from 1931 through 1938. In Paris, she found refuge from prejudice.

When World War II forced Mercer to leave Paris, she looked to the United

States. Difficulties with entry papers becalmed her for several years in the Bahamas; it was during this time that she heard the Wilder octets and was captivated. She said Wilder was the first man she wanted to meet when she reached America. After marrying a black musician, she finally entered the country but did not find it a haven at first. She suffered racial abuse and, according to Wilder, was startled to find that she could not live where she wanted to. "Above 110th Street," she was told.

In 1941 Mercer began appearing at Le Ruban Bleu in Manhattan, and it was there that she and Wilder first met through pianist Cy Walter. "Alec," she was to say, "played Is It Always Like This? and many other beautiful songs of his which enriched my repertoir." After six months she began what turned out to be a seven-year engagement at Tony's on West 52d Street. Every great jazz instrumentalist and singer was to be found there during those years. It was always a magical street to Wilder: "New styles developed there. It might even be said that the seeds of modern jazz grew on 52d Street." The whole area was like a block party; people felt secure and protected, and everybody seemed to get along with everybody else. "It was a great big, friendly world. It has never happened since. And I don't think it will ever again. . . . Fifty-second Street was the last public trust, really and seriously."

In Wilder's opinion Mercer's singing and Walter's playing were untypical of 52d Street:

> For the Street represented all aspects of jazz, while both Mabel and Cy, though singing and playing standard theater and pop songs, performed them in a style which could be termed only jazz-oriented. Neither made any pretense of being jazz performers. They were simply superb musicians who drew on the popular idiom for their sources. I wrote many songs for Mabel and virtually lived in Tony's, which it was called after Cy Walter moved on.

Regal in bearing, physically small and rounded, sitting still and upright in an upholstered armchair, a single, soft spotlight on her face, Mercer made every song her own at the same time that she infused her listeners with the sentiments of the lyrics. Wilder told Whitney Balliett in the latter's *New Yorker* profile of Mercer:

> She transmutes popular song to the extent that by means of her taste, phrasing and intensity it becomes an integral part of legitimate music. When she sings a song, it is instantly ageless. It might have been composed the day before, but, once given the musical dignity of her interpretation, it is no longer a swatch of this season's fashion but a permanent part of vocal literature.

For Wilder, she was the best interpreter of a lyric he had ever heard, including Sinatra. That and her magnetism and essential goodness won him over quickly and forever. Tony's became a kind of temple, a sanctuary, an asylum for Wilder, like a church to a criminal, a place where he felt he could never be arrested for whatever crime he had committed as long as he stayed there.

Wilder wrote many songs for Mercer of which he would later say he had forgotten even the titles, for many were never published. He and others were moved more by admiration than by money. To Mercer as well, the music was everything. She was credited with rescuing and reviving a number of important songs she believed in. One of them was the English medieval carol *The Twelve Days of Christmas.* Another was *Little Girl Blue,* which she thought worth saving from the unsuccessful 1935 Rodgers and Hart musical *Jumbo.* According to Wilder, Mercer did the same thing for another Rodgers and Hart song, *Wait Till You See Her:*

> This was a tremendous ballad that got thrown out of *By Jupiter.* Everyone forgot about it, possibly even the lyricist and composer. But Mabel heard something. She didn't forget. And she began singing it. And then that magical thing happened. Other singers began to discover it. It was a rejected song. But suddenly it was a talked-about song. Peggy Lee heard Mabel and added it to her repertoire. Lena Horne heard it and wanted it. Frank Sinatra listened and went looking for it. Bandleaders began putting it into their books. Single-handed, she was responsible for the revival of many other forgotten songs and for the popularization of songs that would have been forgotten.

Perhaps only Mercer with her aptitude for phrasing would have essayed and captured the difficult art song that Wilder wrote for her in 1947, *Did You Ever Cross Over to Sneden's?* Wilder himself once called it a far-out song, and even the setting was unlikely. Only a few people living around Nyack, in Rockland County, New York, could know that Sneden's Landing on the Hudson River is a spot where produce had once been picked up for shipment by riverboat. Wilder said that after a drunken bout one night he next morning crossed the Hudson with a shad fisherman who sometimes transported people to catch the train on the east side. While waiting for the train, he began thinking of an aunt who he remembered had attended a boarding school at Dobbs Ferry. He wrote the lyric there and then (ironically, he learned later that she had in fact gone to Farmington School, nowhere near Dobbs Ferry). Ronald Prather later praised the lyric's "extraordinary beauty of imagery and subtlety of meaning." It became one of Mercer's most requested songs. Fittingly, when the friends of Alec Wilder gathered in Carnegie Hall to honor his memory in June of 1982, *Did You Ever Cross Over to Sneden's?* was one of two Wilder songs sung by Mercer; the other, *Is It Always Like This?*

The third Wilder song often associated with Mercer, *Goodbye, John* has also proved durable. Wilder said that he once wrote most of the melodies for a musical show by Edward Eager and Alfred Drake. The lyrics were very bright and inventive, but there were none that he felt had the elements or romantic quality needed for a love song. "So I asked Mr. Eager if he would write me one with, if possible, a minimal number of words, since his other lyrics tended to use a great many. I was so pleased with what he submitted to me that I immediately set it, called up Peggy Lee, sang it over the phone and within a few weeks she made a truly lovely recording of it." Lee introduced it, and Mercer made it part of her repertoire of a thousand songs (several hundred of which she could sing at very short notice).

Sinatra apparently picked up from Mercer another Wilder song that Wilder himself would never have thought suitable for him, the "morbid" 1948 ballad *Where Do You Go (When It Rains)*? Wilder's melody and Arnold Sundgaard's words combined to convey a strong sense of melancholy. "Where do you go when it starts to rain? / Where will you sleep when the night-time comes? / What do you do when your heart's in pain? / Where will you run when the right time comes?"© The song was included in Sinatra's *No One Cares* album, and in that setting was perhaps not so inappropriate. Wilder did recognize that this was one album in which Sinatra "did a lot of soul searching and seemed to be in a very depressed frame of mind." *Where Do You Go?* was the song that Stan Getz played at his (Getz's) mother's funeral. Getz also asked Wilder to orchestrate it for his appearance at Tanglewood with the Boston Pops and closed the concert with it. "And," said Wilder, "it all started with Mabel, who had the courage to do songs that no one else would touch."

For three decades, Mabel Mercer would hold court in the supper clubs of New York, sometimes working her magic in theaters and concert halls as well. For many of those years, she lived on a thirty-acre farm in the Berkshires near Chatham, New York, several hours' drive from New York City. Wilder visited her there whenever he could. Mercer talked about Wilder in her interview with Whitney Balliett, noting at one point that a small hickory in the field that flowed downhill from her house was given to her by Wilder for her seventy-fifth birthday. Mistakenly, he had believed it to be a walnut tree. "That was our special joke, that tree," said Mercer. Wilder once said about those visits to her house: "I've gone up to visit her in the country a perfect wreck and in two days felt marvelous. It isn't that she *does* anything—that there is any laying on of hands or such. She just putters around her house, and cooks, and feeds her animals. But there is some quality, some corrective force, in her very presence."

Mercer also told Balliett that she had newly fixed up one of the bedrooms just for Wilder, "but he never saw it before he died. I put a round worktable in front of the window, so that he could look out over the field. I hoped the view would inspire him to compose when he was blocked—which he often was when he came to visit." Theirs was an unalloyed friendship that extended over four decades; its foundation was laid from 1942 to 1949 when Mercer was the reigning star in Tony's. Then and always she represented for Wilder the very best in the performance of popular song.

Despite such good things in his life, the always volatile Wilder, never willing to accept success, seemed unable to take much satisfaction from his career. On June

14, 1946, he was telling Sibley Watson: "I have been very industrious; I have done any and all hack work I could; I have groveled at the feet of the top dogs. And nothing happens. Oh, a few things, but never the dam-breaker." A few months later he was saying that his status in the music world continued to baffle him and others as well. "Reports continue to reach me of Hollywood's great respect, I meet men in power who quite sincerely bow low, I receive letters, and there are many who sit about scratching their heads over the absence of confirmation." Never the dam-breaker.

Part of the problem had to do with the nature of his songs, often too elusive to catch the public ear and often too difficult to be sung well by all but the very best singers. William Engvick saw it clearly:

> Wilder's unusual and, for the time, difficult arrangements and his oddly-shaped, understated and unpredictable melodies caused much antagonism (as they still do), and his progress was difficult. This was complicated by a totally uncommercial dignity and a trenchant wit which left his antagonists sneering, unaware that they were bleeding internally.

Wilder refused to make obeisance in the places where it mattered more than it should have. Dinners, golf games, parties—he detested them all and made his distaste plain. Nor would he have anything to do with the promotion of songs through "song plugging," which entailed being at all the opening nights of the bands and making follow-up visits to the clubs. He told with contempt of one song plugger who did the laundry for a bandleader's wife as a way of ingratiating himself.

Far from being ingratiating in any company, Wilder, when his drinking got the better of him, would sometimes be downright insulting. Writing after his death, Joel E. Siegel recalled the time when Wilder, fortified by far too many Bombay gin double martinis, turned on him in the Algonquin lobby:

> Enraged, because the particular object of his scorn was a mutual friend who had died only a few months before, I made the mistake of retaliating, which led to a public scene and ended with Alec furiously banishing me from the hotel lobby. . . . I think it is important that the lowdown Alec be remembered along with the saintly Alec, who often seemed too good to be true. But he was true, and, finally, that's what shouldn't be forgotten and why Alec's death is so hard to accept.

Wilder stubbornly insisted on standing in his own way. Sometimes it was a matter of principle. Wilder recalled being asked at one point by Mary Martin to consider writing the score for *Peter Pan*. She had heard some of Engvick's lyrics and had wanted him on board as well. However, she then happened to hear some lyrics by Caroline Leigh, a very versatile young woman, and at the last minute shifted ground and wanted Wilder to work with her. Wilder would have preferred Engvick to anyone but, he said, would have worked with some other lyricist if need be—anyone but Leigh. He admired her work but sensed from having met her that they would have trouble collaborating. He realized that the chance to write for Mary Martin was a rare one. "But I have learned to trust my hunches. Great efforts were made to persuade me to agree, including financial ones. I refused and was considered a fool. I'm certain that this refusal convinced anyone in the popular music world who heard of it that I was a loser as well as a fool."

Wilder was often capricious. He once told Engvick that a man had called him about doing a score for a ballet. Wilder had refused. Engvick asked why, and he responded, "I didn't like the sound of his voice." The ballet, says Engvick, was *Fancy Free*, "and put Leonard Bernstein on the map. The voice was, of course, Jerome Robbins." It was an opportunity lost for no good reason. In 1940 Wilder had written music based on the octets for the ballet *Juke Box* (libretto by Lincoln Kirstein, choreography by William Dollar). The ballet was taken on tour to South America the following year, but apparently Wilder showed no interest. He was not always wrongheadedly arbitrary. Engvick also recalls that the noted NBC producer David Susskind thought highly of Wilder, particularly as an arranger, and he very much wanted him to score his forthcoming film *All the Way Home*. Wilder did not want to do it, but agreed in the end because he needed the money. "Then he learned that the main tune in the score was to be one by a teenage relative of one of the managers, and Alec said, 'No way!' And he pulled out. In this instance, Alec was right."

It almost seemed at times that after Wilder had written a composition, he gave it little attention—perhaps for fear of smudging the creative act, or because he wanted to move on, or simply disliked too much business tending. Of all the writers whose songs were considered for *American Popular Song*, he would say that Richard Rodgers showed "the highest degree of consistent excellence, inventiveness, and sophistication." Yet he didn't always admire the way Rodgers attended to his business. Wilder first met Rodgers during the showing of the ultimately unsuccessful extravaganza *Jumbo* at the old Hippodrome across the street from the Algonquin. The cast and the director, John Murray Anderson, were in and out of the hotel every day. Anderson's brother offered to show Wilder the circular curtain that had been designed at great expense. On the way up the stairs to the balcony, they met an angry man rushing down. Anderson stopped him and introduced Wilder; it was Rodgers. He had apparently just learned that copies of the sheet music had not arrived for sale in the lobby, a custom of those days. "He was furious. It wasn't until later that I thought about it. I had been to many musicals and knew fairly well that a hundred copies would be an average sale. So why be so disturbed. I never forgot it, however, and it seems to me a perfect illustration of what I have always called 'minding the store.'"

Wilder could never have been such a man himself. He said he was not sure if it was because he did not care enough or because the drudgery demanded by store minding was more than he chose to endure for the possible profit. Then he added: "I blame no one but myself for the minimal success I have known. I have had to pay this price for keeping myself whole." That minimal success was the subject of a bitter letter he wrote in 1949 to Sibley Watson in which he noted that he was then forty-two with little to show for the previous ten years:

> I have written children's music to order; I have adapted mawkish standard arias and themes and have put calculatingly vulgar lyrics to them; I have written eight complete show scores; I have written over 200 attemptedly popular songs; I have sucked and rubbed around unscrupulous, vicious, corrupt men and women in the effort to crack the wall; I have cut my hair, shined my shoes, pressed my suits, filed and cleaned my nails; I have learned small talk, Hollywood slang; I have buried ideals, held back thought, forgotten poetry; I have accepted lonelinesses, become virtually a victim of masturbation . . . kept myself from shaking to pieces at radio and record rehearsals of my writings and orchestrations—and I have failed.

That letter reflected Wilder's jaundiced view of the world and his place in it. By no means was it the whole story of what he had been doing, in or out of music. His spirits were as often high as low. He told Watson, for example, that he had two songs in the hillbilly department of Decca Records: *Badlands, You've Been Good to Me!* and *Don't Hang the Pictures on the Wall, Mother. We've Got to Move Tomorrow.* Together with Goddard Lieberson and his wife, Margaret, Wilder and Engvick also put out the first of three mocking catalogs called *Touch & Thrash* that poked irreverent fun at just about everything. "It was wartime," said Engvick, "and Alec's friends in the Service loved the gaminess and the slingshot-against-the-world attitude. Most of my quite liberal friends didn't see it at all, and some of the most straightlaced loved it."

The marvelous, skewering Wilder wit was often on display. And he was forever playing a role, putting people on. He often carried cards with bars of music on them, some from Beethoven pieces. When someone he didn't care for asked him about his composing, he would pick out a Beethoven card and show him the music he had written, and watch as the poor fellow cut short the conversation so he could go home and copy the notes.

The eternal loser Wilder presented himself as—in the Watson letter and on many other occasions—was more than a pose, for it masked a fear and an insecurity that could be seen in his alcoholism and in his composing. That eternal loser role, notes composer Warren Benson, was always carried out "with a kind of panache. He was the Errol Flynn of losers. He never did anything without style, even when drunk. Because he had such a lovely affection for the English language, such a joyous use of it, he could put people down in the most elegant way, with a lovely touch, a naughty Cole Porter." Wilder was jealous of people who were doing well in the music world but whose personal conduct was less than admirable. Sometimes he seemed to forget that his own lack of commercial fame came in part from the fact that he was involved in music for the sheer joy of it. He did no capitalizing on such successes as he had. Adds Benson: "Alec never went to the publishers and beat them over the head and had them do the heavyhanded marketing."

Big chances were missed, early and late. Yes, says co-bio-bibliographer David Demsey, coordinator of Jazz Studies at William Paterson College of New Jersey, it was true that Wilder's music and writing did not have the comfortable, predictable label that would have allowed the publicity machine to create a recognizable image for him. But neither was he willing to cultivate and build on a friendship for personal advantage. As Demsey points out, Wilder never even tried to make it in the world and indeed deliberately shied away from "elbow-rubbing" situations as ends unto themselves, "even though he seemed to know everybody who was anybody in New York while at the Algonquin." Adds Demsey:

> As he wrote for Sinatra, he could have cultivated an image of Frank's unconventional alter ego/right hand man/musical guru, continuing to make a name as an arranger/musical director as Nelson Riddle later did, while simultaneously doing his own writing. His popularity with the teenage Sinatra generation is chronicled by his early features in *Downbeat* and the desire of *Seventeen* magazine to write about him—but he pulled away from all that and pursued "classical music" in more of a jazz style.

It was to his credit that Wilder refused to trade on his friendship with Sinatra. But part of the problem was his dislike of Sinatra's lifestyle, a dislike that would grow with the years. Despite the urgings of Lavinia Russ and others that he should try harder to distinguish between the man and the music, Wilder remained ambivalent about Sinatra. He deeply respected the artist and deeply deplored the after-hours playboy. The rupture was never total, and Sinatra would reemerge in Wilder's life toward the end, for the embers were always there. "There was a gentlemanliness about Frank that appealed to Alec," James Maher has said. "And you know very well that Alec probably had a positive effect on Frank in that world with his dignity and bearing and civility, elegance, intelligence and all those positive things Alec wore simply as an aura, like a mantle." Alas, there was never a full forging. As Wilder saw it, the essence of Mercer remained the same but that of Sinatra changed, and never mind that fame is hard to wear. That was simply that.

8

Adventures in Opera and Film

As if further to confound and confuse the critics, and to defy the fixing of labels, Wilder in the 1950s tried his hand at a variety of musical forms. Like a pitcher mixing fast balls and curves, he kept the establishment guessing. In addition to popular and art songs, for there would always be songs even at a slower rate, and in addition to pieces for children and the first of an increasing number of serious instrumental compositions, he also experimented with short operas and film scores. Roughly within the span of the decade, he would write five operas (if *Kittiwake Island* is included in the category), four of them with Arnold Sundgaard and one with William Engvick. He would also work on four film scores, three of them in association with Jerome Hill, and one in collaboration with Engvick.

Wilder's first try at opera was actually made in the late 1940s with *The Impossible Forest*, libretto by young Marshall Barer, probably best known today for *Once Upon a Mattress,* written with Mary Rodgers. Wilder had earlier set to music a Barer poem titled "River Run," and the two of them would go on to turn out some fourteen or fifteen songs, including *Summer Is A-Comin' In* (1952), introduced by Nat Cole. They would also produce *A Child's Introduction to the Orchestra* in 1954.

The task at hand was *The Impossible Forest,* which had its auditions every Sunday night in an unusual setting: the Stratford Suite of the Algonquin Hotel, courtesy of Manager John Martin. Leon Barzin, conductor of the National Youth Orchestra and an unsung hero of music in the United States in Wilder's opinion, was able to provide background orchestral records to which the singers could sing, thereby giving more flavor to the audition. Set pieces from the opera were performed, with Wilder himself singing an aria for basso profundo and playing piano accompaniment for the singers:

Before we knew it, the Sunday evenings had become a fashionable event to attend. All manner of prominent theatrical and literary people came. I recall that one Sunday evening Leonard Bernstein and Mark Blitzstein volunteered to help us get the right balance between the orchestra recording and the "live" voice of the leading singer. I don't think Nancy Walker missed one of these Sunday evenings. Once we held the "curtain" for the arrival of Mary Martin. Oh, they were name-dropping evenings, and I was told much later that all the most elegant rich ladies and gentlemen in town came with investment in mind. One evening I happened to look up from my hot seat at the piano to see William Faulkner and Ruth Ford sitting in the first row of chairs.

Former Hollywood man about town Rogers Brackett, another pivotal person in Wilder's life, about whom more will be heard later, was so impressed by the opera that he undertook to produce it. Early in 1950 Wilder wrote to Sibley Watson in Rochester and told him that the prospects for the opera seemed good. The talented scenery and costume designer Lemuel Ayers (of *Kiss Me Kate* fame) was, he said, impressed with the libretto; choreographer Jerome Robbins was interested in staging the opera and doing the dances. Added Wilder: "I am seeing Henry Fonda this afternoon. He has, I believe, access to money and is very enthusiastic about everything of mine he has heard." In the course of asking Watson if he would consider making an investment, Wilder said he thought the opera was a commercial property that would pay back its investors.

No backers were found, or not enough of them. Barer believes the prospects were never as good as Wilder seemed to think they were, and that Fonda and Robbins, for example, were never enthusiastic. Although he told Wilder that the money was coming from a sponsor, Barer later said that he himself had paid for the auditions and that when he told Wilder he had in fact used his life savings, he was told that he must be paid back. "But I never was." *The Impossible Forest* was given only one professional performance, and that not until eight years later, when the After Dinner Opera Company played it on July 13, 1958, in the White Barn Theater in Westport, Connecticut.

There have been no critical estimates of the work, but the absence of performances must speak for itself. Although a failure, *The Impossible Forest* gave the young Wilder a useful exposure to stage work and would prove helpful in his work with playwright and lyricist Arnold Sundgaard: three short one-act school operas— *The Lowland Sea* (1952), *Cumberland Fair* (1953), and *Sunday Excursion* (1953)— and a more ambitious production more akin perhaps to musical comedy, *Kittiwake Island* (also in 1953). There would be other productions by this team in later decades.

Wilder had first met Sundgaard back in the mid-1940s through William Engvick, though they did not work together until several years later. Sundgaard was already highly regarded as a dramatist and as a writer of opera libretti, and was then a lecturer in drama at Columbia University. One of his earliest plays, *Everywhere I Roam,* had been produced on Broadway in 1938. He would go on to claim many other distinctions, including the libretto for the opera *Giants in the Earth* (1951), winner of the Pulitzer Prize in music, with Douglas Moore as composer. Around 1948 Sundgaard began adapting a play for the stage, *Way Up Yonder,* which is based on the biblical book of Job and set in the Colorado mountains. Author Charlotte Berry, who ran a theatrical camp in Colorado, had depicted Job as a rancher. Sundgaard liked the play very much and believed it could be made into a musical. He wrote the script and lyrics and called it *The Wind Blows Free* (it was later retitled *Western Star*).

But who would do the composing? Dancer Gene Kelly suggested Wilder. Sundgaard, then living on Long Island, liked the idea and reached him in Kutztown. Would he do it? Exploded Wilder: "I'm through with New York. I never want to see it again. I'm not going back to New York, Ever!" (Wilder's booming voice once prompted an Algonquin bell captain to tell someone who had asked if he had seen Mr. Wilder: "One does not see Mr. Wilder; one hears him.") Fortunately, Wilder's bite was often less to be feared than his bark, and he wound up suggesting that the script be sent to him. Less than a week later he called Sundgaard to say that he had written seven of the songs, and he would like to play them for him at the home of tenor Frank Baker, his Eastman School colleague.

Auditions were held later in the year, but not enough money could be raised for production. The musical was finally given its premiere in June 1950, in the Antrim Playhouse near Suffern, New York. Baker sang the lead role of Job, guitarist Mundell Lowe's chamber orchestra played the music, and Dale Wasserman, who wrote *Man of La Mancha,* was the director. Although *The Wind Blows Free* was too fragile to succeed as an integrated piece—"The songs worked fine, but not the play itself," says Sundgaard—two of the songs would take on a life of their own: *Where Do You Go (When It Starts to Rain)?* and the touching folk song *Douglas Mountain,* recorded by popular Canadian children's artist Raffi, Shannon Bolin, and Jan De-Gaetani. So the first professional association between Wilder and Sundgaard was not unfruitful, and it would launch them on a partnership that was often rewarding, albeit sometimes difficult and maddening for Sundgaard.

Wilder moved more fully and formally into Sundgaard's professional life after the death in 1950 of the German-born composer Kurt Weill, who had arrived in this country in 1935 from Paris, where he had gone when the Nazis forced him out of Germany. He had already established himself as a gifted composer of the post–World War I generation in Germany. In theatrical composition, several of his collaborations with Bertolt Brecht were highly successful, and Marc Blitzstein's adaptation of *Die Dreigroschenoper, The Threepenny Opera,* would make Weill almost a household name in the United States, but only after his death. Making the transition from a German to an American composer was difficult, but Weill contributed significantly with the works he took to the Broadway theater, including *Lady in the Dark,* with Gertrude Lawrence, and *One Touch of Venus,* with Mary Martin. He showed his interest in American folk material with the 1948 opera *Down in the Valley*, for which Sundgaard was the lyricist. This was a work written for amateurs and school productions, and was well received.

Sundgaard has recalled that Wilder was in the Algonquin lobby when he met Alan Jay Lerner as he was leaving for Indiana for the first performance of *Down in the Valley*. Lerner's wife, Marian Bell, was singing the lead. This was apparently Wilder's first intimation of the premiere, and he took umbrage on Sundgaard's behalf when he learned that Sundgaard had not been invited. "He never let me off the hook for not protesting the apparent slight," says Sundgaard. "I didn't know what to think. I felt hurt, naturally, but I also accepted it as the price one paid for being a librettist. It has always been an exercise in anonymity."

Sundgaard, a tolerant man, was not inclined to take offense at that discourtesy or at omission of his name from the cover of the Schirmer publication, and has cited several instances of Weill's concern to give him credit for this and other contributions. But Wilder ever after would have few good things to say about Weill. Whether he was reacting to what he perceived as Weill's poor treatment of Sundgaard or whether he was simply expressing one of those endless personal prejudices of his is impossible to tell.

Certainly, Sundgaard didn't admire Wilder for always putting down Weill "as a fiercely ambitious operator in the field of music whereas he, Alec, professed a scorn for the establishment. He said Kurt carried a briefcase and his shoes were polished! However, I don't know what to make of that because Richard Rodgers, whose music he admired, also polished his shoes." Wilder's diminishments seemed as much personal as professional. Says Sundgaard:

> When *Down in the Valley* was given a performance at the high school in Nyack near New City, where Kurt and [Lotte] Lenya [his wife] lived, Alec came to see it. After the performance I was standing with Kurt and several other people in the hallway and Alec—not seeing Kurt in the group—came up to me and said, as I remember it, "You must congratulate Mr. Weill for me. He has done what I thought impossible; he has turned folk songs into middle class music." He heavily accented the "V" for the "W" just as he had done with Fritz Loewe's name. Then he saw Kurt and scurried away in embarrassment. Fortunately Kurt hadn't heard or seen him.

All that didn't dissuade Sundgaard from working with Wilder. After Weill's death, Hans Heinsheimer of Schirmer called Sundgaard to say that with the success of *Down in the Valley*, the publishing house would like him to try something in a similar vein. Did he have a composer he would like to work with? After his experience in collaborating with him on *The Wind Blows Free*, Sundgaard suggested Wilder, and the two men were commissioned first to do *The Lowland Sea*.

With Wilder, more than music was involved in his partnerships. As with Engvick and others, he became in Sundgaard's life a tumultuous, animating presence that extended far beyond clefs and bars. "Alec," Sungaard has said frankly, "was certainly the most important influence in my life." Engvick touches on something important about Wilder when he says that to fail to take the man into account is to miss much of what he was about. "Alec the friend, the benefactor, the witty conversationalist, the critic, the eccentric, and the beguiler of kids, overshadowed his other output. And his range of interests was extraordinary. To many of us, this put the music into second place."

At any rate, Sundgaard, when he started writing the school operas, was catapulted into various wild adventures with Wilder. They traveled all over by train. Sundgaard associates the trains with mostly happy memories of work and good companionship, save for a time when a drunken Wilder called him from Mineola (the Sundgaards lived then in Old Westbury) and said he simply had to talk with him. He said he was in a bar across from the railroad station. Sundgaard drove over and found Wilder in desperate state. He said he wanted to go out to Missoula, Montana, and end his life by jumping into a canyon of snow. Sundgaard talked him into going home with him. But at midnight, Wilder suddenly insisted that he had to leave to catch a train. "Alec, there are no more trains tonight." Said Wilder, "Then I'll wait for one. Take me to the station." About three in the morning, by which time Wilder had sobered up, he called Sundgaard to say, "You're right, Arnold, there aren't any more trains."

At one point Wilder became an ardent bird-watcher. He had learned that in the third week of every April warblers traveled through a particular valley in Asheville, North Carolina. So he equipped himself with a pair of large binoculars and told Sundgaard that they'd just have to get down there for the migration. They rented a car, drove to Asheville and started looking. That year, though, the warblers were late because the spring had been cold. Wilder and Sundgaard kept driving and drifting southward until in Clemson, South Carolina, they finally found a warbler flock. They returned to New York in time for a performance of *The Lowland Sea* at Brooklyn College. Sundgaard and his wife, Marge, attended the performance, having arranged to meet Alec there. "And there he was with that pair of big binoculars around his neck. The tenor turned out to be so terrible that suddenly Alec put the binoculars to his eyes and fixed them on the tenor. Everyone in the audience thought Alec was quite mad. We were seated in about the eighth row."

Writing individual songs and opera numbers with Wilder was both stimulating and frustrating. Sundgaard would become angry with him, and then the storm would pass. "He was not easy to work with, and yet he was so sweet and generous. When the kids were young, one playing viola and the other violin, Alec wrote beautiful duets for them. They were copied beautifully, just beautiful music. Many things like that he gave away, for birthdays and the like." When Wilder looked at a lyric, Sundgaard has explained, it was almost like a mirror, so that the music was reflected out of it. "It came back to him immediately. If it didn't come back at once, it never came. Then he would feel instinctively that there was something wrong with the lyric." When the lyric was smiling back at him, as it were, things sometimes moved fast. Wilder called the Sundgaards one evening as they were preparing supper. He had a title for a song—*Doubt in My Mind But Hope in My Heart*—and he wanted Sundgaard to write the lyric. "I said I'd work on it. It came very quickly for me, and I called him back about 20 minutes later, around 6:30, and read the lyric over the phone. At 7 he called again and sang the song. The whole thing was done in less than an hour."

The first of the Schirmer operas, *The Lowland Sea* (1952), set in a whaling town reminiscent of Nantucket, was written with the help of a grant from the Guggenheim Memorial Foundation. It had a cast of eleven players and ran for fifty-five minutes. The premiere took place on May 8, 1952, in the Hillsdale Junior High School Auditorium in Montclair, New Jersey, with the Montclair State Teachers College Players. According to Sundgaard, Wilder had said he would write his own folk music, as it were, for this production. "And so the songs in that work are all his own. The words for *The Cuckoo Is a Pretty Bird* are traditional, but the melody is Alec's. I soon forgot what the original melody was really like." Roger Carpenter, reviewing the production, described it as a work of modest pretensions, redolent of the sea and its songs, possessing a vaguely Whitmanesque quality of wistfulness. The music, he said, had some wonderful moments, notably a haunting shanty song by the male chorus hauling ropes on board "that might have come straight out of the repertory of Joan Baez." Engvick says he once saw *The Lowland Sea* performed by young people at a fine Quaker school in Pennsylvania: "It was just right, and the young people loved it."

Sunday Excursion, about twenty-five minutes in length, was written the following year for a cast of five players and chorus and was performed for the first time by the Grassroots Opera Company at the National Federation of Music Clubs Convention in New York. It had subsequent performances that year in Interlochen, Michigan, and Minneapolis, Minnesota. When some of the New York critics were less than kind, Mitch Miller jumped quickly to the opera's defense. He noted that its reception up to that summer had been little less than extraordinary, and he was convinced that "the New York newspaper criticisms . . . are invalid in so far as they were flagrantly based upon a frame of judgment in which neither innocence nor simplicity possesses any of the positive values to which I personally feel they are entitled." The third of the school operas, *Cumberland Fair,* was also written in 1953. In that year, too, Sundgaard and Wilder produced the larger two-act work *Kittiwake Island,* closer to musical comedy than to opera but written in the same time frame and stemming largely from the bird-watching expeditions that Wilder had embarked on with Sundgaard. This work did have a brief off-Broadway run of seven performances in the Martinique Theatre but did not do well.

Sundgaard has noted that none of the pieces he and Wilder wrote for Schirmer had nearly the number of performances enjoyed by *Down in the Valley,* the production he had worked on with Kurt Weill. The reason, he believed, was that Wilder paid little attention to the dramatic structure of the libretto—an observation that Engvick would also make. Said Sundgaard: "He seemed so pleased to have words to work with that he skimmed through the pages to see where the music would fit. Once he almost wrote music for a stage direction." Wilder might have disagreed, but he was aware of the limits of the pieces, and he was willing to take blame for the fact that they never had big-city productions or recordings. "There have been other writers who have written similar operas of no greater merit who have had that enviable (and repulsive) aggressiveness which has pushed their small operas into the realm of urban, status-minded society."

The school operas did, however, fill a need, and both Wilder and Sundgaard deserve credit for their efforts. Wilder has said he knew some composers who would have refused such an assignment. "On the one hand, they weren't hack work, on the other, they didn't permit free sway to one's invention. They were for schools and colleges, or more succinctly, amateur groups." But he by no means dismissed them, noting that they posed all kinds of useful disciplines: "The very fact that they were for groups who wished to sing for the fun of it and not to gain another jewel in the crown of their career was incentive enough to write them." He and Sundgaard had fun doing them, he said, people had fun performing them, and invariably some shining talents emerged in some aspect of the productions. "And God knows, they were grateful for them, as the only alternatives were the grand operas, which were impractical, or the hack operas, which were sterile."

Wilder would do other creative work with Sundgaard in the years ahead, but his next operatic endeavor would be with Engvick in the show now known as *Ellen* but originally titled *The Long Way.* Engvick and Wilder had kept working together right along on such musical creations as *Miss Chicken Little* (1953). Now Wilder would also be reunited with singer Frank Baker, who would produce *The Long Way* and also sing the baritone role. Another old Wilder friend, Rogers Brackett, the man who had wanted to produce *The Impossible Forest,* came on board as director. The combination had its problems. Wilder and Baker wound up not speaking, and Brackett was apparently arbitrary in style. But the relationship between Wilder and Brackett would remain solid. Brackett lit up the world for Wilder with a brilliant, nourishing wit.

The Long Way, Wilder readily acknowledged, was out of its time: "It was tender, romantic, funny, entertaining, unpretentious, melodic, harmonious and downright innocent. Not one darn thing to recommend it! Its plot concerns the dreams of a thirteen-year-old girl. Scarcely grand opera! Scarcely Wagspeck." The lead part of the thirteen-year-old was convincingly carried off by twenty-eight-year-old June Erickson Gardner, who had had several successes in revues and shows. In

March 1955, Cuadro Productions put on a revue featuring Zero Mostel and Sono Osato called *Once Over Lightly* at the Barbizon-Plaza Theater. Engvick and Wilder had four songs in it from the 1946 *Chance of a Ghost: So Long to All That, It's Monogamy!, The Osteopathy Rag,* and *Here Beside Me.* Gardner was the singer, and she moved right from that show to the lead of *The Long Way.* She proved to be a quick learner and an adept performer. "You prepared the role in an astonishingly short time," Wilder told her. "You caused no problem in rehearsal. You didn't get panicky when you got laryngitis two nights before we opened. You commuted from New York, you adjusted to a cast largely of amateur actors and singers, and you gave two absolutely perfect performances."

Gardner did not find it easy to handle Wilder's songs because his compositions almost always make big demands. "With Alec," explains Gardner, "you must have it in your head before you can sing it, or you kill yourself. I've done a lot of opera and I've done Shakespeare. He's tough. He's the only composer in my entire life that I couldn't sightread. Once you got it, it was heaven, but I could not sightread him."

If Wilder the composer made the going tough, Wilder the man buoyed and lifted up Gardner, whose first theater job out of college had been with Katharine Hepburn. She toured six and a half months in *As You Like It,* playing Phoebe to Hepburn's Rosalind. "She was such a dynamite woman. Eight performances a week, and you're supposed to have a technique to sustain a performance. She knew when to give me maybe a kick in the ass, but she also knew that I needed help." Help was also forthcoming from Wilder: "He was the one who told me that as a human being I was special, that I didn't have to be anyone else. He was determined to let me know that it was all right for me to be just who I was, and nobody had ever said that to me before." Wilder was often to do that for young performers.

Opera rehearsals were often difficult. Wilder was stressed, Engvick recalls, and threw himself and a lot of money into the production. "But the strain and anxiety led to impatience." Both Wilder and Brackett were apparently short of temper with the cast, "most of whom were amateur performers who would have responded warmly to more considerate treatment." Friction between professional and amateur hindered things. The presence at rehearsal of Sarah Churchill, something of a Wilder camp follower, also turned out to be awkward. Wilder had met the actress through Brackett the year before, and she had been attracted to him. Several Churchill letters to Wilder from London, New York, and Los Angeles made that clear. Wilder for his part maintained a careful rearguard watchfulness against her overtures. In any event, Brackett and Wilder, as Engvick remembers, were not considerate about introducing Churchill all around at rehearsal. That added to the general resentment.

The Long Way, produced by Baker and the Rockland Foundation, libretto by Engvick and music by Wilder, was presented at the Nyack High School on June 3 and 4, 1955. Alas, the critics, to the extent that they took any notice at all, were not taken by the production. "You noticed, didn't you," Wilder commented bitterly, "that never was a word said in the Great City about our little suburban production. And there were plenty of ferret-eyed scouts there just in case. But of course nothing was said or done! Remember that Gogarty said that 'life is an arena without a culture.'" There had been such high hopes. "The music was gorgeous, the lyrics fantastic," remembers Gardner. "We had so much hoped it would go on." Those who saw and heard *The Long Way* greatly praised it. As Engvick has wryly observed, "No one liked it but the audience." With a strong professional supporting cast, with more money for its mounting and promotion, and with a producer of note, *The Long Way* might indeed have succeeded on Broadway. As it is, the opera remains mostly unknown; audiences never reached a critical mass.

What was true for most of the operas—giving great pleasure to small audiences in small auditoriums—would also be true for Wilder's work in film. The small screen of documentary and experimental filmmaking would give him much more creative satisfaction and more to show for his efforts than the world of the big screen. In 1953, just two years before they embarked on *The Long Way,* Wilder and Engvick had worked briefly in Hollywood for the one and only time. It was by all accounts a good partnership, resulting in a film score for a musical that they believed represented some of their best work. But again the world was denied a chance to make a judgment; the score remains locked away in a studio vault.

The call to Hollywood came from Frank Taylor, who told Engvick he was producing a film called *Daddy Long Legs* for Twentieth Century Fox and wanted Engvick and Wilder to write the score. The opportunity was too good to be passed up, although the omens weren't particularly good. Taylor was fired even before Wilder and Engvick arrived on the Coast. The word was that he was too literate, artistic, and trendy for the film establishment. His nominal replacement, screen writer Casey Robinson, advised the two men to write the score anyway; even if *Daddy Long Legs* were never filmed, they would be paid for their work. So they took the script and began.

The Los Angeles area did not impress Wilder, but he was pleased by their workplace, a secluded guest house on the Douglas Fairbanks estate that looked out on the Will Rogers State Park and the Pacific. Engvick remembers it as an ideal place to work and the experience as "one of the pleasantest times with Alec. He was happy to be working and I was happy to have some money in my pocket for the first time in my life. Alec visited the studio as seldom as possible but I insisted on driving through the studio gate to pick up my weekly check." When the scriptwriter found he needed more time, Wilder made a deal with Fox, says Engvick. "We would go to New York until they summoned us. They paid the fares—on the TRAIN of course. And that's just what happened." Had they decided to stay on in Hollywood, the waiting period would have been a bonanza, for they would have continued to be paid, and less scrupulous types would have done just that. "But," said Wilder later, "we decided that if we weren't working we shouldn't be paid. So we decided to go home. We would come back when needed. Now, if you've ever known anything about the ways of the film industry, you know that one *never* passes up such a situation as this." Only a village idiot, he added, would give up a handsome weekly pay check for God knows how long just on a matter of principle.

Leave they did, returning several months later, again to a good working climate. Because Irving Berlin had rented the main house on the Fairbanks estate, and because the guest house had only an extension, no phone calls were permitted. The quiet was conducive to work. Again, Engvick and Wilder might have behaved like many of the other screen writers, padding out their assignment and picking up paychecks with no questions asked, but that wasn't their style. Also, Wilder didn't want to spend any more time in Hollywood than absolutely necessary, and because of that, says Engvick, "we wrote about 15 songs in record time, and got out, never to hear any more about it." The film might have had a chance if they had been more aggressive. Said Wilder:

> We had no press agent, no manager. We went, during the entire time we were there, to only one party, at Fran Ferrer's [then married to Mel Ferrer]. We took no one to dinner, let none of the people I knew in the film business know we were working on a picture. I never asked Peggy Lee, for example, to give me a party, invite Fox executives, learn a few of the songs and thereby make it known that something interesting was being written by two fairly talented people.

After Fox sold the rights later, *Daddy Long Legs* was eventually filmed with Fred Astaire and Leslie Caron, with music by Johnny Mercer. It remains a sad fact that the songwriting achievements of Wilder and Engvick can never be fully judged as long as the original music for *Daddy Long Legs* remains out of the public domain. For a few years at the Christmas season, Mabel Mercer sang one song they had written for the film, *The Family Is Home*. Otherwise, nothing. No one knows what magic may have been lost.

Wilder's disillusionment with the Hollywood scene was all of a piece with his encounters on the East Coast with the aspiring young film star James Dean. The means of their meeting was Rogers Brackett, a "Culver City brat" as he called himself, the son of an early Hollywood film producer and well connected in the film industry. He was an account supervisor with the advertising agency of Foote, Cone and Belding. One of his accounts in Hollywood sponsored the weekly CBS program *Alias Jane Doe,* with Brackett doubling as the show's director. Dean, like so many young out-of-work actors in the early 1950s, was parking cars at the CBS lot and, when money was short, accepting dinner invitations from gay men.

The day came when Dean parked a car for Brackett, and before long Brackett was casting him in small parts in such shows as *Alias Jane Doe* and *Stars over*

Hollywood. They wound up in an affair. Though intuitively intelligent, Dean was ignorant of the sophisticated world around him, and Brackett took him in hand, grooming him in the arts and the social conventions. Brackett worked with Dean in Hollywood until Dean became disenchanted with the "Strip Set." He was urged by James Whitmore and others to hone his acting abilities in New York, home of the famed Actors Studio, good theater, and live television. The real impetus may have come when Brackett was reassigned to advertising work in Chicago. Dean accompanied him, and then was urged by Brackett to go to New York ahead of him.

Eventually, the two of them would live for a time in a studio on the top floor of a five-story loft building in the West Twenties. Brackett meantime called Wilder at the Algonquin from Chicago and asked him to get Dean a room at the Iroquois Hotel, a few doors away. Dean, Wilder remembered, traveled east on the *Twentieth Century* and burst in on him in the Rose Room at the Algonquin. "He almost instantly told me some wild involved joke about a fire engine and behaved even more outrageously than his youth warranted." Wilder wrote some pieces for the recorder Dean was playing, and Dean played them over on the telephone for him. Dean, said Wilder, was "short, physically strong, weak-eyed to the extent he needed glasses, cheerful, uninformed, a prankster."

At the urging of Wilder and Brackett, set designer Lemuel Ayers gave Dean a reading for a challenging part in a new play he was producing, N. Richard Nash's *See the Jaguar.* Dean landed the role. Ayers also asked Wilder to write the incidental music for the production, plus some simple tunes for Dean to sing in the show. Too few funds were available; to save money on an orchestra, Wilder was obliged to write a score using only choral voices that could be put on tape. After short runs in Hartford, Connecticut, and Philadelphia, *See the Jaguar* opened at the Cort Theater on Broadway on December 3, 1952.

Opening night was not propitious. In the first act, the stereo equipment on which Wilder's music had been recorded broke down, and no one could fix it. In the second act, the stage manager missed a prop cue and forgot to fire a gun in a crucial scene. The reviews were bad; Brooks Atkinson in the *New York Times* called the production a "mess." The play ran for only five nights, and Wilder lost the best part of a thousand dollars in the production. Despite the unfavorable reviews, Dean was singled out for praise. Walter Kerr of the *Herald Tribune* went as far as to write, "James Dean adds an extraordinary performance in an almost impossible role." Dean had been plucked out of obscurity.

Although his acting talents grew in New York, Dean was often hard to like. Brackett and Wilder had each played the role of finishing school and had helped him get a foothold in the theater, but both were to be tossed aside as Dean's fame grew. Brackett later lost his ad agency job, and biographer Ronald Martinetti tells of a meeting Brackett had with Dean over a drink to ask for a loan until things got better. "Dean replied, 'Sorry, Pops.'" He also told Brackett that he felt he had "outgrown" him and Alec Wilder, and no longer wished to be friends. To this Brackett replied, "You might outgrow me, but I don't think you can ever outgrow Alec Wilder." Wilder, according to Martinetti, saw Dean as a "neurotic, mixed up kid who tried to con everybody to death. There just wasn't an ounce of maturity in that boy." For himself, Wilder didn't seem to care about Dean's attitude, but it infuriated him that Brackett, who had done so much for the young actor, should be so cavalierly dismissed. And he apparently did something about it. James Maher remembers:

> Jimmy becomes a big gun, comes back to the Algonquin and at this point was going through some kind of religiosity thing. He apparently came into the hotel and was not at all friendly or nice to Tony and Harry (Algonquin staff) and the old gang, and Alec resented that. He resented that kind of attitude, the distancing that had come about. Dean would sit around and read his various guru books and not talk to these people. Finally, Alec one night cornered Jimmy, got him up in his room, and made him sit down, and he dictated a letter for Jimmy to write to Rogers to thank him for all the help he had given at the beginning and such, and Alec mailed it. Quite a moment, for Alec could be like an angry grandfather. I guess he came down pretty hard on Dean. It was Alec at his best.

The friendship between Wilder and Brackett was always solid gold. It made no difference that Brackett was a homosexual and, by the best available evidence, Wilder was not. It has been speculated that if ever Wilder were to have had a homosexual encounter, it might well have been with Brackett, except that the laughter that always enveloped them would have made such an encounter impossible. Brackett was a man of great wit who once described the then Episcopal bishop of La Jolla, a relentlessly cheerful man, as Gregarious the First. Although he said he was never himself a practicing homosexual, Wilder reveled in the company of many such men and was never clandestine or apologetic about those friendships. Whenever he went to Key West, he would almost always spend a few days at Tennessee Williams's house, where the homosexual atmosphere was warm and nonintimidating.

Nothing that Wilder and Brackett did together was zanier than the great doll exchange. "For years," said Algonquin bellman Tony Cichiello, "the two of them had this scrawny little doll they kept trying to palm off on each other. Once Mr. Brackett got it to Mr. Wilder at Christmas by having it baked in a cake. Then Mr. Wilder would find a way to get it back to him, perhaps by having a friend mail a package from, say, Phoenix." They would send it back and forth in orange crates and refrigerator cases, sometimes with a spike through the heart.

His abortive film-score writing in Hollywood and his disdain for such brilliant but brittle Hollywood products as James Dean would always be partly offset for Wilder by his love of Judy Holliday, the enormously talented but precariously balanced star of film and stage. Like two wounded birds, Holliday and Wilder seemed drawn to each other, bound by a common unwillingness to jettison principle for success. Holliday was a woman both timid and aggressive, scarred by tragedy but capable of plucking some genuine happiness from life, never really liking the Hollywood world but willing to stay in it and put down the gossip. She had jumped into the spotlight in true theater tradition. When Jean Arthur, the star of the Garson Kanin comedy *Born Yesterday,* became ill and had to leave the show, Holliday was summoned by the producer and given seventy-two hours to learn the role of Billie Dawn, the feather-headed mistress of a megalomaniac junkman. Both the play and the subsequent movie were tremendous hits. But unlike so many other actors, she never allowed herself to be besmirched by Hollywood, and that alone made her Wilder's friend for life.

Martin Russ has given one small glimpse of Wilder and Holliday as he sat with them in the Copacabana at a Sinatra opening night, with Sinatra substituting "Wilder" for "Gershwin" in *I Like a Gershwin Tune, How About You?* He remembers Wilder's disgruntlement and his own disappointment when, just as it seemed that a brilliant evening was under way, someone brought a white telephone to the table. "It turned out that Miss Holliday's mother, Mrs. Tuvim, was suddenly being very needy, and the extremely attractive Miss Holliday had to leave and go tend to her demanding Ma. My impression is that Alec was seriously smitten with Miss Holliday, and that he was impressed with her intelligence and wit." Wilder has given us this anecdote about a small incident at the Algonquin Hotel:

> Late one afternoon four of us sat at a table in the Algonquin lobby. Three of us were feeling fairly lively, and the fourth was quite amused by our half-seas-overage but remained sober herself. The others were Rogers Brackett, Gerry Mulligan, the great jazz musician, and that truly magical lady, Judy Holliday. The three men in our group were using rather raw language and not in whispers. The proper people at the next table began to stare and then to whisper amongst themselves. It was clear that they recognized Miss Holliday and were torn between making a protest and asking for an autograph. But before they could make up their minds, Judy leaned out of her chair, the one closest to them, and said in her gentle, husky voice, "Stick around for the performance! This is just a rehearsal."

Holliday was always a special person to Wilder. He had an idealized love of a woman both simple and complex. Particularly did he delight in her awareness of what he called the secret places in his music:

> You knew the measures I most loved in every concert piece I ever played for you; I don't know about other composers but I have secret places which are complete expressions of myself. They may last for no more than a few mea-

sures but they're quivery spots. They more often than not are quiet places. Nothing to attract attention, simply special tenderness, special self-revelation. You always knew them the instant you heard them.

In 1958 Holliday cut a record album for Columbia. She chose songs by Berlin, Bernstein, Blaine, Wilder, and others. The album was called *Trouble Is a Man*, after the Wilder song that she sang as the opening number. However, the recording did not sell well and was soon dropped from the Columbia catalog. A short seven years later, at forty-four, Holliday died of cancer. To Wilder, she would forever represent all the strong and gentle, clean and understanding things he had ever dreamed as being part of the personality of a "sometime, someplace woman, girl, female."

Holliday was a person of high courage as well as high comedy, refusing for example to be cowed by the Communist-heresy hunts of the early 1950s. Wilder admired her no less for the way she stood up in his behalf to the powerful Harry Cohn of Columbia, well known for his profanity and vulgarity. William Engvick has recalled that Holliday took Wilder to Cohn's office so that he could sing some of his songs for Cohn. "That was a tactical error, as Alec was not a slick performer. Cohn ran true to form and blasted Alec and his work unprintably. Whereupon Judy told off the Mogul in no uncertain terms." Wilder himself recalled that he had gone through eight bars or so of his first song when Cohn interrupted, saying to Holliday that she was wasting his time. He said he had a thirty-five-piece orchestra to do those things. He was rotten rude according to Wilder, but Holliday refused to be pushed aside. She wanted Cohn to listen, and Cohn was afraid that he might lose a star. Holliday was marvelous, Wilder said. She was willing to put her career on the line for him.

By contrast with the arrogant Cohns of Hollywood, Wilder drew immense pleasure from his later associations with independent documentary filmmaker Jerome Hill. Although he had no admiration for industrial magnates, it no doubt amused Wilder's fancy and delighted the train lover in him that Jerome's great wealth had been inherited through his grandfather, railroad builder J. J. Hill. The grandson was a man Wilder could completely relate to, for he indulged in none of the dictatorial, haughty mannerisms of most of the rich. "It is always amazing to me to see anyone of great wealth become more than a dilettante in the arts." Hill, born in St. Paul, had majored in music at Yale, studied painting in Rome and Paris, and compiled a book of still photography in Greece. Although he maintained homes in Cassis and Paris, on Long Island and in San Francisco, the Algonquin was apparently the epicenter of his film life. It was there that Wilder came to know and to like him.

Wilder scored the music for three Jerome Hill films: *Albert Schweitzer* (1957), *The Sand Castle* (1959), and *Open the Door And See All the People* (1963). His first association, however, was with the 1950 Hill documentary *Grandma Moses*, for which songwriter Hugh Martin (*The Trolley Song, Have Yourself a Merry Little Christmas*) did the music and Wilder the arranging and orchestrating. The film score became the basis for the *New England Suite for Orchestra* and the theater piece *Beauty and the Beast*. Poet Archibald MacLeish wrote and spoke the narrative. The documentary was well received and Wilder's part in it had been satisfying to him. Martin went so far as to say that Wilder's work transcended orchestration to the point where it became a composition. He also recalled the night the two of them drove up to Grandma Moses' farm in Eagle Bridge, New York. Grandma Moses, to Martin's way of thinking, was as remarkable in her way as Wilder was in his. Alec, he said, had the purity and innocence that she had; it was lovely to see them together, a perfect matching of quality.

The 1957 Schweitzer film was a more ambitious, eighty-minute documentary, with Hill doing the producing and directing; Wilder, the film score; and actor Fredric March the narrating of Schweitzer's own words. Hill had once recorded several Schweitzer organ recitals, and he was fascinated, as so many were, that this organist, musicologist, teacher, and preacher should suddenly decide to study medicine in order to become a medical missionary in Lambaréné, Equatorial Africa. One reviewer welcomed the film as a "splendid documentary." As was so often the case with Wilder's music, the critics disagreed about the film score. Henry Hart in *Films in Review* said it was "unimaginative and often inappropriate." The *New York Times* called it "tasteful and eloquent." No matter. Wilder had only praise for the environment in which the music had been made and recorded. The recording sessions, he said, were like reunions insofar as he always asked for the very best players.

Hill could not have been more cooperative. He knew that Wilder had written the music with specific players in mind, so he did not ask him to let the Minneapolis Symphony record the music, even though its annual deficit was covered in most part by the Hill family. Nor did he ask Wilder to consider Charles Munch as conductor, even though he was Schweitzer's brother-in-law. Wilder did not, however, have the same high regard for Schweitzer that he had for Grandma Moses. The reasons are not very clear, though he apparently felt that the famous man was too self-anointed. William Engvick recalls that some time after the documentary had been released he found in his trash can a letter from Schweitzer praising Wilder's score for the film. Also discarded was a photograph of Schweitzer that he had inscribed to Wilder and that had been torn into small pieces. "I asked Alec how he could have thrown these interesting communications away, and he said, 'Why not? I've read them.'"

The Sand Castle, a very different creation, was filmed at Laguna Beach. Hill produced, directed, and wrote it; Wilder did the score and played a fisherman. It is the story of a boy's afternoon at the beach. What happens in his waking consciousness is filmed in black and white; what he dreams is shot in color. When the boy builds a sand castle, the usual holiday crowd gathers to watch him. When the boy falls asleep under an umbrella, he explores in his dreams the interior of his castle and meets the people who had surrounded him while he was building it. *The Sand Castle* was a fanciful, beguiling film that drew some good reviews.

Wilder would do one more film with Hill, *Open the Door And See All the People*, given its North American premiere at the Vancouver film festival. Critics received it less well. Its whimsical moments and sequences of airy nonsense, said *Variety,* were not enough to offset the meandering plot line and sustain interest for ninety-one minutes. The film was about the differing social values and conflicting personalities of two New England families headed by seventy-year-old identical twin sisters, one wealthy and domineering, and the other a happy-go-lucky grandmother working as a cashier in a supermarket. Wilder, noted *Variety,* was cast as an unemployed husband to the poor but happy twin sister "and registers well in an ineffectual part." Alas, Wilder was noticed for a role that was apparently not a good one, but his music received no attention at all. Yet there was to be a happy sequel to the film. Wilder sent a tape of the soundtrack to Engvick, who liked the music so well that he began writing lyrics to it.

(The two men often worked apart, and sometimes with others. Engvick has said:

> I decided that to become professional I'd try any project offered me for a pe-
> riod of ten years. I'm glad I did, because it resulted in *The Song from Moulin
> Rouge, Anna, Kiss and Run, Crazy in the Heart, All Yours, Bonnie Blue Gal,*
> the Dietrich-Clooney japes and others that led to security. But the most satis-
> fying work has always been with Alec.

There was seldom any money in it, but it was with Wilder that he was best able to indulge the sheer joy of lyric writing. From his first professional assignment, Engvick stayed true to the notion that "if you can't write a million-dollar song, write a million songs at a dollar a try.")

The lyric writing to the music from the film *Open the Door* went so well that the result was six of the best of all the Wilder-Engvick songs: *That's My Girl; Mimosa and Me; Remember, My Child; I See It Now; Love Is When;* and *Unbelievable.* The seventh published song from *Open the Door, Such a Lonely Girl Am I,* had lyrics by Wilder. In *That's My Girl,* Engvick did something unique in lyric writing: he used the last word of a phrase, or last syllable, as the first word or syllable of the next phrase, set in a different context. Thus "laughter in the *wind*" is followed by "*wind*ows in the *sun*," and that gives way in turn to "*Sun*day in a quiet town." He used the same device toward the end of the song: "Though I'm over*board* / *bored* is what I'm *not* / *Knot*ted in the good old way."© Wilder said about this:

> It's terribly clever and it works [a word that was always Wilder's criterion for
> success] and it doesn't get in the way. It's brilliant, and he was very proud of

it. And I'm very proud of him for having done it. And I say it's a unique lyrical device never before done even by Mr. Lorenz Hart. Besides which, the lyrics all work.

I See It Now, another of the numbers from *Open the Door,* has been rated by Ronald E. Prather as perhaps the most romantic of all the Wilder-Engvick songs, with the melody using "a series of stepwise ascending phrases of ever-increasing intensity to create an effective musical statement." Gerry Matthews sang the first public performance of *I See It Now* under the title *Making of a Man* in the revue *Dime a Dozen,* that opened on October 18, 1962, at the Plaza Hotel. (*I See It Now* was beautifully rendered by Sinatra in 1965 in his album, *The September of My Years.*)

Mimosa and Me became one of the most requested of the songs sung by two of Wilder's best and most loyal vocal interpreters, the wife-and-husband team Jackie Cain and Roy Kral. Mimosa was the name of the girl in the *Open the Door* movie. Engvick liked the word *mimosa,* Wilder recalled, "and it's a nice one. And he says some perfectly adorable things." Wilder took great pride in Engvick's talents. In the case of *Remember, My Child,* Jackie Cain had always liked the melody a great deal. Engvick wanted to write lyrics for her, but could not find a title. According to Wilder, he kept hunting for a phrase that might include a comma at a point in the melody where there's a suggested pause. Engvick went to lunch at the hotel one day disconsolate because he wanted to please Jackie. "He loved her very much. And out of the blue, as I recall, I fell on this title and immediately the lyric got written, and I think it's one of the greatest lyrics I've ever heard in my life."

> Remember, My Child, remember sunlight and shade
> The laughter, the games, the pretty castles that you made
> How you loved all the little things
> Dragonflies in their paper wings. ©

When Engvick completed the lyric, he sent a copy to Jackie with a note: "Dear Jackie. This song exists for you and because of you." Jackie still has the note. She also has one from Wilder that she holds equally close. When Willis Conover asked Jackie and Roy to do a special show of all-Wilder music for Voice of America, *Remember, My Child* was one of the songs chosen. "It was a song I could identify with, then having two daughters myself," says Jackie. "When we came back to the table from doing the song [at Michael's Pub in New York], I was kind of nervous, for everyone was there. We returned to the table and sat down, and Alec pushed over this little note in red ink saying, 'I don't ever want anyone else to ever sing that song,' I melted. I still have his note."

The *Open the Door* film had made no stir when it was released, but its sequel of songs created its own separate magic. So often in Wilder's career something jumped out of the picture and illuminated the moment. He seldom lit up the entire landscape, but he was always capable of bathing part of it—a field of daffodils, a girl in love, a mimosa shrub—in a special light. And he owed this latest burst of sunshine first to Engvick for his inspired lyrics and then to Jerome Hill. This filmmaker who worked in something of the same avant-garde tradition of Sibley Watson in Rochester a quarter of a century before did not achieve much fame, but he allowed his artists full rein. He nourished Wilder, as Sundgaard had done with the school operas. However, changes were taking place in the music scene that would move Wilder to find other kinds of nourishment. They would affect Engvick also, and indeed all to whom innocence and romance in music were a matter of faith.

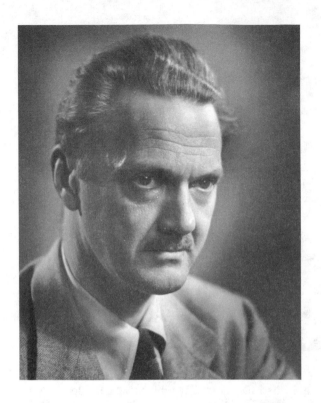

A formal studio portrait of Wilder taken in 1953. *(Copyright © by Louis Ouzer)*

Dr. James Sibley Watson, Jr., lifetime friend, mentor and benefactor to Wilder. *(Photo by Josef Schiff)*

From left, Urling Sibley Iselin (a cousin to Sibley Watson), Hildegarde Lasell Watson, and Alec Wilder in the Sibley home at 6 Sibley Place, Rochester, New York, around 1930. *(Photo courtesy of Nancy Watson Dean and the Sibley Music Library)*

William Engvick and Wilder at work on a song in March 1952, at Stony Point, New York. *(Photo courtesy of Frances Miller)*

Wilder and his MG: *(Above)* Arnold Sundgaard and Wilder out-
side Clark Galehouse's Golden Crest Studios, Huntington, Long
Island, New York, around 1955. *(Photo courtesy of Arnold
Sundgaard)*

(Below) With the Ouzer children, Sandy and Billy, outside their
Rochester home in 1957. *(Copyright © by Louis Ouzer)*

Wilder listening to a tape at Eastman School in 1967.
(Copyright © by Louis Ouzer)

Wilder with his foot on the I-beam that he and Ouzer got from a junk yard and that was used for percussion in *Entertainment No. 1* in an Eastman Wind Ensemble performance conducted by the founder Frederick Fennell in Eastman Theater in May, 1961. *(Copyright © by Louis Ouzer)*

Wilder and some of his favorite performers. *(Above)* With Mary Mayo (left) and Mabel Mercer. *(Copyright © by Louis Ouzer)*

(Below) With the wife-and-husband jazz duo Jackie Cain and Roy Kral in 1973. *(Copyright © by Louis Ouzer)*

Wilder among the books that were meat and drink to him in a used book store that has since vanished from Rochester's Main Street. *(Photo by Jim Laragy, courtesy of Gannett Rochester Newspapers)*

National Public Radio Popular Song series (American Popular Song with Alec Wilder and Friends): *(Above)* Wilder with co-host and fellow-songwriter Loonis McGlohon and singer Thelma Carpenter. *(Photo by Dick Phipps)*

(Below) Singer David Allyn with McGlohon and Wilder. *(Photo by Dick Phipps)*

Marian McPartland and Wilder blowing bubbles outside the Louis
Ouzer studio, near the Eastman School of Music in 1978.
(Copyright © by Louis Ouzer)

(Above) Pianist McPartland enjoys a light moment with Wilder in 1974. *(Copyright © by Louis Ouzer)*

(Below) Wilder with biographer Desmond Stone in the halls of the Eastman School in 1973. *(Copyright © by Louis Ouzer)*

Hotel rooms, particularly in the Algonquin, were often as close as the nomadic
Wilder got to home. Here he has just unpacked in a room at the former One
Eleven Hotel (now East Avenue Commons) in Rochester in 1972. *(Photo by
Jim Laragy, courtesy of Gannett Rochester Newspapers)*

At the Rainbow Grill, 1972, to celebrate the publication of Wilder's *American Popular Song*. *(Above)* Marian McPartland, Willis Conover, and James Maher. *(Copyright © by Louis Ouzer)*

(Below) Wilder, Sheldon Meyer of Oxford University Press, and Walter Clemons. *(Copyright © by Louis Ouzer)*

Wilder listens to a Duke University Wind Ensemble rehearsal in 1974.
(Copyright © by Louis Ouzer)

Wilder in Louis Ouzer's Gibbs Street Studio, Rochester, in 1977. *(Photo by Jim Laragy, courtesy of Gannett Rochester Newspapers)*

Wilder listening to a rehearsal at the Eastman School around 1960. *(Copyright © by Louis Ouzer)*

Boyhood friend Louis Ouzer with Wilder at Duke University, 1974. *(Copyright © by Louis Ouzer)*

Wilder with Mitch Miller on the occasion of the presentation to Wilder in 1974 of the Friends of the Rochester Public Library Literary Award. *(Copyright © by Louis Ouzer)*

Wilder composing in Louis Ouzer's Gibbs Street studio in 1974. *(Copyright © by Louis Ouzer)*

Plaque in the Alec Wilder
Reading Room, Sibley
Music Library, Eastman
School of Music.
*(Copyright © by Louis
Ouzer)*

Wilder watches the children lining up for the performance on May 3, 1969 of
Wilder's *Children's Plea for Peace* at Saint Agnes Church School Hall in Avon,
New York. *(Copyright © by Louis Ouzer)*

A rare photograph of Wilder and lifetime friend Lavinia Russ of New York City taken in 1972. *(Photo courtesy of Michael Geigher)*

In what may have been the last photo taken of him, Wilder listens to a rehearsal at the Eastman School on August 17, 1980, not much more than four months before his death. *(Copyright © by Louis Ouzer)*

9

From Pop to Long Hair

In Wilder's view, the rock and roll movement of the 1950s and '60s was like a blight spreading across the landscape of American music, staining all it touched, turning traditional values inside out. He seemed to take this eruption of youthful mass culture almost as a personal insult. Long after most people had perforce adapted to the noisy new phenomenon, long after most parents had given up trying to stop their teenage daughters from buying the records of Elvis Presley, Wilder was still out there shaking his fist on a lonely promontory. That "rotten" rock music seemed to him to be symptomatic of the age itself. There was plenty to be depressed about. The H-bomb was giving rise to doomsday predictions. The Soviet Union looked menacingly strong, and Senator Joseph McCarthy seemed bent on destroying the political system.

Although the pop scene had its familiar reassurances—*It's a Lovely Day Today, In the Cool, Cool, Cool of the Evening, On Top of Old Smokey*—sea changes were on the way. In May 1955 *Rock Around the Clock* by Bill Haley and the Comets became the best-selling recording in the country. Rock and roll, so unlike anything out of Tin Pan Alley, was cutting across cultural lines into the mainstream. By 1958 teenagers were buying 70 percent of all records, and much of traditional pop music was being drowned out by the thundering sound of rock with its driving, propulsive rhythms, its heavy bass and percussion, its use of electric guitar and other instrumental amplifications, and its suggestive lyrics. Established song forms such as the thirty-two-bar chorus had given way to odd-numbered formations and radical stanza patterns. Now the printed copy of the song was published after rather than before the recorded song. Nothing was the same anymore, although the new sound had not arrived overnight. It had antecedents in the black popular music and country music of the two previous decades.

Elvis Presley was the singer who epitomized it all. Each of his early singles—*Heartbreak Hotel, Don't Be Cruel,* and *Love Me Tender*—sold more than a million copies. By 1960 he had earned $120 million with records, sheet music, movie tickets, and merchandise. The establishment shuddered. To Wilder, highly literate himself and keenly attuned to the sensitive lyrics of Engvick, the words of rock were offensive and downright silly. He said about the whole phenomenon:

> The rock group has just played something on a TV show that is a dreadful insult to music, with lyrics that virtually exhort the kids to turn on with some drug. Following the usual hysterical audience response, the smiling "host" holds up his hands and says, "Wasn't that really super? And would you believe that these boys started to play the guitar only three weeks ago?" Three weeks ago—and they're already earning $500 a week each! Well, it's a familiar story in an age that's been conditioned to instant everything.

It was all fearful stuff, especially to a composer who never assaulted anyone's ear in his life, who believed that fortissimos belonged to circus bands, that nothing good in life could be accomplished without hard work and a long apprenticeship. He resented "the amateur incompetents who become heroes for a few weeks, make a million dollars, and then disappear into oblivion, while others, just as bad, begin to surface." And the worst of it, he felt, was that every young boy in the United States was being encouraged to believe that in three weeks he, too, could become a rock star.

The rock age was both cutting into Wilder's income from popular song royalties and dealing a blow to the aesthete in him. It did not happen all at once, but he began moving more and more into the field of serious instrumental concert music. The decline of market was a more important factor than the loss of money, for he had no expectation of making anything from concert music. In 1959 he testified before a congressional committee that jukebox operators should indeed pay royalty fees for the use of works by composers and authors. He said he had sometimes heard one of his own songs being played for roughly ten minutes of every hour, and the lack of recompense irritated him. At the same time, he drew a sharp distinction during his testimony between his popular songs and his classical writings: "When I write so-called long hair music, I expect little beyond the spiritual reward that comes from having created something, but when I write a song which is sufficiently popular to cause people to spend a great many dimes to hear it on a coin machine, I feel that it is unjust to deny me any return for the repeated performances of my work."

Other forces were also working on Wilder. The changing climate allowed him to indulge a hunger he had had for some time to compose music with deeper roots than songs: longer lines, more complex and more extended forms. However, the strongest push toward chamber music in the 1950s came from his deepening associations with some superb instrumentalists and musicians. Miller had always been there at his side, but now John Barrows, Harvey Phillips, Gunther Schuller, Samuel Baron, and others were providing both the critical launch pad and the framework.

At no time in his career did Wilder turn his back on songwriting. His songs and the songs of others he admired were at the center of his being. A great song in the popular idiom, he always said, made him feel nourished and safe. Life became more tolerable and less intimidating. Song made him feel he was surrounded by friends and that it was all right to be vulnerable, to be scared, to be lonely, and that there were others who felt the same way. And song was the catalyst for all this. As with his train travel, songs wrapped him in a cocoon, so that he no longer felt assaulted and violated. Songs were part of his emotional being. "I've written a ton of concert music," he would say later, "but I go back to songs like I go back to an old friend, a garden, a fireplace, a cat that's come back after being away." But the output grew smaller as he turned more of his attention to concert music. In the 1950s Wilder wrote almost eighty popular songs, but only half that number in the 1960s. His instrumental pieces, on the other hand, grew from a score or so in the 1950s to almost a hundred in the next decade.

Clearly, he had made a new commitment, and it would not have happened without Barrows. James Maher has said that if Wilder was the conscience of a generation, his own conscience musically was Barrows: "Alec worshipped John, and it was John who pitchforked him into things. He said John would never let him look back on mistakes he made in counterpoint, in harmony, in structure." He had a way of saying to Wilder, "Straight ahead"; he was goad and conscience both.

Wilder had first become close to Barrows at the Eastman School. They had caroused together, exulted together in good music, and jousted together against Howard Hanson. When Barrows could no longer abide the authoritarian climate at Eastman, he moved to Yale and completed his education there. Through the years, Barrows became a legendary player who was at home with the NBC Orchestra or Minneapolis Symphony Orchestra, the New York Woodwind Quintet or the New York Brass Quintet, or as a soloist with a string quartet, wind ensemble, or symphony orchestra. He made music with Casals, Serkin, Mitropoulos, Toscanini, Stokowski, Bernstein, Kolish, Schneider, Stravinsky. And he would himself no doubt have added, "Don't forget Woody Herman and Judy Holliday."

Like Wilder, Barrows was a complex man, very private, passionate in his loves and hates, an enemy to all that was false and tawdry. The two men embraced the same causes, marched under the same flags to the same drumbeats. In their conspiracies, they were sometimes two against the world. Wilder loved the man and worshipped the musician. When Barrows died too soon at age sixty in 1974, Wilder deeply mourned the loss of his friend, his mentor, and the source of his musical survival: "No matter what the circumstances or for whom I was ostensibly composing, everything I've ever written since I met John Barrows was written for him." Wilder's drunken bouts would sometimes tax his friend's patience, and there was at least one occasion when Wilder was tossed out of Barrows's home. But the relationship was not imperiled. Flutist Sam Baron said he had never seen a friendship between two men quite like theirs. "There was no way an outsider could get into it, but I observed it often enough. The thing was that each had a tremendous loyalty and a kind of idealism, and the idealism had to do with 'we're not going to get rich or famous, but we give up all to what we do.'"

Barrows, then, was the catalyst, the person most responsible for turning Wilder toward concert music in the 1950s and '60s. Barrows would introduce Wilder to many musicians: to Harvey Phillips, a magician with the tuba; to Joe Wilder, the great trumpet player; to Don Hammond, for whom he composed a flute sonata; David Soyer, later cellist with the Guarneri String Quartet, for whom Wilder wrote a cello sonata. Then there were John Swallow, trombone; Patricia Stenberg, oboe; Bernard Garfield, bassoon; Karen Tuttle, viola; Glenn Bowen, clarinet; Vera Brodsky, piano. Always Barrows was the driving force. Said Wilder:

> If you'll stick with me, keep pushing me, curse me if necessary, then, darn it, I'll do everything in my power to live up to your faith in me. . . . I thought you'd like to know I've started that series of sonatas I told you I might write for every instrument in the orchestra. I take that back as I couldn't face the harp, the bass clarinet, or, strangely enough, the violin. There have been too damn many magnificent pieces written for violin, and unless I could write an undramatic sonata, I'd rather omit it. And when I get to the French horn, I'll write a second sonata for you. I'll do my damndest to make it better than the first. Christ! Have you got me flying?!

That special rapport was never better demonstrated in music than in the Golden Crest recording of Wilder's two sonatas for horn and piano (the first written for Barrows in 1954 and the other three years later) and *Suite for French Horn with Piano*. Critic Irving Kolodin, a lonely champion of Wilder's music, commented in his review of the recording of the sonatas that Barrows was Wilder's constant companion, producing notes that were not in the instrument, bending others with the facility of a sax player, though with no comparable mechanism at his disposal:

> Lest it be thought these are gimmicky pieces of interest only to brass fanciers, let me add my belief that such music could not have existed a couple of decades ago. Not only does it require a player of Barrows's particular command: it rests upon a vocabulary of harmonic, rhythmic, and coloristic effects of which only a composer and performer sharing the same kind of jazz orientation could utilize to such advantage.

Barrows's professionalism and championing got Wilder off to a promising start with his instrumental music. He was encouraged also by the approval and respect of another consummate New York musician, Gunther Schuller, who would go on to become one of the nation's most eminent standard-bearers of American music. Schuller was only eighteen when he began playing the horn professionally. By age nineteen, he had also begun a career as a prolific composer with his *Horn Concerto*

No. 1. By 1962, when he gave up horn playing for composition, he had composed more than forty works. If that were not enough to demonstrate his diversity of talent, he also became a distinguished conductor, writer, teacher, and administrator. His wide compositional rangings over popular and classical traditions, his marvelously informed musicological analyses of jazz, and his publishing and editing of the works of American composers have established him as one of the strongest and most pervasive musical influences in the United States.

As a young horn player and composer in New York in the 1940s, Schuller was aware of Wilder's octets and such other breakthrough music as the airs conducted by Sinatra. Schuller recalls that when Barrows came to town, Mitch Miller ("he was Alec's earliest supporter and arranged for almost all the early recordings that happened"), Barrows, and Buffington "became a little advocacy group for Alec, his music and philosophy of life." Being himself in the midst of New York's musical life as a performer, and also doing quite a bit of freelance recording in a town where "Johnny Barrows was the king of the freelance horn players," Schuller heard more and more about Wilder and eventually met him. "I was very thrilled," he recalls, "to participate in what was certainly for us a kind of amazing, miraculous recording adventure again sponsored by Mitch Miller." This was Wilder's 1951 *Jazz Suite for Four Horns,* with Barrows, Buffington, Schuller, and Raymond Alonge, accompanied by harpsichord, bass, and drums. "It was a highly unusual and experimental venture."

Schuller, to use the musicians' phrase, began "hanging out" a lot with Wilder. Those downtown musicians had some favorite watering holes besides the Algonquin. There were also meetings in homes, and the Buffingtons' apartment in Greenwich Village became a hangout for the Eastman crowd, including bassoonist Loren Glickman and composer Harry Rosenthal. "They had all been students at Eastman and so there was a kind of an enclave of expatriates, and Alec was our hero," says Schuller.

> I was not from Eastman. In fact I was a high school dropout. I never finished
> any education anywhere. But for those Eastmanites, Alec was their hero, and
> he was older. Even with his almost purposely casual dress, there was a sense
> of, a touch of the Algonquin writers in his appearance, dress and demeanor
> and a certain classy distinguished quality. It was just there in his face, his
> eyes, so you could have dressed him in a bathing suit.

Stylistically, Schuller and Wilder were 180 degrees removed from each other in their approach to music composition. Schuller was, and remains, a 12-tone composer, though he made no big issue of that, then or now.

> It's just the technique that I used, and so do thousands of other composers.
> But Alec had a very strong prejudice against that kind of music. I don't think

he knew exactly what it was, and he certainly was not aware of the possible distinctions between various kinds of twelve-tone composers. And I don't think he was aware of the fact that you could be a twelve-tone composer and write uncluttered, unintellectual, accessible music.

Schuller adds that "despite Alec's misgivings of me as a composer, which he was much too much a gentleman ever to express in any overt way, though I knew they were there, he had a genuine admiration for me because I think he sensed the integrity." Schuller, who would later catalog and publish Wilder's concert works through Margun Music, yielded to no one in American music in his faith and admiration of the person and the musician:

Alec was a man of absolutely incorruptible integrity in every respect. I don't think I knew anyone who was as strong and as clear, as pure, as incorruptible as he was. He was able to resist all of those temptations which break through and get to people sooner or later. And that was always an unstated or central theme of any kind of conversation you had with him, no matter what the subject. And I happened to be very much in the same kind of league I think, so that this was a very important, almost inspiring relationship I would say both ways. This is the element I think he most cherished about me and probably therefore forgave me my sins for writing 12-tone music.

What also appealed early to Schuller about Wilder's approach to instrumental writing was his willingness to embrace what Schuller has called the "underdog" instruments, those most neglected by composers through the years. "Who else," Schuller has said, "has been as devoted to the musician in providing a playable, functional literature for those instrumental ensembles most composers generally ignore?" He remarked that it was almost a mission in Wilder's life to "assuage the thirst for good music" for those passed-over instruments, "much in the manner that composers did in the Baroque era, for example." And he did it "at all technical levels, from the beginner to the advanced virtuoso."

Typical of that underdog concern was the literature Wilder helped give to the tuba in the name of tubist and friend Harvey Phillips. His meeting with Phillips came about in 1957 after he had written a brass quintet for William Bell, that "loving man and revered spiritual father of the tuba players." Bell had been with the New York Philharmonic for many years, and Wilder had heard that a brass quintet made up of members of the brass section, in which Bell played tuba, was interested in having music written for it. He wrote a piece, the quintet read through it and seemed happy with it, but then found themselves so busy in the orchestra that they never managed to function as a quintet. Barrows suggested another brass quintet. The fact that the quintet Phillips played in, the New York Brass Quintet, played and recorded the piece was of course a great delight to Wilder, but he placed greater value on the fact that the piece had introduced him to Harvey Phillips, that "stalwart rock of a man."

Phillips had been born far from Wilder's affluent world into a poor Missouri family in 1929, the last of ten children. His mother had been married at seventeen, and did her washing with a scrub board. The young Phillips lived in nine houses before he was ten, and picked strawberries and apples and peaches for a penny a box. When, after high school graduation, he got a summer job playing tuba with a circus, it was figured by some that he was bound straight for perdition. Whitney Balliett in his profile quoted Phillips:

> When word reached our Methodist preacher that I was joining a circus, he came out to the house and Mother received him in the parlor. "That boy will be destroyed if he works in a circus," he said to my mother. "Circuses are full of the wicked and degenerate. He will be lost." Tears came to my mother's eye, and she said, "You don't have much faith in Harvey, do you, Reverend? Well, I do," and she showed him the door. Homer Lee [school music teacher] found me a York BB-flat tuba, and Mother made me a modesty cover for it out of a blanket. The taxi man in town was going to visit a relative in Syracuse, and he said he'd drop me off in Binghamton. From there, I got a bus to Waterbury, Connecticut, where the circus was. I was met at the station by a trumpet player with one leg and a drummer who was afflicted in such a way that he couldn't close his mouth.

Phillips went on to play every state in the union with the Ringling Brothers, eventually won a full scholarship at Juilliard, later joined the Sauter-Finegan band for a time, began playing with the New York City Opera and the New York City Ballet, and joined Schuller as his assistant at the New England Conservatory for some years. He was for many years a member of the Indiana University School of Music faculty, a legendary tubist who is arguably the best in the world, a prestigious figure at instrument clinics, a physically large man with a large heart. He was capable of leveling mountains on behalf of music, and possessed of an almost religious love of family.

Working with Phillips, Wilder would do for the tuba repertoire what he would also do for the marimba, the guitar, the baritone sax, the harp, and so on. His first effort for Phillips was *Sonata No. 1 for Tuba and Piano,* written in 1959. It was a difficult assignment, as he realized very quickly. "Due to the low level of the tuba, the piano part had to be written so as not to clash with it." After Phillips and "that phenomenal pianist Milton Kaye" had run through it, Phillips solemnly announced, "Well, that's the third," or words to that effect. When Wilder asked, "Third what?" Phillips told him he had just written only the third known solo piece for tuba. "The other two were those by Vaughan Williams and Hindemith. I was very impressed by such a realization."

Wilder's concern was for repertoire that was also worth playing. That was shown by his *Effie Suite* for tuba, written for Phillips and for Clark Galehouse, president of Golden Crest Records, who was looking for a children's-album suite that would describe six imaginary experiences of an elephant named Effie. In this piece, the tuba depicts Effie chasing a monkey, falling in love, taking a dancing lesson, joining the carnival, going folk dancing, and singing a lullaby. Remarkably, Wilder was able to do this without ever coming close to making a laughingstock of the instrument. Wilder, said Phillips, "was successful in musically documenting these imaginary events without the usual insult to the instrument occasioned by almost every other application of the tuba as a hippopotamus, whale, elephant or other large creature."

Nearly all instrumentalists, wind players particularly, became indebted to Wilder. After noting that Wilder considered the clarinet to have an agility exceeded only by that of the flute, clarinetist Glenn Bowen concluded his Eastman School dissertation by saying that Wilder had created an important body of chamber litera-ture for the clarinet "which is idiomatic for the instrument and rewarding for per-former and audience alike." Douglas Yeo has said that trombonists may not have Beethoven to haggle over with the musicologists, "but to us, Wilder and other composers who have gone out on a limb and composed for the trombone . . . have given us an important legacy of our own." He also wrote for every instrumen-tal combination under the sun.

Phillips, Schuller, Barrows, and Miller—these were among Wilder's principal comrades-in-arms as he made the change from primarily popular song to primarily concert music. How big and audacious a risk was he taking? Technically, how difficult was it for him to move from the harmonic vertical nature of short-line popular and traditional romantic art music to the many long, weaving, interconnect-ing lines of counterpoint and thematic development? If Wilder were to be taken at his word, risk had nothing to do with it. He simply trusted to his intuitions and steamed ahead. Intuition, good taste, and blind luck, he always said, had been responsible for his best pieces. All his life, he insisted, he had shied away from knowing more than an essential minimum about the creative process. It was possi-ble, he conceded, that had he studied more, his music would have been better. But it was also possible, he added, that too much knowledge would have put his creative muscles into a "permanent charley horse."

He invariably professed astonishment when analytical studies of his music found it shapely, disciplined, and somehow well within the stringent demands of the academic mind. He kept insisting that he was a musical ignoramus. He confessed ignorance when Barrows once told him that he, Wilder, had just written a pas-sacaglia. He also said he didn't understand more than a few pages of the two-hundred-odd-page analysis of his music for clarinet in Bowen's dissertation. "All I can say is that if any of my music is good, its sources are almost solely intuitive."

The fact of the matter is that Wilder was a bit of a fraud when he said he was unaware of what he was doing musically and that his creativity came leaping out of the blue. He was more conversant with form and structure than he ever admitted to. And the reason, surely, for his being less than honest was his profound dislike and distrust of academia and his fear of being put into an academic camp. As one who was self-taught up to a point, he held the educational establishment in low esteem. He hated pedantry and he hated scholarship that encrusted music. As Schuller has said about Wilder's best-selling *Sonata for Bass Trombone and Piano,*

> Alec would have chuckled at the thought of a scholarly edition of his music à la Barenreiter. His healthy distrust of the institutions and establishments of music, his wariness of "fixing" music in some finite form, his abhorrence of the kind of intellectual "justifications" that he felt many publishers (and composers for that matter) engage in—all these made him leery of even having his own music published at all.

Though he was often highly intuitive in his composing, Wilder's work also rested on more knowledge of theory than he owned up to. He was a benefactor of lessons learned and remembered at Eastman, and one gets a sense of that from listening to Eastman composer Warren Benson:

> Inherent in Alec's pop work is an original turn of mind about harmony. As many times as not, he has this lovely melodic harmonic twist. This is brought about somewhat by the linear quality of his thinking, so perhaps the chamber music for him was not so much of a stretch. Alec always thought in lines, moving voices in the piano parts. They're not contrapuntal, but he never forgot his counterpoint lessons. There's an integrity of voicing in his songs. By voicing I mean that the inner voices move very considerably with individual direction to the next notes. The inner voices of the harmony. That came from his study here at Eastman. He often told me how important line was to him.

Benson also reminds us that Wilder listened closely to the great instrumentalists before he ever wrote for them—the men of the New York Brass Quintet, Sam Baron, and the New York Woodwind Quintet. "He had a wonderful ear. He heard what they were doing. When he started to write, it wasn't as if he had not heard those voices moving." Not many composers, not many musicians, have had ears as sharp, as infallible, as Wilder's. He could sit in a session with instrumentalists and call all the wrong notes, even with pieces he had written twenty years before. Says Benson: "He would sit there and say, 'That should be an F-sharp.' He had an absolute sense of pitch." Yes, adds Benson, Wilder was taking a risk when he moved his focus from popular to instrumental music, "but it was an informed risk." It also should be remembered that, although it was not until the 1960s that Wilder began moving heavily into composing for solo instruments and for chamber groups, he had been doing some of that writing all along. He wrote *Suite for String Orchestra* in 1949, *Concerto for Oboe, String Orchestra and Percussion* in 1950, *Jazz Suite for Four Horns* in 1951, *Concerto No. 1 for Horn and Chamber Orchestra* in 1953.

The fact that Wilder did so much of his writing for wind instruments also disposes of the notion that he did not know what he was doing. Because these instruments commonly have some weak registers and weak notes, because breathing control is so critical, scoring has to be highly informed. The demands on the wind composer are heavy. How well Wilder met those demands, often made greater by the combinations he worked with, is demonstrated by his *Suite No. 1 for Horn, Tuba, and Piano,* which had its concert premiere in 1963 when Barrows and Phillips were teaching on the summer faculty of the University of Wisconsin's Department of Music, of which Barrows was then a full-time member. The coupling of horn and tuba was a highly risky undertaking, and indeed Phillips and Barrows themselves thought it improbable that the two instruments could be successfully combined in a single work. But Wilder was up to the challenge. In a beautiful bit of imagery in "The President of the Derrière-garde," Balliett would say of this same piece, "It easily converts the tuba from a two-by-four into a soaring gable."

Wherever he acquired them—from learned knowledge at Eastman, from listening to others with that incredible ear, from his own native intelligence—Wilder had the skills to acquit himself well in his composing for these more intricate forms of music. He himself made no sharp separation between pop and classical writing. One of the reasons he was drawn to Harold Arlen, one of his favorite songwriters, was his feeling that Arlen knew how close vocal writing was to controlled, lyric instrumental writing, "and that the fluid sinuosity possible to a clarinet, trumpet, or trombone, if carefully controlled, would help to suggest more inventive vocal lines." The difference, as Wilder saw it, was more of degree than category. "The seed of a song," he told Balliett, "grows into a small plant with a single flower, but a concert piece has as complex a root system as a tree."

There were, and are, however, several associated problems that had little to do with Wilder's technical and mental capacity but a lot to do with the way all instrumental work is received and estimated by the music world in general: the notion that music for woodwind and brass, rightly or wrongly, is often considered light music, a poor relation alongside the rich literature for strings. Traditionally, even the best chamber works for winds are not considered to reach the highest levels of music composition.

Whatever the validity of that long-held notion there is no doubt that Wilder had difficulty in getting his music taken seriously. Whenever he was on an ensemble program that included works by established composers, whether French, German, English, or Italian, he would usually be reviewed as clever, witty, charming, and ingratiating but seldom as formidable and serious. Still, he was seldom dismissed as a lightweight by those who counted most with him: the performers themselves.

James Maher has recalled a woodwind quintet rehearsal put together by horn player Jimmy Buffington to try out two new Wilder pieces. The performers also doubled in the world of commercial music, and they had extraordinary skills. The good formal musician and the good jazz musician might tend to regard such music lightly, and yet they could not themselves have begun to face the demands made on these "commercial" (a pejorative term in jazz circles) musicians through the years, from the cue music for silent film through television commercials. These were players who met Wilder's every acid test of musicianship and who, by their magic at this rehearsal, transformed him into a suddenly joyful man.

Even this consummation would not have impressed academics unable to give careful thought to Wilder's kind of music. After all, as Maher has perceptively said,

> It is dangerous to like Alec's music . . . because it is, at root, street music.
> It is of the tradition of Ambrosian chant, folk music, blues, jazz, vox populi
> music. It is in the air. All one has to do is listen. . . . It celebrates not the
> box office, not the classroom, not the chancery, but life. Its raw materials are
> commonplace, even banal. Is there anything more banal than a jazz riff, unless
> it is explored with great style and musical wit?

It was hard for the high-domed establishment to take seriously what Maher has so well described as the musical sounds of "the American daily ordinary."

Serious composers wrote for strings; Wilder wrote for winds and brass because the literature for strings was already in place, and because the instrumentalists he composed for badly needed his compositions. In the final result, however, Wilder's risks had less to do with technical mastery or with critical estimates of the wind and brass literature than with the way his move from the pop world to that of concert music was perceived—less to do with the merit of the music than with the problem of fixing a place for it in the firmament. How could he write songs with such titles as *I Don't Want to Go to Bed* and *I Got Big Eyes for You* and then turn around and compose quintets for brass and woodwind? How could he do that and be taken seriously?

As pointed out by trumpet soloist, teacher, and clinician Robert Levy, after a time critics in particular viewed Wilder as mostly a pop-song composer: "He had a label put on him and it stayed and probably will for a long time." It was partly the old problem of uniqueness and what on earth to do with it. "His chamber operas," adds Levy, "weren't sophisticated enough for the opera community despite their popularity at the time, his chamber music wasn't avant-garde enough for the 'new music' scene, and the jazz in his music wasn't 'jazzy' enough for that community either, so where was he to 'fit in'?" If that weren't enough, this composer now writing serious music for longhairs also kept on making music for children. He also refused to give big, sonorous titles even to sonorous instrumental music. He called his pieces for wind ensemble "Entertainments," using the word to make sure that audiences knew "the purpose of the pieces was specifically to entertain and also specifically not to teach." He had no patience with "protest" music or with music that sought to reflect the contemporary scene.

By choice and by designation, Wilder remained the outsider who dared to be different, and he was often put on the chopping block. Today his woodwind quintets (the first six were written between 1954 and 1960) are regarded highly, among his best work, but that was not always so. Reviewing Quintets 3, 4, and 6, one critic noted that the aesthetic Wilder employed his conservative romanticism with "some awareness of modern (up to the 1930s) currents." The slightly jazzy indentions, the reviewer went on to say, were smart and offered relief, though such pertness was to be expected in dealing with woodwinds and their ability to deliver the piquant phrase. Then the haymaker: "Wilder knows the tricks of weaving a good texture but the material is terribly old-hat. This kind of musical stuff is as academic in its way as 19th-century harmony exercises. It can serve for the quiet cocktail hour."

Balliett has observed that the polished, witty, Mozartian Wilder style outraged the contemporary musical establishment because "it is relentlessly tonal and me-lodic in an age that is committed to tone-rows, computer printouts, and random noise." Critics who went prepared for more formal statements were, he added, disconcerted and disconnected by the Wilder faculty "for blending jazz and non-jazz elements into a musical package that has a faintly mocking quality about it." Wilder dubbed the critics "the anointed ones." He liked very few of them and trusted them not at all. They had, he said, drawn the lines somewhere in the 1950s:

> From their judgment seats they had noted my connection with an unproduced
> film, my employment by a rich man to complement his films, my grubbing in
> the pop music market place, my auditions of show after show to no avail and
> the dismissive reviews I received for performances or recordings of my mu-
> sic. The quarantine flag was standing out flat in this wind of rejection.

In exercising that freedom, in the process of crossing back and forth between pop music and concert music, Wilder made and left some tracks that gave example and encouragement to others, just as he had done with the octets a decade or two earlier. Eastman School Director Robert Freeman observes that not many people before Wilder had done both kinds of writing. Howard Hanson would never have approved of anyone who did. Freeman believes that Leonard Bernstein failed to get the music directorship at Eastman and with the Boston Symphony because he was writing Broadway music as well as serious music. "It's no longer an issue but it was a real and lively issue in 1945." It was not, he adds, the only reason that Bernstein did not land those jobs, but it was one of them. "How could you be a serious musician and write this other more commercial stuff?"

Freeman illustrates the change that has taken place with the story of a twenty-six-year-old Eastman graduate who came to town to have a chamber music piece played and who said, when asked by Freeman about his work in New York, that he was making $300,000 a year writing commercial film scores and jingles. While at Eastman, he had studied with not only the serious music composers—Adler, Schwantner, Rowse, Benson, and others—but also jazz arranger Ray Wright, and had learned to write those jingles. "For forty seconds of toothpaste music," the young man told Freeman, "I can earn $30,000 to $40,000. There's an infinite market for that, and I'm good at it." So for two to three months of the year, the young man does that kind of commercial work, and the rest of the year he devotes to his real love, the writing of string quartets. "That's what Alec led to," says Freeman. Here today, he points out, is a young man with no inherited wealth who is doing very well and sees himself as a kind of modern-day Charles Ives; unlike Ives, however, he doesn't sell insurance but writes commercial music. "In Bernstein's time, that would have been seen as a sullying thing. Yes, Brahms wrote Hungarian dances and Beethoven wrote Irish songs, but by the end of the century Wagner had spread the idea that you had to write stuff that was heavy and serious."

Freeman sees Wilder as a forerunner of those who, like the young Eastman graduate, can today move back and forth between popular and serious music and not pay a penalty for doing so. For Wilder, of course, the two kinds of music interpenetrated: the style of the one was the style of the other. He could find no reason that songwriting should not have something to do with woodwind-octet writing. Wilder could not himself have made a fortune from toothpaste music without feeling in some way defiled. But by swinging among various realms of composition and by staying clear of ulterior motives, he made it a little easier for others to be more catholic in their tastes, more flexible in their choices. Yet, trailbreaking was not all of it. In the process, he would also become the most personal and most generous composer in American music history.

10

Music for Friends for Playing on Sunday

The skills and challenges involved in Wilder's shift from popular to concert music have been discussed, but the further dimension of that gradual transition is that nearly all his many instrumental pieces were written for musicians and friends he admired, and usually at no charge, often not even for the copying. It might be supposed that such a large and diverse output could have been achieved only by someone who had entered a monastic cell very early and stayed there until his work was done. On the contrary, Wilder did his writing while he held hands with human-kind, or at least as many of them who met his demanding criteria of excellence and who were not forever put off by his crotchets and eccentricities.

Wilder loved people, but he had little use for fools or bores, and he would make up an incomprehensible new language on the spot to silence a passenger in the plane seat next to him. He had no patience with incompetents, and none at all for those he found pompous or pretentious, no matter how illustrious. Leonard Bernstein, too, had been a pathfinder, believing with Wilder that good music can be found in jazz and popular song as well as in the symphony. As composer, conductor, and educator, he was a major figure in American music. Wilder, however, considered him a tiresome and objectionable self-promoter, and that was that. He would note that *New York Times* music critic Harold Schonberg had once said about his conducting that "Bernstein rose vertically, a la Nijinsky, and hovered there a good 15 seconds by the clock." He would remember that, and ignore all the rest.

Yet Wilder, using composing as his bridge, also reached out and embraced warmly and unreservedly his host of friends. Life was for living and celebrating, and music was for sharing and enjoying not tomorrow but today, not for fame and fortune but for the simple joy of it. William Engvick has put it into words:

Wilder says that he works not for posterity but for an immediate, pertinent and loving communication. When he writes a piece for a friend (a peculiar

120

generosity), it is not reproduced, nor is any listing necessarily made of it. It is, to him, simply a letter, a way of reaching others, and not a pronouncement or a device for notoriety.

For the good musicians, nothing was held back. Once when he was asked how much it cost to have Wilder write a sonata for him, Barrows replied, "A postage stamp." Another friend of the composer has remarked, "He is the only man I know who gives sonatas for Christmas."

To Wilder, it was quite simple. All those whose playing he admired and whom he liked and trusted as people he wished to write music for. Those whose playing he admired but whom he didn't cotton to or trust, he had no desire to write for. They had to be both good musicians and good people. He once said he was extremely proud to be admired by Zoot Sims, Clark Terry, Joe Wilder, Urbie Green, John Barrows, Harvey Phillips, Woody Herman, Count Basie, Samuel Baron, Bernard Garfield, Verne Reynolds, Frank Battisti, Frederick Fennell, David Soyer, Bonita Boyd, Walter Hendl, Eileen Farrell, Ronald Roseman, Harold Goltzer, Karen Tuttle, Gary Karr: "You'll probably have to know the inside of chamber music and music education circles to know any of those names. No, I don't have many as familiar as Eileen Farrell. No Heifitzes, no Ormandys, Zells, no Schneiders, no *Harper's Bazaar,* no *Esquire, Playboy,* not even a Levant anecdote. I have Harold Arlen's telephone number, if that helps ennoble me."

Wilder believed that the top-notch performers did much more than interpret music. They re-created it, and in so doing added a dimension to it. The most noted music in the world, he always said, was only a guide, and it took the sensitiveness of a conductor, a group, or a soloist to put the breath of life into it. He knew that from his own music. Performers such as Barrows, Baron, Garfield, and Virginia Nanzetta seemed able to go beyond the notes and use their musical understanding to bring a "point of view" to the pieces. "They all saw the beauty of the music with their keen sensitivities," Robert Levy has said. "I think Alec was especially taken by these performers because they went beyond his notation to bring the music to life in a manner often missed even by some 'name' musicians."

Most of the critics also missed it. Composer Warren Benson has said that Wilder's music may not have merited more praise by the critics, but it did merit more consideration: "There's a characteristic of critics. They don't review the music at hand, but the music they know. If you write a piece and it goes to New York for the first time, and the reviewer says it sounds like Ravel, that means they had not listened to it. It may have suggestions of Ravel, but they don't listen to find out what the piece is doing on its own." Though he felt the sting when the reviews were bad, Wilder was as little influenced by the critics as they were by him. Instead of changing course or barricading himself, he concentrated on writing personal music for friends who needed it—music that could be played and shared, sometimes there and then; music that could be enjoyed as much for the occasion and the comradeship as for the melodies themselves. Mike (Mitchell) Miller Jr. has observed that Wilder's attitude toward writing music was very much pre-nineteenth-century, "before people started to think that to write something for someone's birthday diminished your work. I think it's the other way around. You think of all the wonderful occasional birthday music Mozart wrote, the domestic music people wrote. That was Alec's attitude, too. It was very much out of keeping, not only with the 20th century, but the 19th for that matter."

Stony Point, New York, about thirty miles out of New York City, was one of the settings for that kind of merry musicmaking. Mitch Miller, his wife, Frances, and their two daughters and son Mike had a home there for many years. Both Wilder and Engvick were important presences in the household, visiting often through the years. John Barrows and his first wife, Pat, were also neighbors, and that added to the appeal of Stony Point. In the spring of 1953, Frances Miller found nearby a converted carriage barn for Engvick to rent for a very small sum. Engvick did some work on it to make it habitable the year round but never owned it. "It was a large tract of land with several barn/houses, a stream, and a swimming hole, all close to stores and bus stop."

Engvick and Wilder had lived together during their brief Hollywood stint; now, for a longer period of time, they joined forces again. Although Wilder's Stony Point days stretched well over a decade, the five years from 1953 were when he was most often in residence, sometimes for a few days, sometimes for a week or two. Two such gifted artists living and working at close quarters were bound to have some fractious days. Arnold Sundgaard remembers a telegram from Engvick from Stony Point: "I've had it. No more." Wilder has said that though he and Engvick were temperamentally dissimilar personalities, they managed to adjust to each other: "My casual ways probably drove him close to madness, while his methodical, rigidly neat ways did the same to me. I threw money around while he saved. But we both liked to drink and we had great respect for each other's talent. And, as an extra dividend, we both deeply loved words, so we had many a cozy evening over a Scrabble board."

At one point, five old Eastman friends were together again at Stony Point. Recalled Wilder: "There we were within howling distance—Mitchell and Frances Miller, Frank Baker, John Barrows and myself, twenty years after our years in Eastman." Miller, he added, had given up playing the oboe for the big money to be made in the recording business. Frances Miller had given up the piano for motherhood and adjustment to the feverish life of her husband. Frank Baker, he said, had married a wealthy girl and continued to sing; Barrows had become a world-famous horn player; and Wilder was trying to prove himself worthy of the title of composer. "They were idyllic years, even though all of us, except Mitchell, drank too much. It was out there at Bill's that I really, totally concentrated, with minimal interruptions, on composition." Wilder wrote a great many concert songs, all for Baker, "the best vocal musician I have ever known." He wrote his first two sonatas for French horn and piano, more woodwind quintets, a piano sonata, two operas, and sixty-odd pieces for players who would gather at Stony Point every Sunday to make music together.

Those convivial Sunday affairs grew out of an elaborate plot by Wilder and Barrows to inveigle mutual Eastman friend Sam Richlin to take up again the French horn he had stopped playing earlier. Building upon Richlin's return to the fold, Barrows persuaded horn player and Eastman friend Jimmy Buffington to make a visit to Stony Point. An impromptu reading of some new Wilder pieces worked so well that the following Sunday Buffington's wife, a violinist, also joined the group. Wilder used whatever time he could find to write pieces for three horns and solo violin. Buffington wrote a tender piece, and so did Barrows. Other musicians heard about the Sunday musicales and asked to be included. In time, the group expanded to three French horns, bassoon, violin, cello, piano, voice, and an occasional trumpet. "Each Sunday," Wilder recalled, "someone new would appear. And each Sunday there would be brand-new music for them to play. I would get the word from John early in the week what instruments to expect and then write and copy parts for as many pieces as I could write before Sunday afternoon."

June Erickson Gardner, the soprano lead in *The Long Way,* the opera Wilder and Engvick were working on, remembers a hilarious night at the Barrows home when *Happy Birthday* was being sung in all kinds of arrangements, with augmented intervals, diminished intervals, and so on:

Whoever came to the party had to write *Happy Birthday* in a different way. We were doing it all at once and making absolute fools of ourselves. A lady who was a concert pianist had complained to Alec because he hadn't finished a sonata he was writing for her. Barrows had brought out his horn, I was playing what I could remember of boogie-woogie at the piano, and there was Alec leaning on the piano and finishing the lady's sonata. He handed it to her, and she sat down later and played it. He did it over all that garbage we were doing. It didn't bother him a bit.

Wilder has said about those happy days of impromptu music-making:

Someone along the line told me that this kind of writing was called "music for use," and he used a German word which I can pronounce poorly and can't spell [no doubt *gebrauchsmusik*]. I suppose overall I must have written 60 short pieces. And though I did rewrite and reuse four or five of them for other groups, all the others have never been heard since. As far as I'm concerned, they needn't be. They served their purpose: fun, friends meeting, laughter, drinking, relaxing and playing, writing. To the average contemporary mind, this would be incomprehensible. Thank God it wasn't to those who participated.

Wilder would look back on those Stony Point years as a time when he felt safe from his fears. Though the operas he worked on were unabashedly sentimental, they were also warm and witty and well put together. Agreeable friends were always close. The charade games were hysterically acted out. Life was good: "breakfast at a window looking out on morning glories and an undisturbed stretch of sloping land. Scrabble in the evening and maybe one more playing of The Wee Small Hours album of Frank Sinatra in which he sang one of my songs." The days were so tranquil that Wilder, the man who never unpacked, started to put things in bureau drawers and on shelves. He even dared to buy himself an MG in which he raced around the countryside. Gardner remembers driving with him one spring evening: "He's yammering away, and you know how loud those motors were. All of a sudden he comes to a screeching halt. 'What the hell are you doing?' I ask him. 'Peepers,' he says. 'I can hear the peepers.' So we have to sit there and listen to the frogs. He heard them even over his own voice and the noisy motor of the MG."

Martin Russ, who often visited Wilder and Engvick at Stony Point, says Wilder was a good driver, but he had the notion that people hated sports cars and were always yelling at him and making rude gestures. Russ, who as a boy had known Wilder, became an author and a writing professor, and Stony Point was an important incidental starting point for his career. In 1951 he had joined the marines, and from Camp LeJeune and Quantico had raced up to Stony Point on weekends to be with Wilder and Engvick. "I always presumed that Alec was delighted to see me, and, bless him, he was invariably gracious, patient and indulgent with a loutish marine."

When Russ was doing advanced infantry training in Camp Pendleton before going to Korea, he realized he was involved in an undertaking worth telling about. The only person in the world he wanted to express himself to in detail was Wilder. So, in Korea he began writing to him. The marines had been told not to keep diaries lest they fall into enemy hands, hence the letters served as a kind of substitute diary. Wilder gave Engvick the letters as they arrived, and Engvick put them in a drawer. When Russ was discharged, Wilder urged him to turn the collection into a book. Ultimately, Russ learned from Dudley Frasier of Rinehart that the firm would publish the book under the title *The Last Parallel* and that it was a Book-of-the-Month selection. It was reviewed on the front page of the *New York Times Book Review* and made the bestseller list for several weeks.

Happy though he was, Wilder had a horror of being detained and trapped at Stony Point or anywhere else. Despite the good friends, despite the music-making, he was a nomad at heart. One of Engvick's anxieties whenever Wilder got the locals irked was that he would hop on a train to somewhere else, leaving Engvick to stay in Stony Point and face a different kind of music. Wilder once explained to him that in psychology *fugue* meant *flight,* flight from trouble, from reality. "I realized that in both music and in personal behavior Alec was a master of the fugue. How else explain the countless trips, the phone-book size railroad timetable under his arm, and the failure to achieve a place of his own." Wilder agreed: "I was constantly leaving Stony Point, taking train rides, visiting friends in strange places, moving. And I knew it [the Stony Point life] was temporary. I knew I wasn't geared for any kind of communal living, even that with a friend engaged in mutual creative work." Trains were his salvation.

Often he would entrain for Chicago to stay with friends Harry and Arlene Bouras. Arlene Bouras had been a pianoforte student at Eastman School. She and Wilder made common cause. "I didn't have the technique but I was a good interpreter and that's why he wrote lots of music for me." At Stony Point or in Chicago, Wilder was always the personal composer. He and Bouras had musical fun together. "I don't know which of us coined the term Hawaiian ending, but whenever Alec wrote an ending I thought was a little tawdry, I'd call it a Hawaiian ending. He used to talk about playing past the end of the piece."

Harry Bouras had gone to Chicago from Rochester and eventually became an artist in residence at the University of Chicago. He had known some of the octets, a few chamber pieces and many of the popular songs—enough to give him something in common with Wilder. Trains also tied Wilder to the Bourases. Together, they rode the *Broadway Limited,* the *Twentieth Century,* the *Zephyr,* and the *Panama Limited.* Arlene Bouras tells of the Saturday when the three of them were talking together in the living room of the Bouras home. This was just before the *Panama Limited* was to stop running between Chicago and New Orleans. "At 3 in the afternoon," she remembers,

> Alec said to us, "You mean you have never ridden on the Limited?" We said no, we hadn't. Well, at 4:20 that same afternoon the three of us were on it. We had a wonderful trip to New Orleans, with Alec proudly showing us the flowers and the good food. So we went to New Orleans together and sat in the Square until the train was ready to return.

Wilder would go often from Stony Point to Rochester, there to visit with his old mentor Sibley Watson Jr. and photographer Louis Ouzer. He also went back to eat blueberry pancakes and apple pie in civilized style at the downtown Manhattan Restaurant (since closed) with its friendly chatter and deferential help. And he liked to talk with the dowagers he had known before; he identified with their mannerly way of life. Yet he was not above betraying his own standards by getting drunk at a house party after a performance of composer Bernard Rogers's *The Warrior* by the Eastman School Opera Department and insulting everyone in sight, notably the composer.

It was with composer Benson that he spent much of his creative time, often getting rejuvenated musically. He genuinely admired Benson for his honesty, for the fact that he was never pushy in his own behalf. "He saw me as really honest," says Benson, "but I continually had to prove myself." Benson wrote very dissonant music from the time Wilder knew him, and Wilder often questioned him hard. "I would go into my office and play some notes and then I would sing the other things (the dissonant music) against what I was playing. I would give him a demonstration that I really heard that stuff. As long as he was persuaded that I heard what I was composing, it was OK."

At the same time that Wilder was making music with friends in Stony Point, he was also hanging out in the same happy, companionable way in the second half of the fifties with the much-admired New York Woodwind Quintet, then and now one of the outstanding chamber music groups in the country. Here, too, he was composing in congenial company. John Barrows, who introduced Wilder to the others, was the quintet's horn player, and the other members at that time were described by Wilder in these terms: "Sam Baron, a saintly, witty, intensely musical man, was the flutist; Jerry Roth, a bubbly, romantic, loving man was the oboist; David Glazer, an urbane, quiet, dignified man was the clarinetist; and Bernard Garfield, another romantic, very funny man, was the best bassoonist I have ever heard." Baron had cofounded the group with Garfield in the late 1940s. A distinguished player and conductor, he made many notable recordings. He was later associated, too, with the American Chamber Orchestra, the New York Chamber Soloists, and the Contemporary Chamber Ensemble. Baron has also taught widely. For Wilder, it was a case of love at first sight.

One of the first things Wilder did was to arrange for woodwinds three composition by Henry Purcell, K. P. E. Bach, and Dietrich Buxtehude. In the early days of its concert career, the group often found itself in need of opening music of a classical nature. "We admired Wilder," says Baron, "for imagining and finding these pieces for the quintet." The group enjoyed them so much that for a couple of seasons they opened every concert with a suite of these numbers. At this early stage of its career, the quintet did not have many dates for formal concerts but did have many requests to play school programs. They took all the work they could get and found that getting up early to play for schoolchildren helped them develop as a performing unit. By this means, they kept themselves going for three or four seasons.

At one point, Wilder wrote a movement in jazz rhythm for the quintet, but the group, playing too squarely, was unable to swing the piece. Buffington and other old friends came to the rescue and got them swinging. That movement became the building block for Wilder's *Woodwind Quintet No. 1* (1954). "We began to enjoy it," Baron has said, "and pretty soon we began to use this at our children's concerts. We were madly in love with that piece, so the next thing Alec did was write three movements to surround it and that became the scherzo of *Woodwind Quintet No. 1.*" Wilder would write thirteen woodwind quintets in all, from 1954 through 1977.

Starting in 1954 the quintet developed a summer program at the University of Wisconsin's Milwaukee campus that became an important part of their lives, and of Wilder's life as well. The climate was ideal, audiences were discerning. The students were taught on flute, oboe, clarinet, bassoon, and French horn, and organized into quintets, quartets, sextets, and octets—small ensembles were made up ad lib. Rehearsals were coached. The Woodwind Quintet had as coplayers the Fine Arts String Quintet of Chicago, and a resident pianist, Frank Glazer (the brother of David, the quintet's clarinetist), an international concert pianist who was later to join the Eastman School faculty. "With these ten people," Baron recalls, "all of chamber music was open to us in varying combinations. The job paid well, and they housed us. It was like a vacation. It developed into a six-week program. We all went out with our families and stayed on the lake, and we talked and played and rehearsed and just lived like that for six weeks."

The Milwaukee program went on from 1954 to 1969, and from time to time the group played Wilder's music, the first two quintets and other compositions. Wilder was part of that happy scene in the summers of 1956, 1957, 1958, and 1959, perhaps five years until Barrows left the group. Wilder had been in his element there—good players, good friends, a rambling house with ample room for privacy:

> I would spend the days composing for the quintet as well as writing wild vocal arrangments for four of them who loved to sing. I remember giving them the name of the Silos in honor of the talented recording singers called the Hi-Los. I wrote new harmonizations of cornball songs, opulent harmonizations of standards, and a few original pieces. Nearly every evening at six the quartet would gather in someone's baronial bedroom to try out the new stuff.

For Baron, those years represented "a peak of a sort for *gebrauchsmusik*. Music to use. Music to enjoy. Music to have fun with. Music to order and on the spot."

Music for playing and enjoying was always center stage in Milwaukee, as at Stony Point, and these were also the years when Wilder and his music were virtually adopted by Clark F. Galehouse and his Golden Crest Records, Inc., in Huntington, Long Island. Both the *New York Woodwind Quintet Plays Alec Wilder* and *The Most Beautiful Girls Sketches* were recorded under his label, as was the 1954 quintet and several score of later compositions. "Galehouse," Baron recalls, "looked up to Alec as to a god, and whenever he could get something of his in his catalog, he would do it." Galehouse recorded Wilder's chamber music for years at what had to be no profit at all. He even sent dozens of recordings at no charge to friends of Wilder who could not get them from retail dealers.

That chamber music from friends was essentially conversational, with the conversation usually carried on at several levels. Only the gifted player and only the acute listener could get below the surface to the essence of what was happening. The music was like the man. Despite his strong public presence, Wilder was also a very private person who had to be sought out in his retreats. So it was with the best of his instrumental compositions. That native, urban, idiomatic, unpredictable music was often difficult to wrest from the notes. As critic Irving Kolodin clearly understood, that was a problem, for not many musicians could play his music well.

The secret discourse could be discovered only by the best of ensembles and soloists, such as the New York Woodwind Quintet, the New York Brass Quintet, the Tidewater Brass Quintet in later years, John Barrows, Milton Kaye, Joe Wilder, John Swallow, Harvey Phillips, Gerry Mulligan, Marian McPartland, and others. It followed from his intimacy with the players that Wilder was at his happiest when he was attending rehearsals. Indeed, he loved them as much as he hated concerts, and he was never more fulfilled than when the players discovered the private language of the music. James Maher has caught this beautifully:

> One summer evening, Wilder was standing against the wall in a recording studio on Broadway listening to a septet of wind players, each distinguished in his musical field—commercial, recital or jazz—rehearsing a new chamber suite he had composed for them. Almost as though they were improvising, they forced the secrets from their parts. Suddenly the pulse was right. The dour set of Wilder's mouth relaxed. The aeolian texture of the piece emerged: the lines began to balance, each with its proper, constantly changing sonic weight and color. The players took on eloquence. Solo passages began to sing. The wintry mask dissolved. Wilder dug his fists deep into the pockets of his tweed jacket and began to smile. He was safe, and his music was safe. He gave into the silent laughter of joy—the open, vulnerable laughter of a boy discovering the white wonder of a windless snowfall.

Wilder put the musicians he knew, respected, and wrote for at the center of his world. In 1960 he received a call from people in the fashion department of *Life* magazine. They were about to do a motion picture based on their fashion photographs since their beginning. "It was a so-called package deal," Wilder recalled. "Had I written for a small combo I'd have made a fair amount of money. But I kept thinking of all those great players I had come to meet through John Barrows. So before I knew it I was scoring a twenty-minute movie for seventeen musicians. So of course I wound up with very little money, but a great deal of joy and beautiful playing." Those musicians read like a roll call of the great players of the age: Sam Baron, conductor; Dave Soyer, Charles McCracken, Sterling Hunkins, cellos; Urbie Green, Merv Gold, Dick Hixon, trombones; John Barrows, James Buffington, Earl Chapin, French horns; Joe Wilder, trumpet; Charles Russo, clarinet; Jerome Roth, oboe; Don Hammond, flute; Arthur Weisberg, bassoon; Bernie Leighton, piano; Milt Hinton, bass; Sol Gubin, drums.

Wilder had met many of the players he was associated with in New York through Barrows in the special bars—more like clubs than bars—that musicians gathered in, such as Jim and Andy's, Charlie's, and others. That was not the way he met Joe Wilder, "a great, especially loving trumpet player," for this Wilder did not drink. They first "met" on a record Barrows played once in a small house he rented before he had made up his mind to move permanently to Rockland County. "It was a record of no great consequence except for the trumpet sound I heard. It was the sound I had always dreamed of hearing and never had. From then to this minute I am lost without his sound whenever I write for trumpets." His playing so beguiled Wilder that he wrote a trumpet sonata for him (1963): "He recorded it beautifully and with as much ease in the non-jazz areas as the jazz." As was so often the case, the respect was mutual, and the record's liner notes affirm that the piece clearly reflects the composer's admiration for the player, just as the performance "movingly declares the player's affection for the music in his high regard for the composer."

With some exceptions, for Wilder behaved differently when he was drunk and broke, the musicians were usually grateful for the music he wrote for them so affectionately, and Wilder also often had the satisfaction of hearing his music played by them quite promptly. If, for example, he wrote a sonata for Glenn Bowen, he knew that Bowen would give it an early premiere and send him a tape if he could not attend the concert. But when his gifts were ignored, a gale warning went up. "When he sent a piece to someone," notes composer Benson, "he expected a performance and a program. If they chose not to do so, that was the end of them. He spanked them every time he mentioned their name."

Sometimes, a composition that landed on someone's desk like a paper dart was the more appreciated for being unsought. One of many recipients of this kind of gift-giving was Frederick Fennell, the founder of the distinguished Eastman Wind Ensemble. Fennell had met Wilder briefly in the early days of the school, and the two saw each other often in the late 1950s and early 1960s. Wilder became interested in what the Wind Ensemble was doing and went regularly to rehearsal. "He just came, sat, and listened." Fennell had not asked Wilder to write anything, and Wilder had given no hint that he was working on anything. One day, however, when Fennell returned to his studio from a rehearsal, he found on his desk a score of *An Entertainment* (ultimately *Entertainment No. 1*, 1960). The piece had its premiere at the Festival of American Music at Eastman the following year, and Wilder attended all the rehearsals.

Entertainment No. 1 is a serious and well-crafted piece of music and had something in it for every soloist in the Eastman Wind Ensemble: contrabassoon, English horn, piccolo, saxes, brass, the whole percussion group, everything. "It was all so typically Alec Wilder," Fennell told Robert Levy in a 1987 interview at Interlochen Music Festival:

> Someone one day will have the time and brains to look at it as a really terrific piece of music. . . . I have played the piece in about a dozen places, plus

some young men who have had some close connection with me have played it also. . . . It's available, but no one seems to know about it. I do what I can do. I just remind people that it's there. They've done it here at Interlochen with a high school band, but of course here a band is the lowest thing on the totem pole.

It's both strange and sad, he feels, that *Entertainment No. 1* is not a part of the repertoire of more groups.

Entertainment No. 1 was notable not only for what Fennell has described as its "terrific music" but also for the first scoring in music history of a steel I beam as a percussive sound. Wilder had been invited earlier by Barrows to a recording session in New York of the Mahler *Sixth Symphony*. In this composition, Mahler makes provision for a hammer blow as the blow of fate. Every symphony orchestra and every recording company had its own idea of how the sound should be produced and recorded, and Fennell remembers that Wilder was deeply intrigued by the whole thing. Indeed, from the inception of the last movement of his *Entertainment No. 1*, he had had in his head the crunching sound he had heard in New York, except he felt that the best way to get the best sound was to drop something heavy, to use gravity rather than the muscular force of a person banging a hammer on a large wooden box. Wilder and Louis Ouzer one day found an I beam in a Rochester junkyard and wound up carrying it along the alley behind Eastman School, up the long flight of steps to the Annex and the rehearsal room. At the performance itself, one end of the beam was lifted up, and, at the critical moment, the other end was pushed down on the highly resonant floating wooden stage of Eastman Theater. The result was one big satisfying crunch, unlike any sound heard in the theater before, or since.

Wilder's relationships with his musician friends often involved their whole families. That was true of no one more than Harvey Phillips. The two men were inseparable in the early years particularly. They ate together, visited together all the time, and when the Brass Quintet made a trip or if Phillips was going to a clinic or making a solo appearance somewhere, Wilder would ride along: "He became almost a companion, more than just being a friend. A very wise, clever, witty, man, very erudite. I would work on crossword puzzles and get stuck on a word, but I never threw a word at Alec that he couldn't give the definitive definition for." More than a companion to Phillips, Wilder became virtually a member of the Phillips family, Harvey and his wife, Carol, have a fond memory of taking Wilder with them on a visit to Harvey's mother in Marionville, Missouri.

The older Mrs. Phillips, Lottie, was a tiny, tough, principled lady who had brought up ten children without fuss, managed without plumbing and electricity until she was about sixty, baked bread every day, and ruled her family without fear or favor. Wilder had talked to her on the phone and was now about to fall in love with her. He was still drinking then, and Phillips told him he would need to abstain in his mother's house. "Alec couldn't quite abide that," recalls Phillips, "so he bought a bottle of vodka and stashed it in the woodpile out back of the shed, in with the old building blocks, bricks, scrap lumber. He would go out there and have a cigarette and pull on that bottle of vodka. He figured you could not smell vodka. Certainly she never said anything." With Wilder, the Phillipses—this was before they had their children—stayed about ten days and then drove back to New York. They were about halfway between Springfield and St. Louis, Missouri, Phillips recalls, "when suddenly Alec roars out from the back seat—'My God, my God, I left the vodka in the woodpile. My God, she'll find it.'" Phillips assured him his mother at her age was not about to go out and poke around in the scraps and stones.

In addition to the many pieces Wilder wrote for Phillips for the tuba repertoire, he also wrote a suite for Lottie Phillips, a sonata for tuba and piano. He would go on and write a piece—indeed more than one—for each member of the family.

As well as for classical musicians such as Harvey Phillips, Wilder wrote important pieces for eminent jazz players he numbered among his friends: Marian McPartland, piano; Stan Getz, Zoot Sims, and Gerry Mulligan, saxophone; Clark Terry, trumpet. Trombonist Bob Brookmeyer and pianists Roland Hanna and McPartland recorded albums of his songs. Jazz is an important element in the pioneering octets; *It's So Peaceful in the Country* is an enduring jazz standard; and the jazz influence is there in his concert music.

Wilder loved jazz players because he felt they had an edge. He also believed that every great classical musician who liked jazz played the better for it, with a looseness alien to the more rigid academic musicians. "All the great musicians, from John Barrows to Bernard Garfield to Sam Baron—I could mention 50 of them—they all love jazz. They don't pretend to be demonstrators of it, and while they wouldn't do it in a club, they loved to join in if a group was playing in the home." He would often say he was not himself a jazz writer. However, as collaborator Loonis McGlohon was to point out, a tune such as *Lovers and Losers* effectively spikes that notion. Wilder in fact was every kind of writer. It always bothered McGlohon that the Beatles were so applauded for discovering seven- and nine-bar phrases and other unorthodox phrases: "Alec was doing that before they were born."

Believing as he did that all music belongs in the same broad stream, Wilder refused to put jazz artists or any other kind of musicians into an isolation booth. He liked jazz musicians for the same basic reasons he liked Jerome Kern, Harold Arlen, Richard Rodgers, Cole Porter, and the other greats of American popular song. He spent hundreds of nights listening to jazz improvisations because he believed that good jazz players take the same imaginative risks in synthesizing materials that the most inventive and sophisticated songwriters take, and that the source of jazz other than the blues and so-called originals is the standard songs.

Wilder did have one big reservation about jazz musicians: their habit of taking off on flights of improvisation without first stating the melody they are drawing upon.

"As a writer of songs," he once fumed, "I deeply regret this insouciant assumption of extraterritorial rights. I am delighted that an accomplished jazz musician should choose a tune of mine to improvise upon. But I am extremely irritated by and even angry at the cavalier alterations made in my or any other writer's melody before the improvisation has begun." He was once delighted beyond measure when alto saxophonist Paul Desmond confirmed his conviction that even the most wondrous improvisation should not shoulder aside the melody. At one point in an intense conversation at Bradley Cunningham's Club (Bradley's) on University Place in Greenwich Village, Desmond said, "Well, the best chorus is the song itself."

In that considered observation, James Maher has said, Desmond, "the superlative improviser, had given to Wilder . . . a fraternal gift by assuring him (despite Alec's almost childlike wonder at improvisation) that the theme itself is the touchstone of good jazz." The jazz world held Wilder in great respect. Perhaps the ultimate accolade was paid by Charles Mingus, distinguished and highly individualistic jazz musician and composer. He was a virtuoso bassist who, like Wilder, could not be pigeonholed. During an evening at Bradley's, Mingus, seated not far from Wilder and Maher, began writing on a napkin, not easy to do. He took his time, really concentrating, got up, put the napkin down in front of Wilder and walked out. It was literally a "mash note" about what Wilder had done to open the way for him and others like him.

Wilder loved jazz players for their passion and vulnerability, but he was also aware that their standards of performance were bound to vary with the improvisations. Except for four measures he wanted played exactly, Wilder told McCandlish Phillips of the *New York Times* that he once turned over an entire movement to saxophonist Gerry Mulligan and left it absolutely wide open for him. This was totally legitimate music, and Wilder wanted Mulligan to make a jazz commentary, knowing his musical sensibilities were so acute that he could never sound like "a patch on a pair of trousers." The first rehearsal of his improvisation was so good that Wilder said that if the piece were ever published, that particular movement would say, "baritone part by Gerry Mulligan." Whereupon Mulligan replied that he had just been fooling around. Noted Wilder: "Jazz improvisation is instantaneous; the musicians never do as well on a record date. Some of the most miraculous moments of jazz have gone right up the flue because no one got them on tape." Once, Mulligan, upon being told by a slightly tipsy lady that she was not very impressed by his playing in the preceding set, replied with his wry Irish smile, "Were you here *last* night?" That, said Wilder, succinctly defined jazz and its evanescence: sometimes it happens, sometimes it doesn't.

Jazz tenor saxophonist and combo leader Stan Getz was another top jazz musician associated with several important Wilder pieces. Getz, who began playing professionally in New York when he was only fifteen, went on to work with such big bands as Stan Kenton's, Benny Goodman's, and, later, with Woody Herman's second Herd—where he and Zoot Sims, Serge Chaloff, and Herbie Steward became famous as the "four brothers" reed section. Getz had a great deal of popular success with his own small combos, but drug addiction in the mid-1950s set back his career and he spent the rest of the decade in Scandinavia. Back in the United States in the 1960s, he drew acclaim when, with guitarist Charlie Byrd, he fused the jazz and bossa nova styles. Wilder deeply admired Getz's ability to remain lyrical even when playing at a very fast tempo, and he felt awed, because of Getz's status as a great jazz player, when Getz asked him in 1963 to write some music for him for a Tanglewood concert. He had been told by others that Getz was a genius who was impossible to work with, but when he took the pieces to Getz, he found him charming, and was pleased that Getz liked what he had composed. *Suite No. 1 for Tenor Saxophone and Strings* was played by Getz and conducted by Arthur Fiedler.

When Getz several years later again asked Wilder to write for him, Wilder was more aware of how desperately disturbed, angry, and unpredictable Getz was. Still, admiring the artist, he composed *Concerto for Tenor Saxophone and Chamber Orchestra* (1968), a work that incorporates both the jazz and classical styles, making good use, as David Demsey has noted, of "the bright, singing upper register as well as the warm, spreading lower range." Says Demsey further: "The melodies tend to be of the simple, singable variety that remain in a listener's ear, or of the darting, chromatic type, reminiscent more of the John Coltrane jazz idiom than the 20th century French style frequently encountered in saxophone literature." Here was a work eminently worthy of Getz's talents. So in spite of some trepidation about the artist's reliability, Wilder secured a superb conductor (former Eastman School Director Walter Hendl) and a good orchestra, and had a copyist's piano reduction of the score delivered three months before the performance so that Getz could rehearse the piece. The undertaking turned out to be a disaster. The week before the performance at Chautauqua was "a shambles." According to Wilder, Getz had gone to Chautauqua, disappeared, been found, got drunk, never practiced, and never performed the piece.

Jazz tenor saxophonist John Haley (Zoot) Sims was another fine jazz practitioner for whom Wilder wrote several pieces. Sims had been a sideman in Gerry Mulligan's combos before becoming soloist in Mulligan's Concert Jazz Band in 1960 and was widely admired for his joyful, vigorous swing style. One of Wilder's works for Sims was *Suite No. 2 for Tenor Saxophone and Strings* (1966). The only place Wilder could find where he could get a performance was in Madison, Wisconsin:

You should know that Zoot Sims was used to large cities and the best of musicians. Yet he willingly came to Madison, didn't make a scene when he was billeted with a very square, non-drinking couple. He had brought the proper clothes to wear at the concert, never said a word (and his put-down remarks are famous) when he heard the blue-haired lady string section. I was the one who got drunk, not Zoot. The professional, to the soles of his feet.

Sims was also the soloist in the premiere of *Concerto for Tenor Saxophone and Chamber Orchestra*, which Wilder had written for Getz, in November 1968 at the University of Miami, with the University of Miami Symphonic Wind Ensemble conducted by Frederick Fennell. Some years later Sims would also be the soloist in a performance in Indianapolis, Indiana, with the Indianapolis Symphony Orchestra, conducted by Sarah Caldwell, a Wilder friend. The two men were both personally and professionally attuned. "He was like an old pipe," Sims would say. "He had that tweed jacket and everything sticking out of his pockets. I met him when he was drinking and then when he stopped. He helped me out once when I couldn't handle myself. A beautiful man."

Wilder was important also in the art and life of accomplished jazz pianist Marian McPartland. Musically, they seemed to challenge and complement each other, and, in their best moments, were able to achieve a close creative communion. Commenting in 1974 on the album *Marian McPartland Plays the Music of Alec Wilder*, respected critic John S. Wilson noted, as others had done, that Wilder's songs and instrumental pieces would be heard more often if they were less difficult to perform. Only a few select performers, he said, could communicate the blend of strength and delicacy flowing through his work. He cited Mabel Mercer and Mildred Bailey as two such exponents and then added: "Now Wilder has found another highly compatible interpreter, this time a pianist, Marian McPartland. . . . Miss McPartland is always a meticulous and imaginative pianist but she seems to bring her richest perceptions to Wilder's music, whether she is presenting his statement of a theme or going off on what Wilder calls 'McPartlandizing.'"

McPartland was still a teenage jazz enthusiast in her native England when she first heard Wilder's octets and was at once intrigued by them—their fascinating combination of classical melodies, graceful and light, played with a jazz beat. The pieces had style, elegance, and wit, she wrote in 1976. Some were tender, some humorous; all were short and perfectly put together. "The melodies were so intricately woven between the various instruments that it was hard for me to pick out the main themes on the piano. I would just listen to the records and let my imagination run riot." That imagination later allowed her to make romantic mind-pictures out of some of his songs. She could see a girl in a crinoline dancing on a sunlit lawn, trees heavy with silence on a windless night, the moon reflected in a dewpond. "The fact that his writing has this pastoral quality, like English folk music, is not surprising. Delius was among Alec's many influences. He is also passionately fond of the countryside and the peace of sleepy villages."

The jazz skills that Wilder so admired in McPartland were arrived at after a long apprenticeship. In England, where she was born Margaret Marian Turner, she began studying piano, composition, harmony, singing, and the violin at age seventeen at the Guildhall School of Music in London. The day came when she stole time from her studies to audition for a position as pianist in a music hall. That led to a tour of vaudeville theaters. In 1943, McPartland joined ENSA, the British equivalent of the American USO, and the following year she became a USO entertainer in France. When there was no piano, she played accordion. In Belgium, sitting in on a jazz session, she played with Dixieland Cornetist Jimmy McPartland, whom she later married. (The McPartlands would later divorce amicably and, toward the end of Jimmy's life, remarry.) After the war they moved to the United States and struggled together to find a footing in the music scene. In the 1950s Marian moved beyond Jimmy's Dixieland music to modern jazz but was always encouraged by him. When she made her debut at the Hickory House in New York, the *Time* reviewer hailed "some of the cleanest, most inventive 'progressive' jazz to be heard anywhere."

It was at the Hickory House that Marian McPartland first saw Wilder, though there was no formal meeting. In 1954 she had recorded *I'll Be Around* for Capital, "a little Bach-style thing," and apparently Wilder heard and liked it. A few years later, McPartland was playing at The Apartment, a kind of piano bar, "not a terribly good room," at Second Avenue and 55th Street.

> One night Alec came in and sat at the bar. I went over and sat down and said hullo, and he was very friendly, very nice. He had a record under his arm of the Swingle Singers, and I said, "I love that group" and he said, "Here, my dear, take it." He wrote on it, "To someone who thinks she should have the record, so she shall have it." Some fanciful thing like that. I have it at home. I was thrilled.

One of Wilder's first gifts of music to McPartland came some years later when she was playing with her trio in the Rountowner Motel in Rochester. The two of them had already achieved an easy intimacy. One night in town they entered into a conspiracy at dinner to get out as fast as they could from a restaurant in which a Hawaiian group was poised to play. "I hate that damned Hawaiian music," Wilder had said after signaling wildly to the waiter for the check. Wilder kept going back night after night to the Rountowner to hear McPartland, sometimes with Eastman faculty members. One night as he was leaving he told her, "I'm going to write a piece for you—I'll bring it in this week." McPartland was pleased but didn't really believe him. She forgot about it until the next time he showed up at the Rountowner: "He airily tossed me a sheet of music, on which was written, 'Jazz Waltz for a Friend—a small present from Alec Wilder.' I was delighted and I couldn't wait to play the piece. It had a haunting melody which had a way of turning back on itself that I found fascinating."

McPartland always had a clear-eyed view of Wilder. She was well aware, for example, that his distaste for the limelight was more professed than real. He was, as she has said, a "closet ham," always scorning the spotlight but often enjoying it when he found himself standing there. He did genuinely detest purely promotional activities and press agentry, and he was bedeviled by shyness and insecurity, but he also liked his moments in the sun, on radio, television, or the stage. McPartland has told of the time he went with her when she was to perform his *Fantasy for Piano and Wind Ensemble* (1974) with the Duke University Wind Ensemble. He had warned her not to get him up there talking at the workshop she was also conducting:

> While I demonstrated a few ideas at the piano for students on stage, he sat in the empty hall, watching. As soon as I suggested he come up and join me in talking to the students, he did so with alacrity, and pretty soon he had taken over the workshop, talking, gesturing, making jokes, explaining the music, making the students laugh with his anecdotes, even playing the piano.

Wilder wrote many compositions for McPartland, among them *Lullaby for a Lady, Homework, Inner Circle, Why.* Together with *Jazz Waltz for a Friend* and *Suite for Piano* written for Eastman pianist Barry Snyder, they represented some of the best of his keyboard work. Wilder thought that McPartland played with great fluency, style, verve, wit, forthrightness, and profound warmth and affection. In three unplanned minutes, he said of her improvisation, she could, and consistently did, invent rhythms, harmonic sequences, and melodic flights "which would take me three weeks to achieve as a composer. And even then, not half as well." James Maher was once witness to that kind of triumph at The Cookery when McPartland played through a new piece of Wilder's. Like most of his instrumental writing and his songs, this was elusive, personal, idiomatic music, deeply challenging to the performer. McPartland was up to it. "Marian searched the music measure by measure, opening out the thrust of its long phrases, trying out harmonic departures implicit in the original changes. The secrets—warm, witty, time-haunted, lyrical, and wintry—slowly emerged."

Despite his vexing, sometimes outrageous habits, McPartland admired Wilder both for his music and for his ability to strip away the layers of adulthood and yield to the boy who was always there in the man. She once sent to a toy shop in London for a clockwork mouse he had been hankering for. She gave it to him at the French Shack restaurant in Manhattan. "He wound it up and ran it across the table, and then he ran it across the floor. Paul Desmond came it and looked at Alec in astonishment."

One morning in Rochester, in Louis Ouzer's Gibbs Street photographic studio near the Eastman School, McPartland found Wilder sitting with a can of bubble liquid, floating bubbles all over the room: "I couldn't believe it. We went out on the street, and the two of us blew bubbles, Alec with his glasses piled back on his head and his tie awry. A little man strutted by from Eastman School, glared at Alec, and said, 'Alec Wilder, you'll never grow up, will you?' And Alec hollered back, 'NEVER.'"

That innocent, childlike, fun-making streak in Wilder, his ability to loosen the bonds and soar with the bubbles, was an important element in his music-making for children. He was somehow able to look at things from a child's perspective and, be it storytelling or flute-playing, understand that children must be met and greeted at their own level of life, not bent down to. Some of his best music would be written for children.

Casting a Spell

In 1965, together with illustrator Maurice Sendak, Engvick and Wilder completed one of their happiest collaborations: perhaps the most charming collection of children's songs ever assembled, *Lullabies and Night Songs,* published by Harper & Row. Since then, this handsome book has given pleasure to untold numbers of American families. But before going into more detail, let us look at some of Wilder's earlier works for children.

Often with Engvick, sometimes with Sundgaard and others, sometimes by himself, Wilder had been writing children's musical numbers off and on for two decades or so. Sometimes for the children of his friends, sometimes for a wider audience, he would continue to compose such pieces until the last year of his life. The compositions were not all exclusively for children but were often drawn from children's classics, such as *Hansel and Gretel* and *Pinocchio,* that have always delighted adults as well. Like Engvick, he had a feeling for what was magical and innocent. It was as if he wanted to do what he could to give children a better childhood than the one he chose to remember.

In 1946 Wilder wrote two musical stories that were recorded. One was *The Churkendoose,* about an animal that was part chicken, part turkey, part duck, part goose. The other was *Herman Ermine in Rabbit Town,* a study in racial tolerance in children's terms. Ben Ross Berenberg wrote the librettos, and two noted theater and film people, Ray Bolger and John Garfield, were the respective narrators. In 1953 the talents of Wilder and Engvick were given a national showcase when *Miss Chicken Little,* a one-act musical fable Engvick feels is closer to a cantata for the theater than an opera, was produced by CBS television on the noted *Omnibus* program sponsored by the Ford Foundation. *Miss Chicken Little* had its stage premiere a month earlier, on November 24, in the Spring Valley High School Auditorium, where it was performed by the Lyric Theater branch of the Rockland Foundation, for which it was written.

Because the original work was written for just two pianos, Wilder had to work at lightning speed, sometimes twenty-four hours a day, to get the piece orchestrated in time for the *Omnibus* production a month away. The talented cast included Jo Sullivan (Loesser), who sang Chicken Little, and Charlotte Rae, one of the hens. Ray Charles did the choral directing; John Butler the choreography; and George Bassman the conducting. Some who saw the *Omnibus* show, with its comic, light operatic treatment, have called it "stunning." There was a second Lyric Theater Rockland County production in Piermont, New York, in 1958, and a TRG Repertory production would play in New York for a month in November of 1983 at the Wonderhorse Theatre. *Miss Chicken Little* was staged elsewhere in the earlier years. At one point, Wilder met actor Alan Arkin, who surprised him by singing whole pages from the cantata; he had played one of the roles in a Chicago production. Several of the songs, notably *It's a Fine Day for Walkin' Country Style,* have survived and continue to have a life of their own. *Don't Deny* is another that's included in one of the Wilder song collections published affectionately by The Richmond Organization (TRO).

With Mitch Miller providing the encouragement, Wilder during these years was writing many pieces for Golden Records, a series of small yellow records that sold for a quarter and contained songs for children. Some of the songs, he said, were quite charming, but others had inferior lyrics that made respectable music impossible to compose. With Miller doing the musical directing of the Golden Symphony Orchestra and the Sandpiper Chorus, Golden Records in 1954 produced something quite different, *A Child's Introduction to the Orchestra,* a novel musical primer that has remained popular. This work describes the instruments of the symphony in seventeen songs and fifteen orchestral arrangements, and in a miniature symphony. Marshall Barer wrote the lyrics, which Wilder thought were adroit and evocative. He cared less for the titles: "Bobo the Oboe," "Knute the Flute," "Antoinette the Clarinet," "Muldoon the Bassoon," "Poobah the Tuba," "Monsieur Forlorn the French Horn," and so on. Still, the whole thing seemed to work as a storytelling introduction to the orchestra for the young.

Again under the Golden Records label, Wilder collaborated with Sundgaard on the 1957 children's Christmas-story album titled *An Ax, an Apple and a Buckskin Jacket.* Bing Crosby did the singing and the narrating of this story of a young boy in the Kentucky wilderness whose Christmas wishes are fulfilled by three wise men of the frontier, Paul Bunyan, Johnny Appleseed, and Daniel Boone. "One of the best things Alec and I did," Sundgaard would say, "was the Christmas album for Bing Crosby." One of the numbers, *How Lovely Is Christmas,* deserves to rank with the best of America's carols, but somehow, even in Crosby's hands, it failed to catch fire and remains undeservedly neglected. Wilder was also at this time writing many small pieces for student piano players that would ultimately be edited by Carol K. Baron, musicologist and pianist, who is an authority on Charles Ives and has a book about him in preparation. Margun has published a graded series in four volumes edited by Baron, *Pieces for Young Pianists*. Some of them needed to be made a little easier to approach, says Baron, "but they're wonderful, vivid, and the individual voice comes through. They're not just another set of pieces for children."

Twice more, in 1957 and 1958, national television showcased the skills of Wilder and Engvick in working with children's themes, and on both occasions the shows, live television specials, were considered hits. Talent Associates' NBC production of *Pinocchio,* starring Mickey Rooney, was presented on October 13, 1957. The cast included Stubby Kaye, Walter Slezak, Fran Allison, Martyn Green, and Jerry Colonna. David Susskind was the executive producer; Paul Bogart the director. *Hansel and Gretel* was performed under the same Talent auspices on April 27 the following year. Red Buttons and Barbara Cook were the leads, with Stubby Kaye, Rudy Vallee, Risë Stevens, Hans Conried, and Paula Lawrence also in the cast.

Working on those two specials would have been a more enjoyable experience for Engvick had Wilder stayed around to attend to the business at hand. Wilder said later that he never knew how he had "shocked and horrified" his partner by leaving for Milwaukee with the *Pinocchio* lyrics in his pocket, promising to ship the melodies back as fast as he finished them: "The thought of my working away from him he rightly took to be a betrayal of the implicit pact of any collaborators to work together. At the time, all I thought of was getting out to that enormous old house and being with those five beautiful musicians [Baron and Barrows and the other members of the New York Woodwind Quintet]." At any rate, the music was written long before the lyrics were finished, and that set up a problem when changes in the script meant that changes had to be made in the lyrics. Wilder, says Engvick, was happy to write the tunes, but he was not going to attend any "meetings" and put up with fussy changes, and, besides, he did not understand why Engvick would be willing to change anything. "So to dodge unwelcome communications, he simply disappeared, and I had some anxious weeks trying to finish the lyrics and trying to conceal Alec's disappearance from the gentlemen in charge."

Wilder acknowledged that he had had no more to do with *Pinocchio* than to see to it that the producers heard and accepted the songs, and to be in the studio when the orchestra rehearsed the music and the actors tried out their songs. He maintained that he never saw the performance itself: "That may seem to have been stretching my isolated point of view a bit too tight." But, he insisted, he had no desire to look at a little television box. He had written the best songs he could and had made certain that they worked. He said he no longer wanted to get mixed up with the show-biz world in spite of the presence "of that lovely lady Fran Allison" and other fine performers such as Mickey Rooney. Wilder believed there were some good songs in the show—which included *The Birthday Song, The Fox's Pitch, Happy News, The Jolly Coachman, Listen to Your Heart*—but because of disagreements between the producer "and my loving friend Howard Richmond," the music publisher, there was no promotion of the songs, "so nothing happened to them." It was a fact, said Wilder, that new songs written for television never became hits, even though the audience numbered millions. However, one *Pinocchio* song, *Listen to Your Heart,* is still admired today for the innocence that flows from its artfully concealed craftsmanship.

Again with the second television special, *Hansel and Gretel,* Wilder showed little interest beyond the writing of the songs, to Engvick's distress and inconvenience: "This time I had to follow him to Rochester, which was under bunkers of snow, to get his cooperation. I realized that his only interest in the project was the money. What should have been an enjoyable project, wasn't." This man who wrote so generously for friends had a different attitude toward more commercial ventures.

Engvick and Wilder's next major collaboration, one of their best and this time an enjoyable experience for both men, was *Lullabies and Night Songs* (Engvick's title), illustrated by Sendak. The forty-eight melodies in the book included such numbers as *Go Tell Aunt Rhody, The Starlighter, The Golux's Song, Baby Bunting, All the Pretty Li'l Horses, Bobby Shaftoe, The Cottager to Her Infant, Douglas Mountain,* and *Wee Willie Winkie.* Many of the verses chosen by editor Engvick were set to music by Wilder for the first time, and all were happily complemented by Sendak's full-color pastel drawings of shady pastures and starry nights and children with faces flushed from pillow fights. Says the foreword: "Some of the rollicking ones are not strictly lullabies, but aim to end the day with laughter and delight. These we call night songs. The collection does not pretend to be definitive. It simply celebrates the magic world of a happy sleepy child." The poems were drawn from such famous writers as James Thurber, Lewis Carroll, Alfred Lord Tennyson, and William Blake. Engvick also lent his own talents:

The Elephant Present

Elephants can be lots of fun—
They're big and warm and pleasant.
Where am I going to find one,
Find you an Elephant present?

Maybe I can go to the elephant zoo
With lumps of sugar to trap him,
Then quickly mail him home to you—
When I find out how to wrap him! ©

In the early 1960s Sendak was not yet the major writer, illustrator, and theatrical-set and costume designer that he is today. The promise was clearly there, however, in such books as *Where the Wild Things Are,* written in 1963 and which by 1985 had sold twenty-five million copies. Wilder had seen Sendak's tiny *A Hole Is to Dig,* and it so pleased him that he would do the *Lullabies* book only if

Sendak would illustrate it. Wilder proposed to do the book first so that Sendak would see it, and Engvick was brought in to find the material. Sendak approved.

Perhaps because of its happy nature, *Lullabies and Night Songs* was always to give particular pleasure to Wilder and Engvick. For Wilder, his best reward came one night in the bar at the Beverly Hills Hotel when he got talking with a man he took to be a businessman. When the man learned that Wilder had written the music for the *Lullabies* book, he suddenly brightened. He said that he and his wife had been having marital difficulties, and that an estrangement had been imminent. At some point, they somehow sat down at a piano to sample the book, and wound up singing it clear through. They both felt better for doing it, and indeed the man said the experience had helped save his marriage.

Twenty years after the original publication, the songs in *Lullabies and Night Songs* were brought as vividly to the ear as they had been to the eye when they were recorded for Caedmon by internationally known mezzo soprano Jan De-Gaetani. Particularly acclaimed for her performance of twentieth-century music, DeGaetani was considered a good choice by Caedmon to give the airs their full, warm measure. DeGaetani, who has since died, was professor of voice at Eastman, and her recordings can be heard on Arabesque, Bridge, CRI, Columbia, Decca, Desto, Nonesuch, Vanguard, and Vox. The liner notes for the album were written by Thomas Hampson, the Wilder estate executor, who also produces a weekly column and radio feature on jazz. He observes that the album is a happy mix of original Wilder melodies and traditional songs known to generations of children. The latter melodies have been around for centuries, the Wilder tunes since only yesterday, "yet it's often difficult to tell which is which; the blend is perfect. Listen, for example, to the pairing of the traditional 'Wee Cooper of Fife' with 'Tiptoe Night,' a Wilder original. In fact, try listening to the whole album before consulting the jacket to verify which melodies are by Wilder and which come to us from antiquity."

Another significant musical initiative involving children was undertaken by Wilder in Avon, New York, near hometown Rochester in 1968. The context this time was very different, for the choral work in question, *Children's Plea for Peace*, evolved from an improbable yet enduring friendship. It was a friendship that embraced Wilder, the affluent aristocratic agnostic; Ouzer, the sensitive Jew of modest circumstances; and Father Henry A. Atwell, the liberal Roman Catholic priest who took an early and prominent role in the ecumenical movement.

Ouzer was the photographer befriended as a young man in the 1930s by Wilder. He later became known for his sensitive portraits of Isaac Stern, Marian Anderson, Vladimir Horowitz, Louis Armstrong, and many other musical notables who performed or taught master classes at Eastman School. (Some of the best of them are in *Contemporary Musicians in Photographs,* published by Dover in 1979.) But Ouzer was more than a photographer of the famous. Constantly documenting social change with his camera and always sympathetic to the struggles of blacks, he had become an important part of the community's conscience.

In Henry Atwell, Ouzer found a soul mate. Here was a small, lean, spry, twinkling man who could usually be found at the leading edge of liberal thought yet did his religious questioning from within the fold and the framework of the church. He did not respect the pope just because he felt he was always right: "In my family home, I respected my father, and most of the time I obeyed him, not because I thought he was always right, but because I loved him and knew I belonged to him." In his newspaper editorials, Atwell never hesitated to take a stand. When a housing proposal for 120 moderate-income families was opposed—purportedly because of school and traffic congestion and tax abatements that would mean less revenue for the city—Atwell's *Catholic Courier* said bluntly: "Simple honesty requires that we admit that just plain racial bigotry is, rather, the real reason."

In 1966, two years before Atwell would become involved with Wilder in *The Children's Plea for Peace,* the Rochester diocese—indeed, the Catholic Church nationally—was startled by the news that the new bishop was to be none other than television's famous "Uncle Fultie," Bishop Fulton J. Sheen, the handsome, dynamic prelate extraordinary, the church's best-known preacher and evangelist. He had converted to the faith such famous figures as Henry Ford II, Heywood Broun, Clare Booth Luce, and Fritz Kreisler. How such a man bestriding a national stage could suddenly be consigned to the provinces was an intriguing question. No, he said at a press conference in New York, he was not being farmed out. "I see it as an elevation." It was widely speculated, however, that Sheen had fallen out of favor with Francis Cardinal Spellman, archbishop of New York. In Rochester, Sheen, saying he was "a soldier of the church," tried to prick consciences on Vietnam, poverty, and racism. He was never reluctant to take bold positions on such issues; in church matters, he was much more doctrinaire.

Almost inevitably, Sheen would have a strained relationship in Rochester with Henry Atwell. Controversy in the columns of *The Courier* was not welcome. In 1967, just as suddenly as he himself had been moved to Rochester, Sheen announced that Atwell would henceforth serve as pastor of Saint Agnes Church in nearby Avon. Like the bishop, Atwell accepted his transfer loyally. His friends, however, had no doubt that Atwell was being sent down for his unorthodox views. Wilder, when he came to know him, was quite sure of it: "Henry is one of the new renegade breed as well as being a very bright, warm, witty civilized man. His editorials were so daring and off limits that he was removed and shipped off to what I suppose his bishop presumed to be the boondocks. It happened to be a lovely little village south of Rochester."

Ouzer had pushed Wilder for a long time to meet Atwell. Wilder, however, had kept pushing back. Who needed a Catholic priest? When he did finally get to meet Atwell in Avon, the two men liked each other at once—to the point that Wilder began arranging his flights to Rochester so that he could drive down to Avon with Ouzer for dinner and conversation. Wilder would say about his new friend: "His principal concern is people, not religion. He is a scholarly man, of great charm and wit, courageous, angry and extremely compassionate. He's no Christer or religious Pollyanna. Yet he believes that people are essentially good. He arrives at this conviction through the confessional." Wilder was so incensed about Atwell's consignment that he determined to do whatever he could to make Avon a cultural center. His *Children's Plea for Peace* (which was also influenced by the Korean War), the opera *The Truth about Windmills,* and the church cantata *Mountain Boy* would all be composed there.

One night at dinner in the rectory, after two of the best martinis Wilder thought he had ever tasted, Atwell handed him a sheet of paper on which he had written five or six statements by famous men on the subject of peace. The cleric's quizzical smile convinced Wilder that he had an ulterior motive. With the help of the martinis, Wilder made a passionate statement about peace. He also said that if Atwell had it in mind for him to write some music for the church using the statements of those famous men, then he would much prefer to have the uncomplicated sentiments of children.

Shortly after that, Atwell arranged for all the children under twelve in the Avon public and parochial schools to write essays about peace. In a short time Wilder received three hundred of them. He found the children's comments "wonderful" and "heartbreaking," perceptive and poignant: "Peace is a horse with a nose of velvet"; "Stupid, Stupid War!"; "Peace is like going wading in the water"; "Peace is a big family of quietness"; "Tomorrow there's peace with opened-up doors"; "The grownups have failed, all us children should not." The chosen passages were then set to music, and *The Children's Plea for Peace* was first performed in Atwell's Saint Agnes Church on May 3, 1969, and was repeated in the Eastman School's Eastman Theater the following day. On both occasions the Eastman Children's Chorus (a select group of youngsters from the school's Preparatory Department) and twenty members of the famous Eastman Wind Ensemble (winds, brass, and percussion) were conducted by Milford Fargo, a faculty member who was close to Wilder. The narrator in the premiere was Wilder's friend, composer Benson.

This was an event as much as it was a musical occasion. "I'm very happy that I composed *The Children's Plea for Peace* for you," he wrote Atwell. "Granted that it was for your church, it truly was for you. Lavinia Russ, whom I'm sure you remember, walked down the block after that performance because she was crying." That, he said, about summed it up. It was not, he added, a great musical work, but everything surrounding it was great: "the beautiful, beautiful children crocodiling across to the church from the school, the perfect spring day, the tender green of the budding leaves, the spring flowers, the friendly spirit of the congregation, Warren Benson's loving narration, you and I up on that little choir loft looking down at it all!"

Thanks in large measure to the missionary zeal of Wilder's protege and friend Robert Levy, associate professor of music at Lawrence University's Conservatory of Music in Appleton, Wisconsin, *Plea for Peace* had several subsequent performances, in Appleton and earlier at St. Mary's College in Maryland. With a text written by elementary school children, Wilder believed that the work could have been a powerful voice in the world for peace. The dream was not realized; Wilder and the children had to settle for making their own personal compact and common cause.

In 1975 Levy conducted a surprise performance of *Plea for Peace* for Wilder at St. Mary's College. More than one hundred elementary children from the Frank Knox and Oakville elementary schools took part. It was, said Levy, "a moving, emotional experience for Wilder, the children and the more than 700 people in attendance." Nine days later, the children wrote to Wilder expressing thanks. Wilder wrote back promptly:

Dear WONDERFUL members of the chorus (including those who had colds and couldn't sing, and those who were supposed to sing and couldn't for one reason or another):

I received all of your letters and they made me so happy that I cried!

I read every single of one of them including the one from Billy Mellott who shook hands with me and Cathy Micheli who thought I was too shy to give her my autograph (it's on the next page) and the girl who met me back by the chairs (Julie Waterman) and all those who wrote "PEACE" in big letters at the bottom of the letters.

It's the sweetest, kindest, nicest, happiest thing that's ever happened to me and I thank you all from the top, the middle, and the bottom of my heart!!!!!!!!

Alec Wilder

P.S. Someone who wrote me doesn't know how anyone so old as I am could write such a piece. Well, I sure am old but my heart and my hopes and my dreams and my love is YOUNG!

Wilder never had much hope that the world would ever mend its violent, wicked ways. Writing about the release of the recording of *Plea for Peace*, he said he fully expected to be visited by the FBI for his pursuit "of that will-o-the-wisp, peace." But even though he believed he was living in an age without style, virtue, dignity, or honor, he was nearly always able to find some blue sky for children. And as often as not, adults as well as children were able to enter into his land of make-believe. That was certainly true of another work he became involved with at about the same time as *Plea for Peace: Land of Oz,* the highly original outdoor re-creation of *the Wizard of*

Oz. Guiding genius for this imaginative show was Loonis McGlohon of Charlotte, North Carolina, the man who would become Wilder's third and last partner in song.

McGlohon is a quiet, courteous, good-humored, diversely talented musician for whom North Carolina has always been home. He grew up in the tobacco-farming town of Ayden, the son of an auto mechanic and a housewife. In an interview with Whitney Balliett, he noted that the family was poor and that the best he could manage was East Carolina University in Greenville. During World War II he was with the 345th Army Air Forces Band in Marianna, Florida, in the middle of a pecan grove in the Panhandle. Said McGlohon: "I was with Jimmy Dorsey's band some after the war, and then my childhood sweetheart and I got married. We talked about going to New York to join Ralph Flanagan's band, but decided they wouldn't have grits in New York and probably wouldn't take kindly to bib overalls anyway. So we stayed in Charlotte."

Until his retirement, McGlohon was producer for Station WBTV in Charlotte. He has accompanied singers of the stature of Eileen Farrell, Judy Garland, Barbara Lea, Marlene VerPlanck, Maxine Sullivan; he is the pianist with his own trio; and he composes music as well as writes lyrics. McGlohon is the kind of man who worries about poverty in Africa, and he has raised money to do something about it. He directs his church choir, and he believes in Big Brothers. He has collaborated with close friend and fellow North Carolinian Charles Kuralt on the record album and show *North Carolina Is My Home.*

Land of Oz was staged on top of 6,000-foot Beech Mountain in western North Carolina, a state that has a strong tradition of outdoor theater. It opened in June 1970 and continued for ten years, and for most of this time *Land of Oz* was included on Rand McNally maps of the eastern United States. "It was a unique piece of theater, a walk-through production in which the audience moved in groups of about 35, first visiting the Kansas farm field, then entering Aunt Em's farmhouse, where they suddenly were rushed to the cellar because of an approaching tornado." The audience was finally led through an enchanting garden to the yellow-brick road, which they followed past the houses of the Tin Man and the Scarecrow, the cave of the Cowardly Lion, and even the Witch's castle, where each of the characters performed. Then it was on to Emerald City to meet the Wizard.

Harold Arlen gave permission for use of *Over the Rainbow,* but Wilder wrote such new numbers as *I Lost My Heart, I'm a Fraidy Cat, Open Your Eyes, Plenty Good Enough for Me, The Witch's Song (How Do I Brew That Stew?).* Singer Mary Mayo did the sound track, and her daughter Lori played the part of Dorothy.

Those were exciting, creative days, though not without problems in the presence of the high-powered Wilder. On a day when McGlohon went fishing just to get out of the way for a bit, Wilder accompanied McGlohon's wife, Nan, and Mary Mayo's mother, Mrs. Franklin Riker, to breakfast. Mrs. Riker had been a famous concert soprano many years before; she was now about ninety-four and still a *grande dame*. At the table she turned to Wilder and said to him in so many words, "Mr. Wilder you know you're a very talented young man but you're very, very [and here Wilder tried to fill in the words for her by saying eccentric]. No, I wasn't going to say eccentric. I was going to say ill-mannered, inconsiderate, rude." She sailed right on: "You've gobbled your breakfast like an animal, and now you're smoking a cigarette and I find that very offensive because Nan and I have just begun to eat breakfast. But more than that, Mr. Wilder, I was watching you as we went through the cafeteria line, and you never offered to pay for breakfast. You didn't even make the gesture of reaching into your pocket." After all that, Wilder simply looked at her, smiled, and said, "Yes, Mrs. Riker, you know, I believe it is more blessed to receive than to give." Wilder was never easily discomfited.

Land of Oz, McGlohon has said, was one of the great experiences of Wilder's life. He visited the place many times, and was like a child as he explored the site. Yet the romantic world inhabited by Wilder and children was not always as guileless as it seemed. Arlene Bouras of Chicago feels that his relationship with children was in fact very complicated, an example of ultimate seduction: "I think he made every child feel that no one understood him as well as he did, that nobody really loved him as much as Alec. He didn't necessarily alienate them against other adults, but he did assume heroic proportions in their lives, and he still does." His relationship with Bouras's daughter, Lorraine, was indeed "a very nice one." He was a "very, very important" man in her life. And yet, Bouras feels, "it was never simple loving. I consider Alec a terribly complex person, and I don't think anything he did was without motives."

Other close friends and colleagues also saw beyond the surface shine. James Maher points out that Wilder would write songs about and for children and talk about them "in such a way that you would be impressed and say, 'My God, this man had a feeling for children that's almost uncanny.' But little by little you would also discover Alec the manipulator of children." Forever dealing in absolutes and proscriptions, Wilder had only scorn for most contemporary children's literature, and he did his utmost to give Maher's son Fred a copy of Thurber's *Story of O*. Maher would have none of it. He considered it unsuitable to force the Thurber book on children and told Wilder, much to Wilder's disgust, that his son was happy with the *The Enchanted Tollbooth*. "I thought," says Maher, "I'm not going to let him intrude, and I never did. He met Frederick a couple of times, and that was it."

Loonis McGlohon confesses that he never could get a handle on Wilder's feeling about children: "He was childlike, and he loved that world, but I don't think he loved very many children." He does remember that Wilder loved the children of some of his friends: "He admired Whitney Balliett's boys very much. He loved singing duo Jackie Cain and Roy Kral's two daughters, particularly the older, Niki. He thought she was an exquisitely beautiful child." When Niki died in an automobile accident at twenty, no one among her friends was more devastated than Wilder. The two of them went back a long way together.

Jackie remembers that once when they were living in New York, Wilder called and invited Niki, then four or five, to go with him to the large and famous F. A. O. Schwarz toy store to choose a gift for herself. Wilder's only stipulation was that it be something that could fit into the backseat of a taxicab. "Apparently," says Jackie, "they covered every floor of the store. Much to Alec's surprise, instead of taking some huge, wondrous toy, Niki ended up choosing six or eight tiny stuffed animals and birds, things she could hold in her hand." Wilder told Jackie later that when they got back to the apartment in a cab, Niki very politely but matter-of-factly dismissed him with a "thank you, bye now." Recalls Jackie: "Alec had a chuckle about that. He always loved the fact that kids were so honest, with no pretensions. Niki was too young, and she didn't yet have manners enough to say, 'Thank you very much.' She just said in effect, 'Thanks, that's enough now, goodbye.' He laughed about that, he got such a kick out of it."

There was also the time when Niki went with Jackie and Roy to a Sunday afternoon rehearsal of a piece Wilder had written for those outstanding guitarists George Barnes and Carl Kress. Wilder wrote later that just before they started playing, Niki walked up to him "with a marvelous blend of pride and shyness, her child hands delicately smoothing down her dress. She stood before me smiling and then she said, 'I'm all in pink.' And so she was, and God knows I've never forgotten the moment." When Niki was killed some fifteen years later, Wilder wrote to Jackie and Roy, asking them: "Would you be kind enough to place the enclosed words under a sturdy shell near the place down the beach where you plan to take part of my love? I hope you will." These were his words:

> *About Nicoli Lisa Kral*
> *Older Daughter of Jackie and Roy Kral*
>
> All of us gathered that Sunday afternoon
> Not for the playing of two dear men
> But more as an affirmation
> As if to say, "How nice to look about
> And see the faces of friends!"
> There was laughter and the opulent
> Sound of sleekly stroked guitars
> And then—and then, dearest girl,
> You walked across the room
> With a radiant smile,
> Smoothing down your pretty dress
> With your butterfly fingers

And you stood before me and proudly said
"I'm all in pink! . . ."
And that's how I shall always remember you
All in pink . . .
You're many safe places now, I know
And among them you are standing here
Inside my reverent head,
Smiling at me
Smoothing down your proud, pink frock . . .

Jackie and Roy placed Wilder's poem under a seashell on the beach at Fire Island where they took Niki's ashes.

With Niki, it had been love at first sight, but Wilder was never tempted to put his arm around all the world's children. His love was discriminating and personal. The children had best be clean and well dressed. They should preferably be little girls rather than little boys, and they should never have runny noses. But when Wilder cast his spell, it often remained unbroken for a long time after.

Harvey Phillips Jr., middle son of Harvey and Carol Phillips, still remembers a train ride on a summer day in France in 1986 when a man walked by him who had the same distinctive personal fragrance as Wilder. "I remember that was very comforting to me. I made sure I went and sat by him in the coach. That's kind of weird, I know, but it made the train trip a bit less tedious. That was a long time after Alec had died, a long time for something to be still in the nostrils and senses."

The children of Louis and Helen Ouzer were no less attracted. Wilder was in and out of the Ouzer household in Rochester half a dozen times a year. Theirs was the only house to which he ever had a key, and he was proud of that trust. Even as a small child, Billy always called Wilder by his first name, the first adult he did that with. Wilder always treated Billy and his sister, Sandy, as adults. "He made you feel you were at his level. He could adapt himself. He became a model in some ways." Billy remembers that Wilder had an intense interest in natural history, and that he was worrying about conservation, about polluting factories and disappearing swamps long before the environmental movement was born. "Alec," says Sandy, "was around all the time, it seemed. When he wasn't around, we were fallow until he came again."

Wilder carried a lot to such friendships. "What kind of things? Bobble birds, anecdotes, complaints, theories, enthusiasms, concern, wonderment, spouting bathtub dolphins, puzzles I've made up, books, strange brands of soap; to magicians, music; to animal lovers, books by Gerald Durrell; to nature lovers, Sierra Club books." But best, he always said, he took with him the willingness to listen, to "honest to God listen."

Wilder arrived on his visits with the treasures of a merchant prince, quickening those who had lain fallow. However, there was receiving as well as giving. "Alec was an enriching presence in our house," says Sandy (Ouzer) Hecht, "but he received much in return by being embraced as family, to the point that he could feel free to dislike my purple bathing suit or whoop it up with us in innocent family activities, like when I would yell out the national anthem from the open car window or use a waste receptacle as a basketball hoop."

Sometimes the spell Wilder laid on the young was broken later in life by his drinking. For Martin Russ, Wilder was "the benevolent giant" of his childhood. During World War II, his mother, Lavinia, a sophisticated woman who longed to be in New York City, had to spend a winter at what was called The Farm outside Portageville, New York. Her husband Hugh stayed the week in town in Buffalo and drove down on weekends. Wilder was the most romantic and exciting figure Martin Russ, then about ten or eleven, had ever encountered. One of the outbuildings at The Farm was called The Cottage, across the orchard from the big white house.

> I spent most of my time over there listening to records on the wind-up
> Victrola and practicing the trumpet. One day as I was practicing, I looked out
> the window and there was Alec with a devilish look on his face, the thick
> woods behind him. I can't think of a felicitous way of expressing the thrill I
> felt at that moment. I hadn't known he was coming all the way out to our
> boondocks, and suddenly there stands His Greatness in my private little
> world. And he had walked all the way across The Orchard just to see me!

Years later, out on the West Coast, Russ became disenchanted. He and Wilder had traveled together to Vancouver by train, and from there to Los Angeles. Russ was twenty-five at the time, and Wilder's drinking habits were beginning to dissolve his hero worship. The old friendship broke apart one night. Russ was to meet Wilder for dinner at the Bel-Air, and he took along with him a McGraw-Hill editor, Bob Gutwillig, who had been courting him for a book he wanted him to write: "Alec took an instant dislike to him and did one of those incredible Mr. Hyde things—suddenly becoming very nasty after a couple of drinks. I felt called on to defend Gutwillig, who didn't know what the hell was going on, and I said some harsh words which drove Alec right out of the bar." His last memory of Wilder, in those days when they were seeing a good deal of each other, was "of Bob and me coming out of the bar on our way to the parking lot and seeing Alec standing behind a tree, glowering at us pathetically." Russ walked on by without speaking. "I probably got the usual apologetic telegrams the next day. He was always having to apologize by wire for doing his Mr. Hyde turn."

Yet no one else had so impressed Russ when he was growing up:

> To this day I hear his Shakespearean-actor voice in my head and wonder what
> he would think of this or that. Would he like Antonio Carlos Jobim or loathe

him? (Did anyone ever speak the word loathe more pulverisingly?) I'm sure I would be a different person, about half of what I am, if I hadn't known him. . . . In many ways, he was like a dream father. Not an ideal father but a dream father. He never corrected, deplored, nor dispensed advice. I wish he had done so. . . . He was by far the biggest influence on my life up to the time I was about 25. I cried when my mother called to say he was dying.

When he was on his good behavior—and even sometimes when he was not—Wilder was hard to resist. Niece Beverly McGinness wrote often to her favorite uncle when she was at boarding school in Dobbs Ferry, New York. Two or three times during the school year, Wilder would breeze in and take her to lunch. He was "devilishly" good-looking, and her classmates were always "atwitter," particularly since she did not call him uncle. It was her farewell to Wilder at a train station that remains one of her warmest memories. On what would be his last visit with her, he arrived in Hamilton, Massachusetts, from New York for a weekend:

> We had a marvelous time, as always, and when I took him to the station to catch his train, he picked me right off my feet and gave me a big hug and kiss, just as the engine pulled abreast. The conductor, thinking no doubt we were sweethearts, hollered out, "Give her another one to make it last," whereupon Alec did, and the conductor pulled the whistle a mighty blast, and we cracked up laughing.

Never a model of consistency, Wilder most times recoiled from physical contact. He was known to visit Arnold Sundgaard with his arms full of books so as to avoid shaking hands. But an attractive niece was different perhaps.

Before she met him, Margaret Russ, the daughter of Lavinia Russ, was fully prepared to dislike this rather weird man she had heard so much about. "Even at ten, I was a very conservative child. I knew I wouldn't like this man. And when we met him at the train station, I was put off by his Bohemianism and his loudness. But hour by hour, I found myself more and more gone on him." By the end of the first day, the forty-six-year-old and the ten-year-old were getting along famously. "That night I went to bed with him. It was like he was a brother. The two of us giggled so hard that the bed broke. We were living then in Buffalo, in a housing project with papier-mâché thin walls. Alec was mortified the neighbors would hear the goings-on." Margaret (Maggy) Turner, as she now is, later set up a successful business in Manhattan in window-box plantings, those defiant little banners of color and hope that help redeem the concrete canyons. Wilder had wanted to stake her when she began the business, but, she says, being young and prideful, she did not accept his offer. However, he did go to some trouble to get clients for her in those crucial first days.

Toward the end of his life, when Wilder was deeply depressed, Turner stopped every week at the Algonquin and left him flowers. They were usually the Star of Bethlehem—clusters of starlike blooms on long spikes, a spectacular, long-lasting flower Wilder always liked. Turner remains grateful to Wilder for treating her as an individual in her own right, not as just a child. "He was wonderful with children. He was like an uncle to me, not a father, for he wouldn't play that role. But he was always part of the family." Wilder was often away, she remembers, but he kept reentering their lives. "It's hard to come to terms with the fact that he won't be back any more. I'm really mad at him for dying."

Although adults sometimes wondered and worried about his manipulations, Wilder's impact on the very young was often magical. Another relationship that prospered through several decades was that between Wilder and Lorraine (Bouras) Bowen, daughter of Harry and Arlene Bouras of Chicago. She was two when Wilder was forty-eight. "I called him Uncle Al, which he hated. My great pleasure in my pestiferation was to call him that. I'd get on top of the piano or sit on his lap while he was writing music, and I'd pester him until he yelled. He was a great yeller." They could never wake her father, so Wilder once got on Lorraine's bicycle—"big Alec on my small bicycle"—and rode around the bedroom ringing the bell, trying to arouse her father. Or he would prevail on her to start blowing the French horn in the bedroom.

Bowen could always count on Wilder's support both early and later in her life: "He became so much a part of my life that he's always with me, even today. My only regret is that he couldn't see my daughter May." Somehow, Wilder was always available when she needed him. She could always call on him, as she did in New York several times, and if she wrote to him, he would invariably reply. "You could never count on what state he would be in, but I was used to that." She shared a good deal of poetry with "Uncle Al" and also went to him one day saying, "I'm going to be a composer." Wilder would say, "Okay." He was very encouraging about the music she played: "I played French horn, and though I was just struggling away he would write me pieces. . . . He was just so enthusiastic, about the poems, about the music. And he loved to hear me sing *My Shining Hour*. I'd sing it all the time."

Even when he was with children and teenagers, the music was never far away. And it was no wonder that he enjoyed hearing Bowen sing *My Shining Hour*, for Harold Arlen was one of his favorite popular-song composers. He dared to put him above Gershwin, and, for its translucence and simplicity, he also dared personally to prefer *My Shining Hour* to Irving Berlin's *It's a Lovely Day Tomorrow*. And even as he listened to Bowen, he was gathering thoughts about Arlen that would become an enthusiastic chapter in his book *American Popular Song*, a work likely to be still around when the personal memories have faded.

·||12

American Popular Song

Almost everything Wilder did in the popular music field was prelude and preparation for *American Popular Song: The Great Innovators, 1900–1950,* a definitive work begun in 1968 and published to applause by Oxford University Press in 1972. Here in this volume is the distillation of a lifetime of study and practice of popular song. All that listening with ears acutely attuned to critical judgment, all that affirmation of life, all that awareness of what makes a great song, all that flooding of the soul with melody—those were the things that finally crested and came together in a pioneering publication in the last decade of his life. This is a book of sustained wit and wisdom, prejudices and perceptions, crotchets and cherishings, and, most of all, honest-to-goodness love and affection, for as Walter Clemons pointed out in the *New York Times Book Review,* the hundreds of tunes we whistle and hum every day are examined by Wilder in this work "as attentively as if they were Schubert lieder."

And for him, indeed they were. For Wilder, the fact that a song was popular by definition "by no means proves it is beneath contempt, as some pompus academicians would have you believe. After all, so were Elizabethan songs, so much revered today, at one time popular street songs." He had fought for years a lonely battle to have popular song elevated to the level where he believed it belonged. His pleasure was unbounded when a musicologist once told him that Harold Arlen's *Last Night When We Were Young* was a better melody than any of the vocal melodies that Beethoven ever wrote: "Now here's a professor in a university making a remark like that. That pleased me very much." He felt it gave to popular song the distinction he had been fighting for all his life: "Not just the squares but the academic mind have dismissed all popular music on the grounds that if it's popular it can't be considered in the same terms with concert music, and I don't agree."

For once in Wilder's life, the critics, in this instance book reviewers who were often musicians themselves, were thoroughly agreed on the merits of his work. After years of being bruised by his falls between different music stools and by his refusal to make compromises, now he was being saluted almost uniformly. One regret voiced by critics was that Wilder had not included in *American Popular Song* some of his own songs for analysis. Yet Wilder's songs never achieved wide public popularity in Tin Pan Alley, in film, or in the theater. Even if they had, he would never have put himself in the company of the "Great Innovators." He would have been forever tripping over the shoelaces of his inferiority complex, and a detached judgment of popular song would have been impossible.

The man who made the book possible was Jerome Hill, the wealthy filmmaker who had earlier commissioned Wilder to write the scores for several of the outstanding documentaries Hill had produced and directed (those about Grandma Moses and Albert Schweitzer) and for his avant-garde entertainments (*The Sand Castle* and *Open the Door And See All the People*). The Avon Foundation that had been established by the Hill family (it was renamed the Jerome Foundation after Jerome's death) had granted money to an Italian composer who had been unable to come to the United States to carry out his work. Hill suggested to Wilder that he submit an application to the foundation for a grant for the book that "you're always talking about." Hill, Wilder said, knew that he was eager to write a book about professionally written popular music, not—quite definitely not—rock music. It was to be about the best of the great songs of the 1920s, '30s, and '40s, and, through serious though not solemn analysis, would give some "patina of dignity and recognition" to a unique but often underrated art form.

How to go about such an enormous project? Wilder at that point threw out a lifeline to perhaps the only person who could have seen the project through, James T. Maher, who became the book's editor and Wilder's indispensable collaborator. Wilder freely acknowledged Maher's "inestimable" contribution—through his knowledge and research, his collation of thousands of facts, his patience and tolerance, his good humor, encouragement, and superb editing: "If ever the phrase 'but for whom this book would never have been written' were apt, it is so in this instance." And it is so for even more than the given reasons. Maher was the man who time and again saved the book from abandonment by Wilder.

Maher began his writing career in the 1930s as a sports reporter on the Cleveland *Plain Dealer*. In the 1940s, and again in the 1950s, he was with the public relations department of Texaco (then Texas Company). He is the author of *The Twilight of Splendor: Chronicles of the Age of the American Palaces* (Little, Brown, 1975), one of several achievements that won him a Guggenheim Fellowship in architectural history; a novel, *The Distant Music of Summer* (a section of which had been published earlier in the *Saturday Evening Post*), which won an award from the American Association of University Women; a number of short stories and magazine articles on popular music, jazz, architecture, and other subjects; and countless liner notes for record albums.

When Wilder first met Maher, he liked him at once: "He was affable and distinguished." Wilder quickly came to respect his erudition; he found that the only area of knowledge with which he was more familiar than Maher was the battlefields of the Civil War. Wilder liked his lack of pretense: "Usually, very informed men have the tendency to be pompous or humorless or both. James Maher is a truly modest and humble man." Wilder knew that he himself was a difficult personality for Maher to adjust to, though he said Maher gave no signs of impatience: "He advised, he suggested, he relinquished his own inclinations graciously, he put up with my unpredictable, intuitive, methodless ways of work. Without him, there would have been no book."

That first meeting, a brief one, had taken place in 1956 at an evening recital given by the New York Woodwind Quintet at Music House, a small private music school in a brownstone on Manhattan's West Side. Maher recalls that only about thirty or forty people were present: "Very cozy, good music and superb musicianship." The program included some of Wilder's music. "During the recital, Alec stood in a corner at the back of the parlor-like second-floor room, tall, tweedy, smiling secretly; rumpled, handsome, holding an unlit pipe. . . . You couldn't help but notice him. Alec was a master of the strange art of 'hiding' publicly."

Through subsequent meetings at the Algonquin in the 1960s, Maher came to know Wilder well enough to sign on, so to speak, as one of a crew devoted to a captain who roamed the high seas like a pirate of old:

Happily, if unwittingly, I entered into a wonderful and spirited conspiracy: *us* (Alec Wilder's friends and sympathetic enthusiasts) against *them* (the music critics, the music publishing and concert promotion establishment, the music academics, the indifferent and uncaring public, and, oh, a host of greedy, selfish "cut-throat hustlers who smoked cigars and wore green eyeshades").

Wilder first pressed Maher into service to write a formal grant application. Maher drew on his expertise gladly enough, but he had some reservations. Yes, Wilder knew as much about the subject as anyone alive, but could he sit down long enough to write a book—"a marvelous composer, wonderful company, a witty and engaging raconteur, a glorious conversationalist, an extremely literate man, but a restless wayfarer, and a bad (wildly erratic) drinker to boot." To their surprise, on December 11, 1967, the Avon Foundation approved a three-year grant of $102,405, later supplemented with an additional $16,000. The money would flow through the New England Conservatory of Music, where Gunther Schuller had only recently been named president, with his new assistant, Harvey Phillips, doing the actual grant administration. Both were devoted advocates of Wilder's music. Maher would share fifty-fifty in the copyright royalties and other postpublication earnings, but he would get only about 30 percent of the grant money. Although this was not a particularly fair split, given Maher's immense labors, he made no demur, for he felt privileged to be working with "the great Alec Wilder" on an exciting project, and he also assumed Wilder to be in poor shape financially.

On January 5, 1968, about five weeks after the grant approval, Ethan Ayer of

Cambridge, Massachusetts, put on a superb dinner at Lock Ober's in Boston to celebrate the award grant. Ayer was primarily a poet who had also published a novel and short stories; a writer of librettos; and a member of an immensely wealthy family. The dinner, in a private upstairs dining room, was lavish. Among those at the table were Ayer, Wilder and Maher of course, and also Harvey and Carol Phillips and Charlie and Terry Davidson of Cambridge. Afterward, some of the party drove to Ayer's architecturally historic house in Cambridge (the Stoughton House designed by Henry Hobson Richardson). Wilder by this time had become thoroughly intoxicated and was beginning to make himself unpleasant. When Phillips announced that he and Schuller had scheduled a press conference at the Conservatory the following morning to announce the grant, Wilder exploded. In a long drumroll of drunken invective, he tore apart the Conservatory and Phillips for exploiting and cashing in on his grant for their own advantage. It was a dreadful display, one that turned Ayer's affectionate salute into ashes. Such a tirade—and his friends had to endure many—was almost always followed by a deep apology and forgiveness. But a signal had been hoisted that the popular-song book would not be easily accomplished.

Back in Manhattan, Wilder and Maher began meeting for lunch at the Algonquin. Once, Wilder invited him up to his room. Such was Wilder's presence at the hotel that Maher assumed he would be walking into a suite. Instead, he found himself in a small room that was completely filled by the bed, and armchair, and a dresser:

> This was the suite of Alec Wilder! No books, no records—no room, for that
> matter. There was a second chair, a side chair, but I couldn't see it because
> there was an opened suitcase on it. Tobacco, some shirts, a bobble bird (once
> he had four going at once and the goddam place looked like an aviary—he
> tried, but never succeeded, to get them to bobble in unison), a jar of special
> honey, some airmail writing pads, and similar odds and ends lay on the top of
> the dresser.

Maher would have preferred a more affordable lunch spot than the Algonquin, and he was annoyed when he discovered later that Wilder, when he was on his own and not trying to impress anyone, would often eat more cheaply at a nearby sandwich shop. Maher, a superb organizer, arrived at those first meetings with bunches of file cards and endless notes, and proceeded to lay out some of the options: theater music, popular music, the effect of jazz on popular songs, and so on. "Alec sat there as much as to say, 'My God, I've found him.'" And so he had, and the team was born.

A focus was still hard to find, for the subject was enormous, and could be approached in so many ways—sociologically, culturally, musicologically. Maher also had to survive the first real crisis in their relationship: Wilder's adamant refusal to have anything to do with theater music. It's impossible to find any rational reason for his hatred of Broadway musicals. Perhaps it flowed from his own failure to make it there. Certainly, his insistence on doing things his own way would have ruled out the kind of collaboration necessary to successful theater. At any rate, Wilder clearly had to be talked out of his fixation as far as popular song was concerned. Any survey that excluded Broadway numbers would be a joke. Maher finally was able to get Wilder turned around by appealing to his professionalism; *American Popular Song* includes much eloquent writing about Broadway music.

The two men decided to explore further the framework of the book in Florida in undistracted meetings at the Atlantic Shores Motel in Key West, where Wilder usually stayed. There they talked around the clock for days. Maher, when he showed up at the motel—he was staying elsewhere—would walk back and forth under the balcony whistling one of Wilder's songs. He knew that if there was one thing Wilder loved to hear, it was his own music. Finally, they found their focus and framework, and returned to New York.

Maher was now about to confront his second crisis: Wilder's drinking. He spent a full week typing up the notes he had made in Key West, organizing them into sections and chapters, making copies, and putting two sets of the outline into spring binders complete with separators and an index. The project was ready to go. Wilder and Maher were to have dinner that night in the Rose Room at the Algonquin—"the one," says Maher, "that Oliver Smith, the theater set designer, did and redid perfectly by practically not doing anything, which was the right way to keep the spirit and beauty of the room." When Maher walked in, Wilder was seated in his favorite spot in the far corner. He could see the whole room from there and nobody could see him if he didn't want to be seen. Edward O'Malley, a bookseller of whom Wilder was fond, was with him. He was a pleasant and well-informed man to spend time with, Maher recalls. Even as a teenager, O'Malley had saved his nickels and dimes to go to musicals, and Jerome Kern was his god. Thus he had many memories and many useful notes.

Wilder that night half pulled himself up from behind the table, and as Maher approached, O'Malley signaled wildly to him. He did not understand the gestures, but it was soon obvious what was wrong: Wilder was drunk. His necktie was tied around his neck and not under the shirt collar. He was not a pretty sight, for "he was an absolute slob when drunk." Disturbed, Maher sat down at the table and handed Wilder the spring binder that represented so much work on the project: "He paid no attention to it. He knocked it off the table onto the floor. I knew it was on the floor, and when we left I didn't say a word. I was furious. We walked out. Like everybody, I was in awe of Alec." Next day came a phone call from Wilder and a tremendous apology. Someone had retrieved the binder from the floor and taken it to his room: "When he saw what it was. . . . He just went on without letup to me on the phone for fifteen minutes. . . . My God. . . . It kind of scared him [that the project might have been scuttled]. It was very touch and go, but we got started finally."

Wilder's drinking was not again a major threat to the research and writing of *American Popular Song,* though Maher had to do some heading off from time to time.

Maher and Wilder faced two big challenges in organizing the project: finding a place to work, and finding a source for the immense amount of sheet music Wilder needed to examine. The man who came providentially to the rescue was music publisher Howard Richmond (The Richmond Organization, TRO), who had already turned upside down Wilder's conviction, born of bitter experience, that music publishers were a shabby, worthless breed. In fact, Wilder insisted, Richmond could never be mistaken for a music publisher: "He is too distinguished looking and too civilized. He has believed in me since we met and has been more considerate and generous than anyone I've ever known in that otherwise disreputable business. He was as concerned as much about my state of being as about my work. He recognized instantly that I was an unaggressive, untypical writer of songs." He told Wilder that he was obligated to print his songs no matter what their potentiality "because until they were in print, they would still be taking up room in my mind. This would be wrong, as a creator's brain should be as uncluttered as possible. A popular song publisher?!!"

Together with Al Brackman, the general manager, Richmond had founded TRO in Manhattan in 1949 in a very modest way: paying $105 a month rent and using a rented phonograph. Wilder recalled that he set up in a cubby hole on 57th Street with Irene Kelsey, "his great secretary," as his sole help and a song called *Polka Dot Polka* (actually, *Hop Scotch Polka*). Wilder no less respected Brackman, who brought his own strong credits to TRO. He had begun in the music publishing business in 1933, when he helped form the American Academy of Music. He had also been involved in promoting such performing artists as Duke Ellington, Cab Calloway, and Milton Berle. He was coproducer of more than four hundred jazz recordings, most by Ellington.

Perhaps because it did not fit the traditional hard-headed publisher mold, TRO was not expected to make much of a dent. Instead, said Wilder, "they found hit after hit, moving as their success grew to larger and larger offices." Richmond and Brackman, who were important in facilitating the immense labor that went into *American Popular Song,* had used well their experiences in promoting performing artists and plugging songs. They became the publishers of songs written by Pete Seeger, Woody Guthrie, Huddie Ledbetter (Leadbelly), Kurt Weill, Bill Evans, Bart Howard, and others. They succeeded in turning many folk-type songs into popular-chart successes, among them *Goodnight, Irene, Tom Dooley, If I Had a Hammer, Kisses Sweeter Than Wine.*

An early TRO song was one Wilder wrote with Marshall Barer called *Whippa Whippa Woo* (1950): "It was brilliantly recorded by Sarah Vaughan and that was the end of it." Although Wilder was contributing only in a small way to TRO's large catalogue, the partners continued to treat him with love and respect. At one time, Richmond drove to New Jersey to see one of the operas Wilder had written with Sundgaard:

> On the way back to New York he offered us an advance for a new opera which he would pay for, sight unseen, music unheard. Since then he has paid me sums of money not owed me, he has had printed songs which had little likelihood of success, and he has phoned me often simply to ask after my health and state of mind.

In the first forging of a relationship that would be important to the writing of *American Popular Song,* they invited Wilder to make TRO a depository for his work. That in itself was a godsend, for Wilder's habit was to scratch out only one copy of his music and give it to a singer or instrumentalist. His music had never had any real home. "And so," remembers Richmond, "it became a ritual for Alec to bring his works to our TRO offices, where we made copies and lead sheets and started the wondrous file of Alec Wilder material." When the firm expanded, Wilder would often stop in to use any available piano, and Richmond would forever urge him to leave his writings there, not to carry them around and risk losing them. Later, Wilder would sign a contract with TRO and receive a monthly stipend, and TRO would get all the music copyright renewals (under copyright law at that time, songs came back in twenty-eight years) and anything new. Richmond was not sure that he himself belonged on the pedestal Wilder had placed him on: "I hope I was always a step or two ahead of my contemporaries, but I felt I was never as good as Alec believed me to be. But Alec felt so positively and warmly about me that he forced me to be a better person than I was. He brought out the best in me."

So when it came time to get down to work with *American Popular Song,* Richmond put at the disposal of Wilder and Maher a rehearsal room with a piano that became their base of operations. Critical help was also given by Abe Olman, who had achieved fame as a songwriter in World War I and the postwar years with hits such as *Oh, Johnny, Oh* and *Down Among the Sheltering Palms.* By the 1930s, he was in the publishing business, and he talked often with Richmond through the years about an idea that would ultimately take shape as the Songwriters Hall of Fame. What the two men were also doing in those early days was gathering up and saving the sheet music of all the great composers: Kern, Gershwin, and others. Olman had an enormous treasure on his shelves, and he gave Wilder and Maher access to it. Even with that kind of help, the size of the task was daunting. Maher has estimated that about 300,000 popular songs of every variety may have been deposited for copyright between 1900 and 1950, the period chosen for their study. Wilder actually examined some 17,000 of those songs, citing 300 of them, with brief comments, in the book. In the musical examples, he quoted from nearly 500 more. The quotations were autographed in some 700 "examples" comprising 4,000 measures of music.

Both men knew that a major difficulty would lie in getting copyright permissions to quote from the music of the composers whose works were being examined. No precedent existed for such permission from music publishers for that amount of book material. In their preliminary digging around to find out what they were up against in terms of the money they might have to pay, they were told that the cost could run to $10 a bar. That would make the cost of the book prohibitive.

Up to a point, some resistance was understandable. It was the nature of popular-song writers, Wilder would say, to worry about being pirated. It happened to them often with song sheets for which they were never paid royalties; hence they were not a trusting bunch of men. Wilder's problem was to get someone to listen in terms of logic to what he and Maher were trying to do, to understand that the book would have absolutely no performance value of any kind. To that end, they planned to eliminate all complete songs and all lyrics, and use only brief examples. Fortunately for the project, Philip B. Wattenberg, counsel for Chappell and Company, one of the biggest and most important theater-music publishers, was ready to listen. So with Chappell serving as a kind of bellwether for the copyright arrangements, a reasonable scale of payments was worked out with most of the industry. (When unwarranted interference toward the end of the project threatened the copyright clearances, Maureen Meloy, who had worked with both Schuller and Phillips and was experienced in the music-publishing world, came to town and saved the day with her tact and intelligence. The book would not otherwise have gone to press on time.)

Wilder had set out his criteria for good songwriting—originality, the singing line, honesty, control—long before *American Popular Song* was thought about. Although the book itself would burst suddenly on the music scene, he had been writing and talking about the subtleties of the subject for many years. In 1966, for example, he was telling Loonis McGlohon:

> Sometimes an involved tune (which needs its harmony to clarify it) justifies itself simply by its extraordinary ingenuity (many Kern releases—*Sky Lark,* the middle section of *Blues in the Night*). But generally, I believe that a great tune should sound great without a note of accompaniment. Harmony and fill-ins should be dividends, bonuses (*Let's Fall in Love, Stormy Weather, Ill Wind, All the Things You Are* to quickly grab a few).

The groundwork, then, had been laid.

In his introduction to *American Popular Song,* Maher explains that the book evolved from two assumptions, the first being that at some point, perhaps just before the turn of the century, American popular song took on distinctive native characteristics. The second assumption was that these unique qualities have derived continuously from the innovations of a few outstanding song composers. Jerome Kern, Irving Berlin, George Gershwin, Richard Rodgers, Cole Porter, and

Harold Arlen were the major songwriters to whom separate chapters were devoted.

Very early, *American Popular Song* makes it clear that the impact of black music was perhaps the most critical formative contribution to the "Americanization" process. Wilder, at the conclusion of the first chapter on the transition era from 1885 to World War I, speaks of the early anonymous Negroes who had managed to create the early stages of an entirely new music: "But these weren't all just beginnings. For some of the spirituals, work songs, blues and ragtime songs can never be improved upon." That acknowledgement flows from Maher's concern that early black music be given its rightful place. Wilder did not disagree. His feelings were accurately reflected, but it was Maher who did the initiating and insisting. And he makes the point emphatically himself in a chapter footnote, saying that "the straight line from plantation music to the earliest recorded jazz (1917) runs through ragtime; the impact of Negro syncopation is the major force in the Americanization of our popular music." That should serve to answer those critics who say today that the white music world has ignored the historic role of the black musician.

When it came time for Wilder to examine the composers he had chosen as "The Great Innovators," he looked for especially loved turns of phrase and identifiable patterns, strictly the composer's own, and, beyond that, for "a fugitive essence and personality" that stamped a song as American. In the work method they devised, Maher would pull together the raw material—the sheet music, the shows the songs had been in, the movies, whether a song had been dropped from a show, and so forth: "I would lay out the music according to the periods of the composers. Alec had grown up with the music, but he hadn't thought about it in historical or chronological terms." They would sit down and talk a bit, then Wilder would start to play the music. Maher would sit about a foot and a half behind him so that he could read the lyrics himself if he wished to. Wilder would make comments, and Maher would ask questions on behalf of the nontechnical, nonmusician reader. Wilder would answer the questions, Maher would take notes of all his comments, transcribe them, and return them to Wilder for revision. Wilder readily accepted Maher's criticisms of his writing along with his suggestions for improvements.

Gradually, Maher and Wilder built a solid relationship based on a deep commitment to the value of the common song as a part of daily life. They recognized that it stretched back to Gregorian chant, elevated to be sure by its liturgical nature but still song. For both men, the song was the heart of the matter, and as the partnership deepened, they developed an almost secret language. For example, they both discovered that they had a great favorite from the Benny Goodman days in the person of Helen Ward singing *Restless*, published in 1935, with words and music credited to Sam Coslow and Tom Satterfield, a pianist and arranger. The curious thing about the song, says Maher, is that it's very instrumental, with an extremely difficult bridge to sing: "It was a piano player's song, one that Helen Ward sang marvelously." Wilder says about *Restless* that it's much too good to be as little known as it is: "However, its obscurity is understandable insofar as it's murderously difficult to sing. . . . None of it's simple; all of it's good. The chorus has the deterrent of a very wide range, an octave and a minor sixth. This would be asking a lot of even a theater song."

In any event, Wilder and Maher both loved *Restless,* murderously difficult though it was. Came the night when the two of them stood on Fifth Avenue at 34th Street "looking like a couple of idiots" singing *Restless* back and forth to each other and going over and over the difficult bridge. "So we then used that as a kind of touchstone," recalls Maher. They were sitting in the Algonquin one night when George Barnes, the superb guitar player, walked in. Maher looked at Wilder and grinned and nodded his head, so Wilder said, "OK, George, right from the pickup notes, the bridge from *Restless.*" Barnes didn't miss a beat. His big grin said he knew they had been trying to trap him. Those subtle inside connections and common sympathies made working together that much easier.

Whenever he was in residence, so to speak, at TRO, Wilder had the help of a knowledgeable and sympathetic staff, notably TRO music editor Judith Bell, another of Wilder's special people. She was able to see him clearly enough to understand that he attracted wounded birds such as Judy Holliday and was in turn attracted to them. Bell sensed as not everybody did that the public Wilder concealed many hurts and fears, that he was quick to recognize others who were also vulnerable. They became good friends. "One author we shared," remembers Bell, "was Rumer Godden. She was English, and Alec was an Anglophile. He would give me the Godden books and borrow them back, and the only one I managed to keep was the last one, *China Court.* Alec once left an out-of-print Godden book in a cab, and was inconsolable for days."

There was always an extra effort by Wilder to identify himself with the interests of others. "He knew I loved Block Island off Rhode Island," says Bell, "so he joined me there once and asked me to show him the things I liked. . . . We often lunched around the corner from TRO, and Alec got along well with the woman who ran the place. Her legs bothered her, and he never failed to ask about them." In gratitude for one of the TRO songbook collections she produced with him, Wilder gave Bell a window box for her New York City brownstone apartment, and had it installed by Maggy Turner. Every season, Bell plants her flowers in a box that has become a living memorial. Later, Bell would go on to do Trojan work in compiling the list of compositons and the discography in Margun Music's 1991 *Alec Wilder* booklet. She also gave indispensable help in the preparation of *Alec Wilder: A Bio-Bibliography* by David Demsey and Ronald Prather.

The show would never have stayed on the road but for Maher's limitless patience, tenacity, tolerance, and understanding. He kept Wilder on the job when, as the labors grew longer, he would just as soon have walked away and stayed away.

Directly or indirectly, Maher estimates, Wilder quit the project twenty times. But Maher was up to it all. At one point, he became a coconspirator with Rogers Brackett in the struggle to keep Wilder harnessed to the plow. Maher would get a call at, say, six in the morning from Brackett in California. He would tell him that Alec, who was often out on the Coast, had been up all night drinking. Brackett was one of those men who could drink forever and yet remain articulate and focused: "Rogers would say to me, 'Now Alec will be calling you a little later this morning, and he's going to quit.' Rogers did that at least three times. I would get the call from Alec, and, immediately, before he had a chance to say anything, I would say to him, 'Alec, my God, I'm glad you called. Listen, let me read you this paragraph' and I would read the last thing he had sent me. 'That is superb,' I would say to him. 'Right on the nose. It's moving, analytical but very understandable.'" Maher let all the air out of his balloon before he had even blown it up: "I had to do that again and again and again."

Maher's successful salvaging kept the book on line. There was, however, one major roadblock they had to go around: the absolute refusal of Irving Berlin, alone among the songwriters and publishers, to allow even a bar of his music to be reproduced for purposes of illustration. Nor, after promising to arrange a meeting, would he even agree to an interview. Berlin also made an abusive telephone call to Maher in which he called the book a lot of crap, reviled both Maher and Wilder as "stupid bastards," and left Maher astonished and shaken by "the sour malevolence of a mean spirit." The story is told by Berlin biographer Laurence Bergreen. Berlin's outburst, Bergreen explains, came after Maher had complied with a request by one of Berlin's lawyers for an advance copy of Wilder's section in the book about Berlin. According to Bergreen, Berlin took such violent exception "because, with its scholarly tone, its Oxford University Press aegis, and its penchant for comparing songwriters with one another, it hit on nearly every worry that Berlin had about his musical abilities."

Berlin was particularly outraged by Wilder's comments about his song *Always*. "Who the hell cares what he thinks! That's just his opinion. Who the hell is Wilder, anyway?" In fact, Wilder's criticisms of the 1925 song are quite mild. He simply says it is not a favorite of his, that a writer with a less distinguished reputation would probably have been asked to rewrite the A section. His comments are not capricious but thoughtfully grounded in careful analysis. Thus he said there is simply too much insistence in *Always* on the rhythmic device of the opening measure, that of a dotted quarter note followed by three eighth notes. But nothing could pacify Berlin, who also told Maher that "that song of mine he thought sounded like Harold Arlen— that's all wrong. I'll show him and get him straightened out. . . . I wrote *my* songs first: *get that straight*." But Wilder makes no accusation of plagiarism or anything else. He simply says that Berlin's *It's a Lovely Day Tomorrow* is "a pure, hymn-like melody" recalling Kern at his purest or Arlen in *My Shining Hour*.

What made the whole episode so bizarre and so unnecessary was that Wilder in his writing expresses only respect and admiration. He notes, for example, that many popular music enthusiasts do not seem to be aware how remarkably wide and varied is the range of Berlin's writing: "His output was extraordinary." Wilder concludes his chapter by saying flatly that Berlin is the best all-around overall songwriter America has ever had. "In this area or that, I will say, and have said, that I believe so-and-so to be the master. But I can speak of only one composer as the master of the entire range of popular song—Irving Berlin."

A saving grace for the book itself is the universality of Berlin's appeal. His songs are so well known that it was not really necessary to reproduce any of the bars of music by way of example. The obstacle thrown up by Berlin was not, then, a fatal blow.

American Popular Song was completed and published by Oxford University Press in 1972 to deserved praise. It won the Deems Taylor ASCAP Award in 1973 and a National Book Award nomination the same year. It is an entertaining and informed celebration of American popular song, never dull and never pedestrian. The discussion is serious but not solemn or portentous. There is no descent into gossip or anecdote. And yet the witty, civilized nature of the writing makes the whole thing eminently readable. What's more, *American Popular Song* countenances no sacred cows, for Wilder does not hesitate to quarrel with conventional estimates of popular songs. *Over the Rainbow* disappoints him because it is not distinctively Harold Arlen. When Judy Garland sang the song, says Wilder, he was always deeply touched, "But I was never listening to an Arlen song; I was listening to a very good, well-made ballad." Wilder finds Richard Rodgers's *Some Enchanted Evening* "pale and pompous and bland. Where, oh, where are all those lovely surprises, those leaps in the dark, those chances? I'm in church, and it's the wrong hymnal!"

As a matter of fact, Wilder is unenthusiastic about all the melodies from *South Pacific*. He finds them self-conscious. "I almost feel as if I should change into formal garb before I listen to them. . . . Something's missing: fire, impact, purity, naturalness, need, friendliness, and, most of all, wit." Yet Wilder yields to no one in his admiration of Rodgers's work as a whole: "Of all the writers whose songs are considered and examined in this book, those of Rodgers show the highest degree of consistent excellence, inventiveness, and sophistication."

Wilder does no genuflecting before even such a universal favorite as Jerome Kern's *Dearly Beloved*. The song is played at many weddings, and that, notes Wilder, would have pleased Kern, for he wanted to see *Oh, Promise Me* replaced with *Dearly Beloved* as often as possible. For Wilder, however, *Dearly Beloved* lacks the appeal of Kern's *I'm Old Fashioned*. And he pinpoints the problem: "I truly do not like the fourteenth and fifteenth measures insofar as they completely destroy the diatonic character of what has preceded and what follows. . . . The verse is literally a throwaway of eight measures and has no character. I apologize for speaking ill of a song which to many, by now, has the stature of a hymn."

American Popular Song is both discriminating and opinionated. Wilder's peeves and prejudices are not, however, loose, random arrows but are backed by specific technical example. Agree or disagree with it, the criticism is always informed. Thus he does not just say that Berlin's *How Deep Is the Ocean* is expertly written; he demonstrates precisely how:

> Though it is a melody of small steps, never resorting to an interval more than a fourth, it makes one totally unexpected move in the B section, dropping to a *g* flat at the end of the first phrase and then restating this note twice more in the last half of the section. . . . It is a superb example of what can be done within the confines of popular music form.

Wilder's lively, entertaining, informed writing is well demonstrated by his analysis of a 1920 song called *A Young Man's Fancy*. There is, he says, a much higher degree of creativity in this song than in *Whispering*. "Bone simple as it is, it has an air about it, a pastoral gaiety. And, indeed, it was known as the Music Box Song." At only one point, he adds, does the "rough hand of manufacture" reveal itself. "And it comes as a bit of a shock after the daintiness of what has come before . . . [and he cites the relevant three bars]. That F sharp and the syncopation are like a belch at a formal dinner party. Other than this slip, it is a special, almost distilled song, unlike any other of its or any other time." That kind of statement combines good writing with illuminating analysis. When Wilder gets through with a song, you know exactly why it does or does not appeal, and you know where it stands in the developing line of American popular song.

So ambitious a project, and one that makes as many comparisons and judgments, was bound to draw down some fire. There were those who believed, for example, that Wilder does not give enough praise to Cole Porter and George Gershwin, that he pays too little attention to the contributions of performers in giving songs their ultimate shape, that he neglects black composers such as Duke Ellington, Fats Waller, and Eubie Blake. Yet no one denied the analytical brilliance of the work. And only a master of the medium could use just a word or two to make clear distinctions among the great song composers. Thus at the end of the chapter on Cole Porter: "Overall, I find Rodgers warmer, Arlen more hip, Gershwin more direct, Vernon Duke more touchable, Berlin more practical. But no one can deny that Porter added a certain theatrical elegance."

For Maher, it had been a long journey on an often rough and rocky road. In addition to bringing a monumental work safely into harbor, he was under great pressure to continue working on his own manuscripts. Somehow, the partnership survived. Sometimes, laughter relieved the travail and the tedium. Maher notes that occasionally in the book "you will see reference to canoe music. This is where

I'm putting in a good word for some marvelous piece of schlock I've always loved. I fancy I'm one of the great authorities on schlock in popular music. And Alec would say, 'Well, indeed you are.'" The teamwork, the quick mental communication, that made it all possible was nicely demonstrated at a meeting with Oxford's sales force about the marketing of the book. When the very nervous Wilder was asked to speak, his agitation vanished: "All Alec usually needed was to hear the sound of his voice: it was like a down beat," recalls the amused Maher. Wilder spoke briefly, charmingly, and self-deprecatingly: "I don't really know that much about the popular songs; all I really know is that *Lulu's Back in Town* [the song introduced by Dick Powell and the Mills Brothers in the 1935 musical *Broadway Gondolier*]." To which Maher, when it was his turn to say a few words, was able to rejoin: "One of the reasons we got along so well is that whereas Alec knows *Lulu's Back in Town,* I know why she left in the first place."

Together, Wilder and Maher had produced a work that will be around as long as songs are written and sung and whistled. Gene Lees summed things up as well as anyone. Never, he said, had he seen such a book:

> It is not a collection of anecdotes [but] an analysis of major American com-
> posers and their "popular" music by a peer. The book needed to be written,
> and fortunately when at last it was, that work was not done by some pedant,
> or, worse still, some over-zealous fan, but by the erudite, brilliant and unpre-
> tentious Mr. Wilder.

With his cool intelligence, his mocking wit, his enormous sophistication, his deep knowledge, and his sheer love of melody, Wilder had, with Maher's indispensable help, pulled off a masterpiece.

American Popular Song would also lead to other celebrations. The year after its publication, it directly inspired a Newport Jazz Festival concert, Jazz Salute to American Song. As McCandlish Phillips pointed out in the *New York Times,* "If credit is given where it is due, the editors of the Oxford University Press (specifically Sheldon Meyer, Senior Vice President/Editorial) would have to come out and take a bow. They published the book on which the concert was based."

A more ambitious sequel was launched in 1976 when Wilder began hosting a series of forty-two weekly one-hour radio broadcasts under the title *American Popular Song with Alec Wilder and Friends.* The series, made possible by a grant from the National Endowment for the Arts, was produced by the South Carolina Educational Radio Network for airing on the 190 stations of National Public Radio. Loonis McGlohon, then director of community relations for WBT, Charlotte, North Carolina, was the music director and the cohost with Wilder, and the series director was the late Dick Phipps, public relations director of the South Carolina Educational Radio and Television Network. The program originated with Phipps. The first thirteen broadcasts were produced during a series of weekends in the late spring

and summer of 1976, in the living room of Phipps's home on a lake outside Columbia, South Carolina.

Each program in the series paid tribute to the songs of an individual composer or
lyricist, or to a body of songs associated with a particular period or singer. Wilder
set the scene and tone with his informal, informed analyses of selected songs,
happily indulging his enthusiasms and prejudices. The stage itself was given over to
a parade of outstanding guest singers mostly handpicked by Wilder: David Allyn,
Tony Bennett, Mabel Mercer, Barbara Lea, Teddi King, Jackie Cain, Dick Haymes,
and many more. The singers were paired with particular songwriters or performers: David Allyn with Jerome Kern and Harold Arlen, for example, Barbara Lea
with Willard Robison and Lee Wiley, and so on. The format gave full play to Wilder's
rich insights, his conversational candor, his illuminating wit.

Many exciting musical encounters took place in South Carolina, and Wilder gave
every appearance of enjoying himself. Although he often expressed distaste for
holding forth in public, he seemed at home in this setting. Speaking on radio was less
demanding than a concert appearance or a speaker's platform. Even so, precautions
were taken. The microphones were hidden deep in some jungle scenery, and the
producers made sure Wilder was surrounded by friends and admirers at all times. It
amazed Marian McPartland that McGlohon had been able to keep the peripatetic
Wilder long enough in one place for the forty-two hours of the program. Said
McGlohon: "We sat him in a chair facing a lake and lovely green trees and invited his
friends Mabel Mercer and Tony Bennett and Marlene VerPlanck to sing his songs."
That was about the size of it—Wilder was lured by his peers and then laved with
love. And whereas *American Popular Song* does not include any of his own compositions, Phipps and McGlohon made sure that at least one Wilder song was featured in
each program. It all worked, to use one of Wilder's favorite words, and the series
would eventually win the George Foster Peabody Award.

True to his habit of shrugging off success, Wilder once dismissed the merits of
American Popular Song to Bill Engvick in a casual reacquaintance with him on the
West Coast. Engvick was no longer seeing much of Wilder by the start of the 1970s;
Wilder was always somewhere else, and Engvick needed a one-on-one working
relationship, not a long-distance one. In New York, too, "all the affordable small
clubs had given way to the rock disaster, and there were very few people left in
New York that I knew." On the Coast, Engvick's mother was now upward of ninety,
and he had felt it was time to go home. It was there, in San Francisco, that he had his
last meeting with Wilder: "I had just read some interesting acknowledgments of
American Popular Song in the *New York Times,* and I congratulated him. His response was, 'Oh, that's a lot of newspaper s—.' He was consistent to the end."
Wilder's credo did not allow him to profess much pride in his achievements. Beyond
the posturing, however, there had to be satisfaction, both with the book and the NPR
series.

American Popular Song had also shown Wilder to be a writer of some stature. He had great natural talent, and under Maher's patient and expert tutelage, he had honed his skills to the point where he was often limpid and luminous. Looking back a quarter of a century, Maher says there was no musician, and certainly no academician, of Wilder's generation who could have carried off such a probing and loving contemplation of American popular music. He remembers the expectation excited by Wilder's chapter-by-chapter writings:

> The green spiral-bound notebooks that came in the mail from all over, tracking the fearful wanderer on his endless journeys to nowhere, were like little firebursts of surprise, mixing thoughtful insight and affectionate caprice (even the carping was considered and filled with glints of almost sinister wit). Oh, that prose; so personal: the voice of the man. A tweedy huff of Edwardian urbanity.

Respected writer and teacher William Zinsser would later say that he had taken *American Popular Song* as his model for his book *Writing to Learn*. *American Popular Song,* he said, was a book he had been waiting all his life for. Wilder, he noted, had written his way down into the most minute essence of his subject—down to the individual note. "It's an immensely hard kind of writing, combining a scholar's precision with an artist's wonder, and in bringing it off Wilder is both learner and teacher."

That kind of praise came as no surprise to the scores of friends Wilder had corresponded with through the years. Gunther Schuller has said of him that he was "a glorious letter writer." Indeed, his letters are so prized by his friends, kept so close to their hearts, that many remain securely hidden from public scrutiny. Even the Wilder archive may never see them. However, enough of his writings are accessible so that the wider world can also be entertained.

The Letter Writer

The letters of Alec Wilder to his friends are legion and legendary. Reading them is sometimes like walking into a confessional, sometimes like listening to an orator on a soapbox, sometimes like sitting in the shade of a tree whispering with the wind. Whatever the circumstances, whatever the tone—fiercely denunciatory or warm and tender—they are nearly always evocative and entertaining. The best of them are the stuff of autobiography. And the habit of sharing even his intimate thoughts was formed early. In March 1939, Wilder was writing from the Algonquin to tell Sibley Watson: "The phone rings with crazy persistence. People burst in and out of the room like drunken impulses. Appointments are so many and involved that long lists must be kept, daily. No more reading, which is bad. Very little sex, which is good, but increasing masturbation, which I'm told is bad. Much drinking and smoking. Little sleep. Constant worry."

Music was Wilder's bedrock, but literature was also integral to his life. "I'm better fed by a well-written book than by an extra dividend (though I own no stock). I am better fed by Dylan Thomas than by the products of General Motors (I don't own a car)." When the *New Heritage Dictionary* was published in 1969, he bought copies for all his close friends. He wanted to open up the world for those he loved. Books were his constant companions. Although he would countenance only hard covers in the beginning, he broke down later and began to buy the paperbacks he had once abhorred. They were easier to carry. Hard cover or soft, he only wished that more people would do more reading. He once said sadly to Lou Ouzer, "Don't bother to lock the car, there are only books in it, and no one steals books."

Like many self-educated men and women, Wilder read widely and incessantly. He had his established favorites: James Thurber, Robert Ardrey, John Cheever, Rumer Godden, Peter De Vries, Bruce Catton, Lawrence Durrell, Albert Murray. He also enjoyed E. F. Benson, P. G. Wodehouse, Mary Norton, Georges Simenon, Sara Woods, and others. It sometimes seemed that he admired craftsmanship more than genius. Among the books and authors he dismissed as bores were *Moby Dick*,

War and Peace, most of Dickens, most of Henry James, *Henry Esmond, Tom Jones, Moll Flanders, Don Quixote* ("I'm terribly sorry"), *Precious Bane* ("oh, that regional language"), Ernest Hemingway, over half of Fitzgerald, Kafka, Kierkegaard, and "quite a lot of Shakespeare." Indeed, you would have to say most of Shakespeare judging by what he told Sibley Watson: "One of my life's saddest losses is my inability to comprehend more than scraps of Shakespeare." Ignorance of scientific theorems did not alarm or surprise him, "but after all the reading I've done, why do I find it impossible to find the meaning of so much of that great man? Some of it, I know, is due to obsolete words and phrases. Yet that doesn't account for my abysmal inability to find the meaning of all those marvelous words."

For the most part, Wilder kept his distance from academe and from the books and music that no well-educated person could supposedly survive without. Sometimes, he was playing the role of the heretic, something he always enjoyed doing. In music and literature both, he refused to do any genuflecting.

However much he may have veered from the traditional paths of learning, Wilder wound up with a mind as well stocked as the shelves of a good library. With his soaring intelligence and his unsurpassed knowledge, he was forever surprising even those who knew him well. He had many unsuspected depths and layers. James Maher remembers once talking with him about a trip that he, Maher, had made to Venice with Ethan Ayer, who lived in Cambridge. "All of a sudden, Alec was talking about Tiepolo [a painter of the Venetian group whose murals became popular in Europe during the 1700s], and that to me had been the big moment of the trip." There were many magnificent things to look at in Venice, says Maher, but the Tiepolo ceilings were the only ceilings that truly made sense to him—"the whole renaissance bravura of flying off into space, of course to God. Alec started talking about Tiepolo, and I said, how do you know him? And one by one he told me the places where the Tiepolo paintings could be found. After he left, I had the strangest feeling that there were parts of Alec I would never know."

Another who was witness to Wilder's far-ranging knowledge was the physician he placed so much faith in, William R. Ploss, of Gainesville, Florida. Ploss was sitting with Wilder one day in a seafood restaurant and saying something about Nikos Kazantzakis's *The Last Temptation of Christ.*

> He immediately compared my point with a similar thought train in a previous Kazantzakis book. He criticized the author's lack of consistency between his books. I was amazed, and didn't trust his memory or wanted to check up on this guy (Kazantzakis was consistent; he'd simply matured in his thinking.) I quickly wrote the reference on my napkin under the table, and checked in the library in the next few days. Alec was "right on."

Although his reading had told him much about the world around him, Wilder sometimes surprised people by what he did not know, particularly if popular television programs were involved. Once he wrote to Sibley Watson about walking as rapidly down a Boston street as his age would permit and catching sight of some large block letters that spelled out ARCHIE BUNKER, nothing more. Intuition, he told Watson, kept hinting to him that Bunker was a schlock Aryan religious martyr like Mr. Dooley. He said he did recall that the Bunkers owned a hill near there sometimes referred to as Breed's Hill, and he had once introduced a Jennifer Bunker to Augusta Dabney, the actress. "But as for Archie Bunker, I shall ask a fount of useless information this morning, and, if successful, inform you immediately. PS: Archie Bunker, I just learned, is the character of a bigot on a television program called All in the Family." Wilder had to be the only adult in the United States who had never heard of Archie Bunker.

When it came to what he considered important matters, Wilder was seldom caught out. His knowledge was encyclopedic. And more than his friends benefited from his immersion in the literary world. Mike (Mitchell) Miller Jr., today a distinctive and successful children's book illustrator, made many train trips with Wilder. He was often witness to his egalitarian habits in his contacts with railway porters and others who worked on the trains. Always, Wilder carried a stack of books with him on the train, and, says Miller, he gave away each book as he finished it. "He would ring for the Pullman porter and say to him when he appeared at the door, 'I don't know how you feel about the latest Elizabeth Bowen,' et cetera." Miller would wonder what was going on. "It turns out that these porters were sometimes writing novels themselves in their odd hours with their strange sleeping schedules. They were reading the books Alec gave them, and a few were writing themselves. He accounted for the most literate train crews. They were as much beneficiaries of his reading habits as you or I might be."

Some of Wilder's highest flights of invention, fancy, and creativity were reserved for the word puzzles of which he was such a master. He was the great craftsman of the puzzle world, particularly the enormously challenging cryptic crossword. The best witness to his puzzle-making genius was Frances Miller. These two undying friends, each with a sharp intellect and an irrepressible sense of humor, exchanged, composed, and solved hundreds of cryptic crosswords. By mail, by telephone, and in person, they were brilliant exponents of one of the most complex of word games. Miller notes that friends who saw him in the last quarter of his life had to be aware that Wilder was never without a dog-eared dictionary under his arm: "Since Alec himself was a walking encyclopedia, it was impossible not to speculate why this gentleman who scorned all earthly possessions felt compelled to carry this burden everywhere."

The answer was in those puzzles that tugged at him constantly. "What began as a casual interest," says Miller, "swiftly burgeoned into a consuming passion. Periodically, he would experience an unproductive, anguished, dry spell when his musical springs seemed to dry up and disappear." That was when he turned more than ever to puzzle making and solving. James Maher remembers one such dry spell when Wilder sat in a hotel room in Rochester for days on end doing nothing but puzzles:

"On the phone he sounded like the only visitor he had had that day was death." Miller worked on hundreds of Wilder's puzzles, all of them witty, "and some of them as bawdy as anything in Rabelais. After the first shock of discovery when the answer is revealed, I find them outrageously funny." Concludes Miller:

> As long as he lives in the thoughts of his close friends, he will be remem-
> bered as a man who was obsessed with cryptics; who was unable to carry on
> normal conversations because he was deeply engrossed in words; and who
> will never be forgotten by the waiters and bartenders of some very fine res-
> taurants as the gentleman who always ate his dinner with the dictionary on
> the table and the beam of a flashlight trained on its pages.

This man who never signed a mortgage or a lease, who never took out a garbage can or mowed a lawn or dried a dish, did make time with his correspondence to enrich the lives of others with his wit and wisdom. He stands out as one of the last of the great letter writers. Wilder's words were so warmly personal and particular to his correspondents that his letters became prized. Harry Bouras of Chicago has pointed out that those letters were mostly of two kinds. The first kind were "the gentle, wonderful, long, pally and gossipy letters in that big, generous, open hand of his, never varying, so clean, no shift in the angle of the letters, never sliding into verticality and intransigence, never wobbling back and regressing." The other kind, sometimes written when he was drunk, were those that excoriated and denounced and harangued and despaired, or apologized for some transgression. But they were still unmistakably Wilder.

To Allen Kelly, he wrote: "When I have to travel, I carry a cane and limp, heavily, in order to get better service. It works! First on and off planes, meals served in roomettes on trains, red caps less surly. . . . I did it so much that my knee started to ache!"

To Harvey and Carol Phillips: "The worst thing about age is not growing old but being more than ever aware of youth. Your family and farm fairly shout with fanfares for youth and joy. To add springtime to it all could be heartbreaking to one as old as I, but miraculously it gives me only hope and faith in the glory of life."

To John Barrows: "I'm as immobilized as a burnt-out tank. . . . I'm like Benny Goodman, who never could learn to play the new way. I can't live the new way. Most of the people and places which make me feel a degree of safety and hope are gone. I thought if I stayed away from this bus station hotel and this mugger's paradise, New York, I could find a place. I can't. The hell broth people are out in force."

To Bob Levy: "When I try to go to sleep, I try not to remember all the failures and lost lives, but rather those people like yourself who give dignity and profound meaning to the sad journey of life."

To no one did Wilder write more often over a longer stretch of time than to

Sibley Watson in Rochester. Hundreds of letters poured in from the 1930s through the 1970s, and the subject matter was infinitely varied. On despair: "I feel much as primitive man must have felt wandering through the African savannah armed with no more than the bone of an impala while all about him roared the carnivores." On Los Angeles: "It's almost as new as BeBop and quite as sterile. An endless suburb. Clumsy unframed wealth vying with other unframed wealth. Pseudo-anything at all. Slashed hills that run off to the sea at the merest shower." On Wagner: "Wagner blazed a trail straight to the supermarket, the super-star and Holiday Inn furniture. His gods were all Thor. I'm not saying that the solution was Debussy or Ravel but I am saying that they took the children out of the school room into the playground."

Yet it was his poems, not the letters, that Wilder prized the most. Like the coloratura soprano who wanted to be a pop singer, Wilder, deep down, wanted to be known as a poet. Significantly, this man who kept nothing kept the verses he wrote—"hundreds of poems, poems on menus, scraps of paper, backs of letters, torn, smudged, cracked along folded edges." He copied out the best of them and sent them to Watson. They were all, he said, very personal, passionate statements, pleas, questions, speculations, a compensation for the absence of those in whom he might otherwise have confided. They were, he added, "of great consequence to me as they constitute catharsis, probably more revelatory than the maunderings that ensued for three years on an analyst's couch during the early 1940s." Both mordant wit and gentle reflection were to be found in them:

> In between sunshine and shadow
> In between breathing and dying
> In between the exultation of larks and sparrows
> In between the see-saws of friends and foes
> I'm certain there is one perfect statue of myself
> In plastic!

> Never fear forgetting!
> Your only concern need be
> What you remember
> Then you will note
> That all the forgotten things
> Are of little value,
> While all the things remembered
> Are those to do with love and laughter,
> Constancy and compassion.
> And should you speak to me
> In any language other than my own,
> I shall make a point
> Of learning yours.
> Then we can remember together.

Many of the hundreds of poems he sent to Watson for safekeeping spoke to the magic and miracle of life. Although his poetry was more tethered and earth-bound than either his music or his prose, it was always true to the character and the spirit of the man. Yet the personal letters were somehow more encompassing, more sharply focused. If enough of the best of them could be pried from their owners, they would make an entertaining and publishable collection. But ironically, virtually the only Wilder letters that have passed into the public domain are those that were written for publication rather than for purely personal perusal: the letters to Whitney Balliett that were at the heart of his July 9, 1973, profile in the *New Yorker*, "The President of the Derrière-garde"—the best piece ever written about Wilder— and the letters that made up the 1975 Little, Brown book *Letters I Never Mailed.*

Wilder complained more than once that the *New Yorker* piece had breached his defenses against publicity and that the exposure was spoiling his life. He protested too much, for he had to be well aware that Balliett intended writing about him. And the letters that began arriving on Balliett's doorstep were surely sent in the knowledge that they might well be published. It's good that they were, for, as Balliett noted in the profile, the letters had a fine, eighteenth-century timbre: "Some were broadsides, some were inchoate, some were confessional, some were mystical and some very funny. And they were rhetorical; no answer was expected, or even possible."

Although he never knew exactly how Wilder felt about his *New Yorker* profile, Balliett suspects that Wilder was not displeased. Secretly, he was probably flattered. It was Balliett, more than any other person, who brought Wilder to the attention of press and public in the last decade of his life. Balliett admired his music without stint; he respected the morality of the man; he loved the humor; and he liked the range of his friendships: "Alec didn't have a high-falutin' bone in his body. He was never snobbish toward people unless he felt they were shams."

Two years after the *New Yorker* profile, Wilder walked before the footlights once again with the collection of letters entitled *Letters I Never Mailed: Clues to a Life.* There was some understandable confusion about the contents when the book came out. Gene Lees pointed out that, characteristically with Wilder, it filled no known category of literature, that it was not an autobiography, a diary, or a compendium of correspondence: "Wilder lives everywhere and nowhere, and these letters are all he has kept in his nomadic life." In fact, the letters were written not as personal letters penned through the decades but as essays composed as an autobiographical device. It is a legitimate device, but some of Wilder's friends refused to read the book for that reason. Yet it is still authentically Alec Wilder, marked by the same contradictions, ambivalences, and eccentricities that ran through his life like a mother lode. Here is this most private man going without clothes in public, retailing his sexual adventures (though not telling tales), and baring his soul embarrassingly.

The book is a richly entertaining, highly idiosyncratic account of his journey through recording studios, jazz joints, hotel lobbies, rehearsal halls, and train stations. Much of the time he lays about him in royal fashion, including guppies and wives among the possessions he distrusts and fears, pouring scorn on amateurism in music, loving flowers only if they are grown with organic fertilizers. Wilder reserves one of his best broadsides for "Mr. Income Tax Man," saying in part:

> Will you believe me when I solemnly swear that I go to Key West to write music, that I've never fished in my life, that at most I spend an hour a day on the beach and then only if my work is going well? No! It's like set concrete in your head that all people go to Key West to fish! Hell, that's what *you* would do! . . . You told me I couldn't compose if I didn't have a piano in my room. So I told you you couldn't add figures without an adding machine! Up yours!

True to his principles, Wilder does no trading in his book on his friendships with the famous. Readers have to pick up the clues to know that Mitchell is Mitch Miller, that Frank is Frank Sinatra. So it goes. The Mabel of the letters is singer Mabel Mercer; Cuzzin is writer Thornton Wilder; Bruce is Civil War historian Bruce Catton; Peggy is singer Peggy Lee; Al is writer Albert Murray; Whitney is Whitney Balliett; Marian is jazz pianist Marian McPartland; Tony is Tony Bennett; Judy is actress Judy Holliday; Z is actor and comedian Zero Mostel. Had he chosen, Wilder could have piggybacked on the shoulders of many important persons, for he had the connections and the stories. Perhaps because he felt so warmly about their writings, Wilder does break the insider pattern of *Letters I Never Mailed* by identifying some of his favorite authors. In addition to the letters he wrote just for the book, Wilder also kept up a flow of genuine correspondence with his favorite authors, for he firmly believed that no one was so popular and successful as to be indifferent to a reader's thanks and appreciation. Often the authors wrote back.

Appropriately, in view of his literary interests and writings, Wilder in 1974 was honored by the Friends of the Rochester Public Library with its Literary Award, then given each year to a Rochesterian "who has made significant contributions to the field of literature and other branches of the humanities." Wilder accepted the honor with professed reluctance—fidgeting, squirming, and smoking through the whole ceremony. Mitch Miller was there to do the principal honors. The tributes seemed to get to the essence of the man. Wilder, said Milford Fargo, was just a thorny cream puff. "He can pierce the phony with one indignant stab, but he will literally weep at the beauty of a phrase." Warren Benson put it this way: "He's honest, sweet, tough, loyal, loud, rich and deep as good soil, tender, profane, respectful, precise and juicy with words, well-weathered as an old standard song— he's been around—and when Alec comes to our house, all the children glow."

The award was made on the basis of Wilder's *American Popular Song*, but it might also have embraced the letters that were savored by so many people. Somehow, he had a gift for suiting his words to the person and to the occasion. Gunther Schuller, sometimes alone among the eminent in music, never ceased to be a champion, and Wilder in one of the letters he really did write told him that his support had been like a reprieve from the governor to a criminal headed for the long mile: "You've made me feel as if this long search has not been fruitless, that my fumbling for not only self-expression but musical aspects of a truth less temporal than myself has not been pointless or without dignity and a curious kind of absolute discipline." And so he humbly thanked Schuller for refinding him. "Yours is a large canvas, a multifarious contribution and I would have been only sad, not offended, had you missed my island. I have only a candlelit lighthouse and no bell-buoys. But here you are again and I hope fiercely that I never lose you." Schuller included that letter and one other in the 1991 booklet published by Margun Music, *Alec Wilder: An Introduction to the Man and His Music.*

That glorious soprano Eileen Farrell is no less proud of Wilder's autographed words in her copy of *American Popular Song.* Unlike many of the singers who sang Wilder's standards in the 1940s, Farrell has stayed with him and kept singing his songs. Wilder loved her for that, for the way she crossed the boundaries, and for the fact that success left her unchanged. "She never became grand or full of herself." Said Wilder in his book inscription:

> I respect you enormously. I love you even more. I'm profoundly rewarded by knowing you have this book. It means that the respect is reciprocated. And the way you have sung songs of mine not to be found in this book tells me you love me too. What a marvelous thought to have dancing in my heart as I wander about the somewhat lonely landscape.

It may have been a lonely landscape, still Wilder did much peopling of it with his letters and comments, so varied in nature. Here he is writing at about the same time from a room in the Atlantic Shores Motel in Key West:

> There is a cross breeze due to opposite open windows. There is the sound of a gentle surf and the sursurration of palm tree branches. There is none of the human racket that exists later on in the winter season. There is a two-burner stove so that I can cook breakfast. This ritual pleases me. The motion of the curtains calms me. The unlikelihood of the telephone ringing lessens my normal tensions. The occasional burst of a mockingbird's song makes me forget that I'm old. The consciousness that I exist, even though only temporarily, on the last of a string of small coral islands makes me feel as if I had escaped from a horde of slavering barbarians.

It really makes no difference whether Wilder's letters were mailed or not, written singly and personally through the years or all at once for publication. They were all seamless, all speaking to the same man, all illustrating one facet or another of his infinitely complex character. Together, they make a colorful tapestry. But the strands that most catch the eye are those that relate to music, particularly the promising young musicians who kept restoring his faith. There is one letter in particular in *Letters I Never Mailed,* this one addressed to Lavinia Russ, that says a great deal:

Right after you told me of the cheery young men who were touring the Village in a pickup truck selling pumpkins in which they had carved absurd faces and how uplifted you were by their rollicking spirits and genial calls to the passing public—the same day I visited a group on the Upper West Side which was about to perform a trio I had written for clarinet, bassoon and piano. . . .

The small apartment house was run-down, the halls looked as if the building had once been used for some unmentionable purpose, so much so that when I had trouble finding the right door I sensed the echoes of evil. Then I found the door, pressed the bell and it was opened by a young innocent-looking boy, followed by an affectionate gray cat.

As I passed down the gloomy hall I happened to look up and the high ceiling was a mass of large curls of flaking paint. Then I was in a room, equally gloomy, where two more young people sat in front of their music stands, one a bearded boy and the other a thin, intense girl. They were the bassoonist and clarinetist. . . .

They played.

They played exquisitely. They played not only musically but with conscience. They played as if that was the whole point of living.

I nearly wept. . . .

Sure, they'll be dust, all three of those inspired children. Sure, there'll be no pyramid built in memory of them!

But not even the devil could deny what took place in that room though the belief, the faith, the conviction permeating it would have driven him back to hell!

Forgive the melodrama, but, Lavinia, I was in a Presence. Such ineffable moments defy and shout with glorious laughter at mortality and the waiting worm.

I remember once in a book written by a self-elected voice for the California hippie there was a remark made by a bearded young man who had been asked what he supposed he'd be doing when the Bomb dropped. He replied, "Oh, I'll be right here painting."

Skin of our teeth, yes, but the miracle is still all around us.

There would be other such moments of exaltation with young musicians Wilder would become much closer to.

14

The Young Believers

In the 1960s and 1970s, Wilder became an important generative force in the lives of many young American musicians he knew both professionally and personally. He was their conscience artistically, and sometimes their father confessor too. The striking thing about that conscience was the range of it: from formal music to jazz, and through the great middle ground of popular music. Always urging them on to higher endeavor, Wilder had a profound impact on these talented young men and women.

This music partnership with youth probably had its clearest and most continuous expression at the Tidewater Music Festival at Saint Mary's College of Maryland, located sixty-eight miles southeast of Washington, D.C. Founded in the early 1970s by then college faculty member Robert Levy, the festival included a performing faculty in residence, a public concert series, and music-camp experience for students at the junior and senior high school levels. As its music director for seven years, Levy, a gifted trumpet player, gathered about him a group of fine young musicians from as far away as Vancouver. Each year he invited a visiting composer to the campus—composers such as Aaron Copland, Warren Benson, Samuel Adler, David Cope, Fisher Tull, Vincent Persichetti, John Watts, and Alec Wilder. Even when he was not a visiting composer, Wilder went again and again to the Tidewater Festival, stimulating the young players by his presence, writing music especially for them that expanded their horizons, reveling in the rehearsals, and being buoyed in turn by their respect and affection, by hearing his music played in concert and recording. In the process, he formed a deep personal bond with Levy in particular. Indeed, he was to have no more ardent young disciple than Levy, who would blaze many trails for Wilder's music.

First, however, Wilder had to regain a measure of faith in the world about him. He had always had that special kinship with the very young, as shown by all the music he wrote for, about, and because of children. The rock explosion of the 1950s, however, had shaken him mightily, confirming some of his worst fears about society. All that new permissiveness, that slacking of reins, had to be bad. Nothing disturbed Wilder more than what he saw as the prevailing lack of apprenticeship to music and to life. Whether it was instant coffee or instant genius, everything seemed to be arriving full-blown in the modern world. He did not believe he was speaking out of old-fashioned pique. No, he told Rochester bandleader and songwriter Carl Dengler, he was not bitter about the ball being tossed to young people. All he asked was self-discipline, good taste, and professionalism, and those things did not exist anymore. The studio where Dengler worked with young players was "a chapel of hope," but he took little comfort from the larger picture. Television's Ed Sullivan, he said, was a nice guy but not very bright, and he had no business showcasing immature talent. Work, excellence, self-discipline, perspective, wit, fun, joy, wonderment—those were the qualities and virtues that had to be revived.

Wilder's worries and forebodings were offset, however, by the young people he began to meet in the 1960s as he traveled about the country and came to know some of the students in the music schools and the college music departments. He was forced to revise some of his earlier characterizations and opinions. Yes, he would always detest rock for the explosive noise that displaced music, for the manic superstars, the Nuremberg-type rallies, the beads, the hair, and the facelessness of the rock generation. Perhaps his strongest condemnation was reserved for the magazines and newspapers and television stations that concentrated on the hippie/rock culture of the 1960s and ignored so many talented other young musicians. Wilder was familiar with a very different world in which thousands of young people kept good music alive in the "stage-band" movement in the high schools and colleges (the term "stage band" was deemed to be less offensive than "swing band" would have been to the upright, God-fearing boards of education of the day). These were the young people, the musical hope for tomorrow, he felt had been lost in the rock frenzy of the media.

Looking back in the *New York Times* in 1972 on the rock hysteria, Wilder admitted he was at first repelled and appalled by the students' dress, especially their hairstyles:

> When some lank-haired girl would come up to me in a school and say, "Hey, you wrote a tenor trombone sonata and I'm rehearsing it and I'd like you to hear it," I'd think, "Oh, my God." But I'd go up to the practice room and THEN the magic would start. The girl would play it beautifully and the accompanist play perfectly. So now I say to myself, "I've got to forget about the hair." I have written a great many pieces for these young people and in every case the reward for me has been limitless.

Wilder, then, was learning to look beyond the hair and the dress when he first met Levy in the early 1960s at Ithaca College in upstate New York, where Levy was a music student. It is also the college where Warren Benson, later to become professor of composition at Eastman, was then professor of music and composer in residence. Ithaca High School band conductor Frank Battisti worked with Benson on the commissioning of pieces for the band by American composers, of whom Wilder was one. Wilder often traveled to Ithaca from New York City, or else friend Lou Ouzer drove him there from Rochester. Wilder also visited with the New York Brass Quintet when it held a recital and workshop in Ithaca. When Levy began his studies at Ithaca in the early 1960s, jazz was almost taboo in colleges; jazz programs were mostly underground. Benson, however, was supportive of having jazz at Ithaca and started up a jazz workshop band. Levy, then a sophomore, asked to rehearse it. "He did so well and earned so much respect from older students," Benson recalls, "that I turned the group over to him." The jazz climate, Levy remembers, was difficult. The band had to rehearse off campus and had to settle for performing in the student union rather than in the music building. Nor was the group allowed to take part in the Villanova jazz festival. They were finally able to give a lunch-hour concert in the college's music building downtown.

Wilder, of course, fully shared the jazz sympathies of Benson. Through their Ithaca associations, the two men developed a healthy respect for each other's music and person. Benson's Eastman years were to strengthen the tie. Wilder, noted Benson, was at odds with the music world after 1950: with both rock and roll—with its oversimplified melodic and harmonic content and its deafening amplication—and the incredible sophistication and expansion of the world of dissonance and linear complexity. To his thinking, much of the new composing and playing was being done in a disordered way, without framework.

Wilder believed that the composer should always be in control, and Benson respected the narrow band of intensity that Wilder worked in, using a harmonic language fundamentally consonant and chromatic: "He was the sunshine down the middle—piquant, sad music, a little touch of lament, but basically a sunny, forgiving kind of music." Wilder for his part admired Benson's ability to build substantial structures and yet keep the music lyrical. He warmly praised Benson's composition *Helix,* saying that "its phenomenal control, its glorious sense of freedom, its astoundingly personal revelatory moments, its juxtaposed wit and passions, its gossamer delicacy and sun-burned sinew, all make it a masterpiece."

In 1964, Robert Levy wrote to Wilder at the Algonquin that he had heard and liked some of his music, and asked if he would consider writing a solo work for saxophonist Donald Sinta, the Ithaca faculty adviser, and the jazz ensemble. He was interested, Wilder replied, but could not undertake it at the time. Unbeknownst to Levy, Battisti, the Ithaca High School band director, had also written to Wilder asking him to write a solo for Sinta and the band. In any event, Wilder traveled to Ithaca for rehearsals. He attended Levy's senior recital, and he also heard him directing the jazz band. A dark, intense, bearded youth with blazing enthusiasms, Levy at the time was confused about his future. He shared that concern with Wilder, who took a shine to the young man and lost no time demonstrating it.

A day or so after he had talked with Wilder, Levy was walking by Sinta's office when he saw a note on the bulletin board asking him to see Sinta urgently. Sinta told Levy that in the next few days he should call a musician named John Barrows in Madison, Wisconsin, and find out when Barrows would be available to meet with him to help sort out his future. He should then make a plane reservation; his expenses had been taken care of. The surprised and grateful Levy asked to be given at least some handle on the sudden circumstance and prevailed on Sinta to be more revealing. It came out that Wilder was the benefactor, that he admired Levy and his playing, and that this was his way of trying to help.

Levy made the flight and had the meeting. Barrows was later to help him with a music-clinic appointment in two summers at Madison. According to Benson, Wilder also arranged with the assistant chairman of the department to provide $50 a month to aid in Levy's keep, though Levy has no knowledge of this. Always generous, Wilder once paid for Levy to stay at the then Sheraton Hotel in Rochester. In 1967, Levy asked Wilder to write a suite for him; *Suite for Trumpet and Piano* was performed by Levy at the University of North Iowa and the University of Iowa. It became the first of a number of pieces, all gifts.

A closer association with Wilder began when Levy joined the faculty of Saint Mary's College and established the Tidewater Music Festival. Wilder had to be humored a little on the job during his several stints as visiting composer. Because Wilder was reluctant to stand formally in front of a class, Levy found a basement area and arranged the furniture and the students in such a way that the setting resembled a living room. In 1972, Wilder contacted Levy about a possible reading of his *Brass Quintet No. 4*, which he had written for and dedicated to Harvey Phillips but had not heard. He had been taken, he said, with the playing of the resident Tidewater Brass Quintet (Levy, trumpet and flugelhorn; Gary Maske, tuba; Martin Hackleman, French horn; Loren Marsteller, trombone and euphonium; Chris Gekker, trumpet and rotary valve trumpet). The quintet work was premiered successfully that year. Wilder felt the group had a special sympathy with his music, which it did, and he said the only way he could thank them was by writing them another quintet. Over seven years, he wrote four brass quintets in all (*No. 5* through *No. 8*) and all were recorded by Tidewater Brass for Golden Crest Records.

In the Tidewater Brass Quintet, Wilder had found a new generation of musicians who were fully worthy successors to the New York Woodwind Quintet he had composed for so happily in earlier years. Superlative performances of his music had been too rare through the years, but here now was another desperately needed affirmation of faith. In a personal letter to Levy, James Maher made the point that because of the condescension of the critics and Wilder's failure over the previous thirty years to find more players of the high caliber of John Barrows, Wilder had blunted his compositional daring: "He could let go when he wrote for John. He now knows that he can let go perhaps even further when he writes for your quintet or for Virginia [Nanzetta] or Gordon [Stout] or Steve [Hart]—or for any of the Robert Levy family-repertory company." Added Maher: "The reflexes of fear, of frustration, of defence against being demeaned, and of age run very deep. But at least now he knows that, for whatever mysterious reason, there is a generation of young musicians who can sense and can create what he has written and will write. And that is marvelous."

Wilder's non-pop music, such as the brass quintets, was not easy to play well, mainly because of his uniquely personal style and approach. Believing as he did that good performance lay heavily and properly in the hands of the performers, he provided few markings and notations on the score. "He often said," remembers Levy, "that the secret was in getting past the notes and kicking open the door behind them. Many times people didn't get past the notation to see what was on the other side."

In his richly textured liner notes for the Tidewater Brass Quintet's recording of *Brass Quintet No. 7* (written in 1978 and dedicated to Frances Miller), Maher told of listening in the recording studio as the group wrested "from the barren calligraphy of notation the creative intentions of Alec Wilder." Too often, Maher asserted, musicians failed to go beyond the surface of Wilder's music, winding up bemused and becalmed by "charming solos, sonorous textures, and striking cadences, leaving the music beyond the notes to the silence of failed perceptions." But in the control room that afternoon, he sensed a discourse flowing under the music. "Composer and musicians had become one: thought and voice, impulse and reflex. The surfaces had vanished. The noteless poetry of the composer's vision emerged." Levy and company had been able to kick down the door to his secrets, and Wilder exulted.

Wilder's formative influence was strong. Quintet trumpet player Chris Gekker said that when he was in school he would now and again write to Wilder with a question: "He would always write back to me. There was no reason [for him to do that]. I have had trumpet teachers who would never answer letters. He always really answered, not just a scribbled acknowledgment. He actually dealt with the question." Wilder, Gekker points out, was fully engaged with each person. And that was true not only for the quintet members. Judith Pauley, a clarinetist who was then the wife of another clarinet player, Steve Hart, was another young musician who met Wilder at the Tidewater Festival through Levy. Wilder later wrote several compositions for the two clarinetists. Hart was to say: "It was Alec's influence on me, his love and dedication to music, that helped me find new meaning in being a musician." Nor have the years diminished Pauley's feelings about Wilder. "I love him," she says. "I wish he were here now. I wish I could talk to him right now." She learned much from Wilder just by the witness of his life: the way he lived, riding on trains, going to see friends, free of spirit, not tied to things and places. But Wilder also spoke to deep personal need. He had such an ability, says Pauley, to look inside a person, past the shell. "He helped me to really look honestly at myself. He could see the way I was—what was there to be brought out."

Gordon Stout, who became percussion teacher at the School of Music at Ithaca College and specializes on the marimba, also came to know Wilder at the Tidewater Festival, also through Levy. Wilder in 1969 had written a solo guitar suite for a guitarist who promptly pronounced it unplayable. Levy had a copy and showed it to Stout, suggesting he try it on the marimba. So Stout prepared it, and when Wilder visited the festival that year, played the suite for him. "He loved it. It was idiomatically so correct for the marimba." Stout changed a few figurations and patterns, but it nearly all fitted well. Wilder said it was the only time he had written a piece for one instrument only to learn that it was really suited for another. Later, Wilder wrote a trumpet and marimba suite for Levy and Stout, and that spurred them to establish the Wilder Duo for trumpet and marimba. Each already well known in his own right as a performer, both wanted not only to perform as a duo but also to develop a new literature for these instruments. With Wilder showing the way, other composers turned their attention to pieces for marimba and trumpet.

Wilder also had a warm relationship with flutist Virginia Nanzetta. Through the mail and by telephone, the two of them, the older man and the much younger girl, conducted a kind of long-distance love affair, with Nanzetta knitting sweaters and sending poems, and Wilder writing little compositions and sending poems as well. Wilder's name was already known to Nanzetta before she met him at Tidewater. In graduate school at the University of Illinois, the instructing musicologist had invited the students to make themselves familiar with the works of American composers such as Wilder, Bernstein, Copland, and others. It used to bother Nanzetta that she heard so few performances of Wilder's non-pop music that sounded right. It seemed to her that jazz people did a certain kind of pitch bending to the harmonics that made them work and move to the right place, whereas the straight people did not, either because they did not know about it or because they did not think things should move that way. The chords just did not flow. It also troubled Nanzetta that some people see Wilder's work as light music:

It's very serious music. His music reminds me of Mahler because of the intensity. You know that in Mahler there's a great joy but also this edge that
you know it's going to be snatched away. There's something about that combination, the awareness in one individual of both a very joyful and happy
something and also the opposite thing. Maybe to have that incredible joy
there has to be that awareness of the other. There's something of the pre-
ciousness of life about it.

At Tidewater, Levy had invited Wilder to hear a concert by the faculty of a whole cross-section of his music. Nanzetta worked up *Sonata No. 2 for Flute and Piano* (1968) but did not feel she was able to get remotely close to the way it should be played. With her love of music transcending a deep shyness, she went up to Wilder after rehearsal and told him how inadequate she had been. She wanted him to know she had special feelings about the piece and would continue to work on it: "I knew the way I was playing would not convey the feelings I had for it. I didn't want to leave it like that. Alec was supportive and understanding and knew I was concerned. He was never a person to put anyone down."

Later, Wilder wrote for Nanzetta some unaccompanied pieces for flute. She played them at the college, but forbade Levy to send the tapes to Wilder; they were not good enough. But Levy persisted and mailed them off. Wilder promptly called Nanzetta and told her how well they had sounded. His encouragement came at a critical time. With her musical future in doubt, and with small children to care for at home, she was about ready to hang up her flute. Then came the call: "I thought if he could hear something in my music, maybe there was something. . . . I still remember standing in the phone booth [at the college] and hearing him say all these wonderful things. After that, we talked on the phone a great deal and he would write and send things and I would play them."

Nanzetta has many sharp snapshots of Wilder from the years she knew him. She sometimes called on him at the Algonquin during her visits to the city to study with Sam Baron of the New York Woodwind Quintet. She would tell him everyday things about the children, about the mushrooms of incredible color that she had found growing near the blueberry bushes. She would call from home to say that the Canada geese had just passed over. She would tell him how you knew it was really spring when the blueberry bushes came into full leaf: "When I told him the spring things, he was very happy. When I told him the fall things, that made him sad. He hated to think about fall, my favorite time of the year with the colors. But he said it just reminded him of death."

There were earlier links with students around the country, notably in 1968 during the January–May semester when Wilder was a teacher-in-residence at the University of Wisconsin at Madison, where Barrows and Glenn Bowen were both on the faculty. Barrows had wangled the appointment. "Students," says Bowen, "liked his honesty, his musical honesty, and his caring for people." He was always generous. The story is told of Wilder one day meeting in the corridor a flute teacher who was bubbling over because his new bass flute had finally arrived from France after a long wait. A week later the teacher walked into his office and found there a piece for bass flute and piccolo that Wilder had written especially for him.

Although Wilder touched the lives of many students in many places, it was his Tidewater family that remained at the core of his involvement with young talent. And Levy was the person who sustained him and kept the associations vital. Levy's daughter Randi was also Wilder's affectionate friend. He wrote three French horn pieces for her when she was ten. No one among Wilder's young band of followers had done more, or would do more, than Levy on behalf of the non-pop music. Although not questioning Wilder's contribution to music as a phenomenal songwriter, Levy deeply regretted and resented the passing over of his instrumental output during the later decades—"all that wonderful chamber music, the solo sonatas and suites, and the Entertainments." Too many musicians, he has always thought, tend to "read through" Wilder's music and miss the point: "Instead of seeing the lovely simplicity for what it is (its charm, grace or elegance) . . . they will dismiss it as overly simplistic and/or lacking." He has always viewed Wilder's music as a set of "clues." As a performer or conductor, "I may have to give it a more self-directed point of view or interpretation than with the works of other composers. But I respect the craftsmanship and substance that is there."

Levy not only was indefatigable in promoting performances of Wilder's music but became a gadfly in his pursuit of music publishing houses, pointing out to them that much of Wilder's work had not been accessible for years. Since the early 1960s, Harvey Phillips had been suggesting to Wilder that because publishers were not printing his work, the two of them should consider establishing a company just for that purpose. In 1964, Wilder Music, Inc., was registered as a corporation in the State of New York. Some of the smaller chamber works were printed early on with the aid of some small personal funds invested by the two men and some advance royalties. And Wilder was no longer having to bear the full cost of having a professional copyist extract the parts and a "master score" from his original manuscripts; this was no small expense, averaging some $4 a page for each part. Wilder would then pay—again out of his own pocket—the reproduction and mailing costs for supplying copies to those professional musicians who happened to hear about a piece.

Wilder was touched by Phillips's efforts to make his music available: "It is one of the very few unselfish gestures ever to have been made to me in my life." He also knew the project would run into difficulties, given Phillips's staggering workload and the huge, scattered nature of his own music output. In time, it did indeed bog down. Writing to Sibley Watson in 1970 for financial support, Phillips noted that no advertising or catalogue mailing of the music had yet been made because it would be impossible to satisfy the resulting orders and inquiries. Up to that point, he said, he had been able to reply only to "chance" requests, and inadequately at that:

> While I am committed to serving Alec, I must at the same time serve many others in order to provide for the needs of my immediate family. I shall not bemoan my personal situation—except to say that the term "overcommitted" is an understatement. In any case, some solution must be found to the problem of getting Alec's music printed so it can then be distributed and performed.

Levy did what he could to help break up the traffic jam, and Phillips appreciated his efforts. He himself had tried hard. He cared when few others cared about Wilder's music, and he had tracked down over a period of five years many Wilder suites, sonatas, concertos, art songs, and chamber music compositions. But he could not keep up.

He and Wilder, Phillips would say later, were both relieved "when Gunther Schuller formed Margun Music, and we then consigned Wilder Music to Margun Music." No one was happier with the turn of events than Levy. For years, he had been bending his best professional and personal efforts to getting more of Wilder's non-pop music into the public domain. Now Schuller had come to the rescue. In the late 1960s and early 1970s, Schuller's sporadic contacts with Wilder had broadened into a deeper relationship. Although his own music was so different from Wilder's, stylistically and idiomatically, Schuller began to feel more and more strongly about Wilder's music, its importance, its beauty. He was also troubled by the whole notion that Wilder had been writing for years for people, his friends, never accepting a dime. Every other composer Schuller knew received proper commissions, "but Alec just wrote all that remarkable music, and in most cases it was languishing around on somebody's shelf or music room." He recognized that although they had done much for the popular songs, the commercial publishers, even those who were his friends, were not interested in Wilder's instrumental music, seeing it almost as an aberration.

It was that neglect that moved Schuller into action, just as Phillips had been spurred in the beginning:

> Harvey was the first to take an interest and to take pity on Alec's condition
> and try to help him by forming a publishing company, and trying to run it out
> of his basement in Bloomington, where he had gone by then. I became aware
> of the fact that Harvey, who runs 90 miles an hour, and juggles 18 balls all
> the time, couldn't handle it either.

People began to turn to Schuller as a friend of Wilder's and as a musician known to be interested in new music and in performing it. They asked him to help them get copies of Wilder's music. Once before, Clark Galehouse and Golden Crest Records had taken some of Wilder's music into their subsidiary publishing company, and did indeed publish some of it. But Wilder wrote so much music that Golden Crest wasn't equipped to keep up either.

The catalog that Schuller took over from Wilder in 1976 turned out to be about 90 percent of what he had written, but because there were hundreds of works, 10 percent still represented a substantial amount of music. It took Schuller some eight or nine years to get some of the compositions "into the vault." There were pieces Wilder wrote that he didn't even remember writing, pieces he had given to some wonderful musician somewhere in the country. "That person," says Schuller, "was not necessarily aware of my publishing company and would not necessarily have thought about getting the music to me. But the word began to trickle through the land, through the Alec Wilder network, that Gunther has undertaken unto himself all of Alec's music, and if you have anything, please send it in."

Schuller's task was made more difficult by the fact that little of Wilder's music was completely finished. Nearly always he was composing for performers he knew and admired—whether Bob Levy, Virginia Nanzetta, John Barrows, Glenn Bowen, the New York Woodwind Quintet, or others. Such was his respect for them that many of the markings a composer would usually put on his music—phrasings, dynamics, tempos, little subtleties—he would omit out of respect for the players. That, Schuller points out, was "an absolutely inseparable part of the phenomenon of Alec Wilder." But once the music went beyond the players for whom it was composed, those missing instructions posed a problem. So a large part of Schuller's job was editing the music to the best of his knowledge and putting in those things Wilder left out. Schuller emphasizes that he went about it carefully and still does, not wanting to intrude himself into the original but needing to make the music fully available. Levy was now also doing all that he could to help Margun spread its net. "My greatest concern and highest priority," he told the Margun people, "is to locate ALL of Alec's music." With publication now more assured, Levy edited some of the brass music, and he also coordinated editing by Nanzetta, Bowen, and others.

With Schuller showing the way, Margun Music's harvest has been a good one. Today most of Wilder's solo, chamber, and large instrumental works are owned and published by Margun. The commercially available works (some printed, some rental, and some available from copyists) have been growing at eight to ten pieces a year and numbered some 150 pieces in 1995. New Wilder pieces, such as a small work for three bassoons, are still coming to light. Margun in 1994 released new editions of Wilder's *Sonata for Euphonium* (written for John Swallow) and has supervised newly printed versions of *Suite No. 2 for Tuba,* written for Harvey Phillips in 1975, as well as the *Suite for Horn,* written in 1956.

Even in his lifetime, Wilder's friends and supporters helped him put behind himself, at least for a time, some of the demons that had bothered him since childhood. That kind of unqualified faith did much to sustain him as he went about changing the landscape of music and human affairs. His remarkable intelligence, his undeniable presence, his total independence, and his incorruptibility were somehow harnessed in a force that was both wand and staff. More often for the better, sometimes for the worse, but never without impact, he seemed to quicken into life all that he touched. He lifted people up, musicians and nonmusicians, and sometimes he let them down, but they were never again quite as they had been. This man who could be endearing on Monday and exasperating on Tuesday almost always left a mark.

15

Defender of the Faith

Although music always took precedence, Wilder never believed that it should be isolated from the rest of experience. His concern was with all of life: life had to be lived passionately. He had nothing good to say about people who stood at the edge of affairs with their toes in the water. They had to immerse themselves, be fully engaged. They had to be able to laugh and cry. As music critic Richard Freed has said, Wilder was offended by few phenomena as much as by a cold heart, "and [he] could be heard admonishing a young adult in tones one might associate with an Old Testament prophet, inflaming each syllable, 'Let yourself be vul-ner-able!'" His friends had to be willing to follow their star and hold to their visions. Complacency and inertia infuriated him.

The days had to be affirmed, never just marked off on the calendar. In the course of a radio interview with Marian McPartland, Wilder cited singer Ray Charles as an example of a special human being. The man, he said, had everything wrong in his background—"enough to make him a basket case"—and yet he had come out of it smiling and happy. "He's constantly affirming the glory of life." Later in the same interview, McPartland noted that Wilder's tastes ran from Ray Charles to Gunther Schuller to George Barnes. "That's what I love about you. Your tastes go in every direction." Responded Wilder: "Wherever there's the sound of life." The sound of life could be a conversation with a bellman in the Algonquin, a train ride to nowhere, or a lovely spring afternoon on Columbus Circle when "the trees in the park were still in their first pale unsullied green."

In his insistence that others, too, should welcome and embrace life, Wilder cajoled and implored and pushed and, often, led by example. Even so, he was not always able to meet his own moral injunctions, especially after a drinking bout. He frequently meddled, and he ended one friendship, ostensibly at any rate, because the man had bought too cheap a bottle of wine. He could be generous and mean-spirited, too. But even when his deeds didn't match his exhortations, he was almost always involved in life, seldom standing idle—even when he might better have done so. If he couldn't drive in a nail, or claim any home as his own, or paper a wall, or take a photograph, or use a typewriter, or diaper a baby, he could, and did, carry great personal care and regard and communication to his friendships.

He was concerned with the essence of things. In his music, he kept in what was buoyant and true and not rigid, and shut out what was dry and cerebral and shallow and dissonant and too grand. He valued friends no less for the same kinds of qualities: for freedom from cant and hypocrisy and braggadocio, for integrity and for intellectual honesty, and, above all, for their celebration of life. Those friends also had to be extraordinarily tolerant. "Alec was witty, erudite, rude, warm, cantankerous, and he was all of those things when he was a house guest," Loonis McGlohon has said.

Looking back with clear-eyed affection at the Wilder she knew during his many visits to her home in Chicago, Arlene Bouras remembers the good days when Wilder would spend his time composing, always with his pencil sharpener in his pocket. There were also the days when he drank, when his dark side was uppermost, "and it was pretty ugly." Drunk, he was impossible; sober, he was perfectly fine. "When he was not fine, he violated everything he could, he really did violate people and objects and relationships." Bouras felt that his blackouts, when he could not remember what he had done the night before, were genuine: "His behavior was so bad that I don't think he would have been so destructive had he been aware." She recalls a summer music festival at Aspen where Wilder met some young musicians: "It was during his drinking period, and he had a wild night. It was my first observance of his tendency to pick someone, a woman, safe and unavailable, and then intellectually and psychologically seduce her, and then walk away." Sober, he was always enlisting friends in this or that cause, even involving them in collecting matchbooks for Algonquin bartender Carlos.

Nothing seemed to be too small or too incidental to escape Wilder's attention. He stood one day for ten minutes on a Chicago sidewalk and watched the synchronized movements of a policeman directing traffic at one of the main intersections. Finally, he went up to the officer, told him what a wonderful job he was doing, and likened his performance to that of an orchestral conductor. He admired people who did things well, whether it was a trumpeter mastering jazz rhythms, a bookseller who knew his stock, or a train engineer who managed stops and starts skillfully. He liked his trains to be run efficiently and on time, although they were more than a means of transportation. Bouras once traveled by train to Aspen with Wilder, who sat there composing most of the way. He liked the isolation of the roomette. He always had a first-class compartment, and he enjoyed the ritual. "He loved the fact that he had a staff to wait on him, and no really close relationships were possible. But he considered that in a way a very good personal relationship. Sitting there in the roomette, it was Alec's space as much as anything was ever his space."

Wilder was ardent about preserving wildlife, and he prodded others to be ardent also. He was a passionate supporter of the wildlife refuge that Gerald Durrell started on the south coast of England and moved to Jersey Island, and he insisted that Bouras support the preserve as well. One year when she had been slow to send off her contribution to the Jersey Wildlife Associates, she was sitting in her office at *Playboy* magazine with her editorial director when she received a telegram urging her to send off the money at once. Wilder had signed the telegram with the name of her editorial director. Algonquin bell captain Tony Cichiello remembers that three-quarters of the mail addressed to Wilder had to do with the Audubon Society, "Save the Seals" or the whales or the mongoose: "Wherever there was a cause to help, there he was." Marian McPartland once visited the Chicago Zoo to see two polar bears she helped to support as a zoo parent: "The zoo had a great big board up with the names of dozens of various creatures and supporters, and to my astonishment Alec's name was up there. I said, my God, there he is again. He was donating money for the upkeep of a grass mouse among other things."

One way or another, Wilder was always involved. Rochester attorney and veteran bird-watcher Thomas M. Hampson was once struck by the melodic lines in a song Wilder had composed for McPartland. He told Wilder that the song sounded like the call of the olive-backed thrush: "He was nonplussed, a condition in which I can never recall having seen him in our many times together after that." Wilder exacted a promise from Hampson to take him to hear the thrush when he returned in the spring. "I did, and he was very pleased. More particularly, he said, 'I'll be damned, you're right.'" There were other birding expeditions. Although he had not studied bird calls and could not identify many birds by song alone, his sharp ears made Wilder a quick learner: "He sorted the birds out in a hurry. I especially remember his enthusiasm for a field full of bobolinks which we found along Lake Ontario one May day."

Wilder in turn introduced Hampson to the books of his beloved Robert Ardrey, whose *Territorial Imperative* tells how important territory is to birds, animals, and people alike. Hampson and Wilder put that idea to good use one year when they took a portable tape recorder to a swamp near Scottsville, New York, and used it to play the call of the Virginia rail from a spot along the road adjacent to the swamp. "The Virginia rail," says Hampson, "is a highly secretive bird which is almost impossible to see because it spends its entire life skulking about the cattails and marsh grass. Yet as soon as we played the call of what to him appeared to be another rail intruding on his territory, the bird walked right out of the swamp to within three feet of us and began pecking away at the tape recorder." Wilder was highly entertained.

No one ever knew what compass point Wilder would come from next. He once wrote to Sibley Watson about a visit he had made to an Alabama prison full of first offenders. The work being done to rehabilitate them and to remove the taint of punishment was, he said, extraordinary—unexpected in any prison, but particularly so in a southern prison. The warden, the guards, and the trustees all shared an enlightened attitude. The illiterate prisoners were being educated so that their high school graduations would be accepted by the outside school system. They were ravenous for knowledge, but the library was pathetically small, so that any book on any subject that Watson could make available would be joyfully welcomed.

He wrote again to Watson about a black family he had befriended in Georgia. Although quite capable of common white and majority prejudice toward both blacks and Jews as groups, he seemed to have no hesitation about embracing individuals. He told Watson that he had helped this black father from time to time through the years. He was a man whose luck had never been good, "who is a dedicated parent, temperate, a religious, tender, unaggressive and gracious man." Now he had been given six months to live, and Wilder's desire, he said, was to see that he died with the single comfort that his family would at least have a home and furniture: "His oldest boy has turned in his small savings [in the hope of college] and is working, as is his wife. Anything you can do will, God knows, ease his agony, and his wife's panic and my profound sorrow." Wilder did not leave it to Watson to do all the helping, but gave generously enough to see the oldest boy through college, as he had once helped poor students through Eastman School.

Wilder was always stirring the pot, and just as he opened the gate to many kinds of music, so did he mix with many kinds of people. Although he was never an intimate, he was often part of the group that gathered around playwright Tennessee Williams in Key West, a place he liked for its down-at-heel charm. Most of Wilder's ties there originated with Bradley Saunders, a nephew of Lavinia Russ's. One friend led to another. Physician William Ploss had treated Saunders and had become known to Wilder. Lemuel Ayers, the producer and designer for *See the Jaguar*, for which Wilder had written the incidental music, and his wife, Shirley, who was close to Wilder, visited often. Ayers and playwright Williams knew each other well.

But it was architect Dan Stirrup whom Wilder most liked to visit in Key West. The two men were good companions. Wilder wrote a great deal of music at Stirrup's house, as well as at the library and at the Atlantic Shores Motel where he usually stayed. They ate together every night Wilder was in town, at Stirrup's house, at a restaurant, sometimes at Tennessee Williams's place. Life around Williams was often turbulent. On the surface at least, Wilder and Williams maintained a good relationship, but Stirrup remembers a time when Wilder became angry and composed a series of brilliant black lyrics about Williams and his family to the tune of *Hello, Dolly*. He went on writing them for months. "They were devastating," says Stirrup. Although far from being unredeemedly salacious, the lyrics contain some of that small-boy lavatory-humor writing to which Wilder was prone and that seemed so much at odds with the elegant, civilized facade he presented to the world most of the time. This was always a puzzlement to Stirrup, as it was to others. This outwardly refined, distinguished gentleman had an eye for the lurid and for the explicit.

Perhaps the only shadow across the Key West sun was the death of Bradley Saunders, whose last days were spent in a coma at the U. S. Naval Hospital. Stirrup remembers that Wilder was very bitter about life's raw deal to Saunders. He would go out in the morning to the bars and order a water glass of gin. Frances Miller was visiting at the time, and the three of them would go to the hospital to visit Saunders. "The place was full of captains and old retired admirals," says Stirrup:

> We were all standing there this day when one of the admirals came along and Alec stuck out his foot to trip him. I was appalled. "Alec, why did you do that?" Well, he explained, at a time when Saunders was dying in midlife, the old admiral had no right to be still full of life. The next day when we visited again, the admiral saw us coming down the hall and promptly turned and went the other way.

That was one of the few occasions when Wilder visited a sickbed. Rogers Brackett was one of Wilder's dearest friends, but when Brackett was dying of cancer in California, Wilder could never bring himself to go to his side. Ethan Ayer, who did so much for Brackett at the end, went out with James Maher just to be there with him. Wilder never went. He also once deeply offended Terry Davidson, the wife of Charlie Davidson, the genial proprietor of the Andover Shop, the men's clothing store on Garden Street in Cambridge. It was he who gave Wilder his trademark flannels-and-tweeds appearance. When Davidson had a serious throat operation in 1964, he and his wife had phone calls and cards and inquiries from everyone from everywhere. Wilder, who had been a guest in their home many times, was the only one they never heard from. "I thought it was unbelievable," says Terry Davidson, "that everyone Charlie had ever known either called or wrote or said something to his mother, and yet someone I considered to be a very good friend couldn't even acknowledge that Charlie was ill."

If Terry and Wilder didn't kiss and make up after that, they did pick up, for Wilder's presence and impact were impossible to deny. Whenever he was in Cambridge, Wilder was almost an institution at the Andover Shop, sitting there on the inside steps where he could see all the people, making endless phone calls on the line that Davidson had reserved for him, not paying for the calls but quickly picking up the check in restaurants. The Davidsons, however, always had to be alert to Wilder's meddling tendencies, for he would often drive spikes between men and women, husbands and wives. He would stir up marital confrontations where there had been none, and he would exploit confrontations where they already existed. With sly subtleties, he might also encourage divorce, and then run.

Even in the securest of households where there was no marital discord, his friends, particularly the wives of his friends, often had to survive some tough tests.

No household was more enlivened by Wilder than that of Loonis and Nan McGlohon in Charlotte. Yet the early going was made rough for Nan McGlohon by Wilder's habit of relegating wives to a corner. In many cases, though not in all, he resented their infringment on his time with their husbands and treated them accordingly, sometimes as maidservants, sometimes as nonentities. Nan McGlohon became very tired of being greeted and treated as "Mrs. Mumble Mumble." Wilder's rudeness made her feel that there was something wrong with her, that she was somehow giving offense to him. It was a tremendous relief to her when she got talking with Zena Hampson, the wife of Thomas Hampson, and with Helen Ouzer, wife of Louis Ouzer, and learned that she was not alone in her experience with Wilder.

Ouzer's daughter, Sandy, remembers that typically in the early days Wilder would mostly ignore Helen. If Lou was not home when he called, Wilder would leave a message with Sandy but would say nothing to her mother. Sandy resented his rudeness, but she says that Wilder gradually developed respect for Helen: "His clearest admission of that was when he started taking books to Helen as well as to Lou." He had to be persuaded. Nancy Watson Dean says Wilder suspected her of golddigging when she became Sibley Watson's second wife. But, she adds, when he became aware of her genuine feeling for Watson, and when he saw how she had been able to coax him out of his withdrawals and silences, he changed his mind. He wrote and told her so.

Wilder was not always fair in his judgments. He told Bill Engvick that John Barrows's absences from home were because his first wife Pat was a poor housekeeper. "Not true," says Engvick. "She was a dedicated housekeeper who cleaned, painted and worked on the house constantly. She was also a marvelous cook, and loved to entertain." Part of the problem was that Wilder was always at war with himself about women. On the one hand he was a misogynist, and yet many of his closest friends were women, notably Lavinia Russ and Frances Miller. He tended to throw some of the blame on the demands of creativity. "It's lonely stuff"—you had to give up a lot of friendly moments. The creative art, he said, was enormously rewarding, but it was lonely. He had stayed away from the intimate world because his first love was music. "I can't really share it."

But for those who were prepared to stay the course, who were willing to accept the fact that Wilder would never be housebroken, an understanding was usually arrived at. There was, after all, much to admire about this paradoxical man who was snobbish enough to run his fingers over business cards to see if they were embossed and yet had no hesitation in turning down invitations that would be coveted by most. Nan McGlohon remembers being asked by him how he should respond to a formal invitation he had received. She told him that if his presence had been requested at such and such a function, then he should reply in the same formal way, by saying that he sincerely regretted he could not attend. He should use the same vernacular. And where, she asked, had the invitation come from? From the White

House, Wilder said, in the form of an invitation to dinner with President Johnson (October 10, 1963). No, said Wilder, he had no intention of attending: "I don't give a damn about eating barbecue off Lenox china."

President Truman was a different matter, a man to be admired. One evening at dinner Nan McGlohon asked Wilder who, among all the people he had never met, he would most like to meet. Wilder said he regretted that Montaigne, the French philosopher, had lived in another age, for he was one of his heroes and someone he would like to have known. Among the living, he said that Pablo Casals, whom he had met, was probably the greatest living human being. The discussion moved to Schweitzer and Grandma Moses, and then Wilder asked Loonis McGlohon who his hero was: "I said Harry Truman. This was just after he had left the presidency. Alec then asked me, 'Have you told him?' I said, 'No, I don't think Mr. Truman is holding his breath to hear from me.' Alec promptly told me: 'You're wrong. He wants to hear from you. He wants to know that you admire him.'" Then Wilder went into a long harangue about people never being too busy or too important to be told that they're admired. After being plagued for days by Wilder, McGlohon finally wrote to Truman. "It was a very short note explaining about Alec and heroes and Casals, and it concluded: 'So, this, Mr. Truman, is to let you know that you are my hero and to get Alec Wilder off my back.'" Truman answered immediately, saying: "Mr. Wilder is correct. You should always let those people know that you admire them or their work." He also told McGlohon that Wilder might be correct in believing that Casals was the greatest living human." Said McGlohon later about this incident: "That's the quality I loved about Alec. He would always take time to tell people he loved them."

But Wilder himself was often not an easy person to like. Even his best friends had to suffer through his lapses. Physician Ploss says that, initially, his coarse approach to personal relationships ("his directness and honesty") delayed his wife Lois's acceptance of Wilder's personality. "He was in a phase of intermittent dependence on alcohol, during which (all of us who knew him understood) he *was* difficult to like. His total acceptance, indeed our deep love for him, and for all his idiosyncrasies and inconsistencies, was complete for years before his death." His friends kept on loving him because they sensed and respected his genius. Wilder, James Maher has said,

> was one of those marvelous people who had a profound effect on others.
> . . . Those of us who were close to him were drawn to him because, and
> this is the key to the whole thing as far as I'm concerned, he was a very tal-
> ented, a gifted man. He had a rare gift, and his gift was melody. Alec was a
> singer. He was always the poet in that sense, the lyric sense. He somehow in
> his life, and this was of his own nature I imagine, became a sort of protector
> of certain central traditional values.

Friends and musicians close to him understood that Wilder saw music as a trust not to be betrayed. Music critic Richard Freed once went to the essence of it in the course of noting what Gunther Schuller had said about Wilder's unique style, the absence of clichés, the honest sentiment. "What could not be further defined," said Freed, "came to be represented by his name itself, early in his career as a song composer. 'Alec Wilder' meant sophistication, in the very best sense; it meant urbanity, craftsmanship, taste, discipline, originality, genuineness—and never, never sham or mere cleverness."

And he gave to his friends the same undivided attention that he gave to music. Balliett and Maher and others have told how intensely Wilder went about the business of listening to performers. His head was usually down, sometimes his back was turned, and always his eyes were closed. Totally attentive listening was the key to his critical judgment about music, and it was also the best of all the gifts he gave to his friends. They, too, of course had to pay attention. Douglas Colby, grandson of the former owner of the Algonquin Hotel, Ben Bodne, can vouch for the fact that conversation always had to be given its full measure of weight and respect. Colby, who had known Wilder since he was a child and looked on him as virtually a parental figure, had dinner with him at the Algonquin almost every night Wilder was in residence. Colby says his own mind is apt to go off on a tangent at times, and when that happened one night at dinner he missed something Wilder was saying and had to ask him to repeat it. Said Wilder solemnly: "A conversation, Douglas, is not a smorgasbord." You had to pay attention.

In music as in life, Wilder was demanding and persuasive. "We who worked with him felt a greater range of elation and frustration," says William Engvick. "One worked with him or in spite of him, but always because of him." He always seemed to understand what his collaborators wanted to say, and "with his charm and irresistible, if not juggernaut, persuasion, he made us outdo ourselves." And, adds Engvick, the laughter he generated was a bonus: "A clutch of his goofy songs, like *Badlands, You've Been Good to Me,* and *How Can I Long for Your Sweet Return When You're Sitting on My Lap?,* have made me happy for a long time." The search for quality was the key to it all. It made no difference how the music was flagged.

Engvick had it right when he noted that Wilder made no distinction whatsoever between excellence in the idiom, popular or classic: "Excellence is, to him, quality of intent, genuiness of statement. Dislike of social and musical sham leads him to label most of his works 'Piece' and he attaches no explanations, no dates. If a title is insisted on, he is likely to affix one like 'Mama Never Dug This Scene,' or something less printable."

Wilder was always his own man. In Schuller's words, "Despite the odds for a very broad or deep acceptance always being against him, Alec never, never gave up his quest for what he believed in." If that entailed tilting at windmills, so be it. He was unrepentantly defiant, saying for example about grand climaxes, "Anybody can write a double forte." He himself would sooner be a master of intensity. The biggest climaxes of his life, he said, had been a silence, somebody walking out of the room, a whispered goodbye.

Wilder carried his pursuit of excellence beyond selfish interests. In instrumental writing, for example, he was concerned to embrace players of every station. Clarinetist Glenn Bowen made that point in the program notes for a concert of the Madison Symphony Orchestra that included a performance of Wilder's *Concerto for Clarinet and Chamber Orchestra* (1973). After referring to the colorful orchestration, especially the richness in each instrumental family, he went on to say: "I would also draw attention to Alec's concern for individual performers in the orchestra; there are lovely soloist passages for players of second and third parts who are sadly neglected most of the time. The concept of a large chamber music ensemble is enhanced by this thoughtful technique."

At the same time, Wilder showed little mercy in the technical demands of his writing. He noted at one point about a woodwind quintet sought by Art Dedrick of Kendor Music for the Fredonia College faculty quintet that Dedrick had asked him not to take the horn above a high concert D: "So I didn't. But God help the hornist all the rest of the time." Wilder liked the challenge of it all. Writing to Harvey Phillips about a new piece,

God knows what music from the Gobi desert sounds like but at least, damnit, I've finished it. The berceuse is simply that, an uncomplicated bone simple melody. The last movement should go like a bat out of hell and just maybe it will work. If the last three octave F at the end is too hard to grab, forget it. I kind of like it if it's possible only because the trapdoor opens and the audience is dropped into the river.

Wilder did not hesitate to take to task those performers he felt had messed up one of his pieces. This happened more often with popular singers, for his songs were more often recorded and played than his so-called serious music. McGlohon played for him one night a recording Wilder had not heard before of Jack Jones singing *While We're Young*. Wilder jumped to his feet when he heard a wrong note, demanded that the record be stopped, went at once to the phone, and called someone in California to ask that a message be passed to Mr. Jones:

Tell him I just had the misfortune of hearing his recording of *While We're Young*. Tell him if he had not known the song, he should have listened to the band, because they played it correctly. I understand he's thinking of doing an album. If you get this message to him, that will probably do that in, and I shan't care because I would like my songs treated with a little more respect than he showed.

Again, according to McGlohon, Wilder reacted just as fiercely to an interpretation of one of his songs by Fran Warren, a singer in the big band era who became a Broadway star doing *Pajama Game* and other shows, and who then became a fine solo performing artist. She had made a record for RCA Victor, *The Great American Composers,* in which she had chosen her five favorites, including Harold Arlen, Richard Rodgers, and Alec Wilder. All were living at the time. She heard from two of them: Arlen and Wilder. Arlen expressed his gratitude for what he felt was a nice job, but Wilder sailed into Warren for the way she had sung his song *Who Can I Turn To?,* saying she had sung wrong notes and left out one important suspension. He carried on in these terms:

> You know, you could have done one of several things. (1) You could have called the publisher and he would gladly have sent you free of charge a professional copy. (2) You could have called me and I would gladly have sent you a copy free of charge. (3) You could have bought a copy of the music for 85 cents at any music shop. (4) You could have listened to any one of thirteen recordings done before yours, and correctly I might add.

That was rough treatment even by Wilder's stickler standards. But he waved the same banner of vigilance over everybody's music. As noted by Marian McPartland in *Down Beat,* it was not only his own songs he worried about: "He is as much a watch dog about the songs of other composers."

Wilder was also willing to give a leg up to promising new performers, as he did with those two sophisticated vocal professionals Jackie Cain and Roy Kral. Jackie first sang in public when she was five. In the 1940s she joined Charlie Ventura's Bop for the People combo, and there met arranger-pianist-singer Kral, who would become her husband. In Chicago, Jackie and Roy met Rogers Brackett, who became both admirer and friend. Later in New York, Brackett set up a meeting with Wilder in Sarah Churchill's apartment, to which he had the key while she was out of town. Says Jackie: "We were introduced to this tweedy-looking man. We were thrilled to meet him. We had always admired his music, so when we met him we were in awe." It was a beautiful, spacious apartment. A parakeet was flying around. Brackett asked them if they would please sing a few songs. "We said we would. There was a little spinet piano and we got around it. But Alec crossed the room and sat down with his back to us. And we thought, gee, that's strange. It kind of mystified us. None of us said anything, but in our minds we were saying, why is he turning his back on us?" Adds Roy:

> We started doing some things and when we finished a song, all we would hear from Alec was, OH NO, OH NO. We thought he didn't like us, didn't care for us. Here I was playing the piano and on top of the piano is a family photograph. And who is it? Sarah and her parents, Winston Churchill and Clemen-

tine. My God, I said to myself, Alec Wilder and Winston Churchill in the same room. I almost died.

Both singers were in a state of shock, because of the setting and because of Wilder's reactions.

It turned out, however, that that was his way of saying he loved what he was hearing. He had turned his back the better to listen. The OH NO meant OH YES. Once he knew what they were capable of, Wilder felt that the singers should be working in some of the New York supper clubs, and he said he would try to set up an audition with Max Gordon and Herb Jacobi of the Blue Angel. An audition was arranged; Jackie and Roy drove in from their home in New Jersey and landed a job.

Wilder's exhortations and enthusiasms took many forms. Marian McPartland remembers that he would go to The Cookery practically every night for a period in the early 1970s to hear Jimmy Rowles:

> Alec wanted to see Jimmy Rowles recorded. I had my little record company, Halcyon. I had recorded a couple of little pieces Alec wrote for me. "Why don't you record Jimmy Rowles? I'll put up the money for the record date." Which he did. He gave me a couple of thousand dollars, and as soon as I got it back [from the recording] I gave it back to him.

The encouragement he gave to musicians who met his standards often sustained them for a long time. Jimmy McPartland valued dearly a letter Wilder wrote to him about the way he had played a set one night at the Carlyle:

> I've heard you play many times and always pleasurably. But the other night a whole new world opened up. Your ideas were looser, wittier, warmer, more complex, more elegant, both harmonically and melodically, than I've ever heard. It was as if you had crossed a bridge you had never dreamed of setting foot on. And you sounded safe and sound on the other side.

He was not a performer, he added, and all improvisation was a miracle to him. "But I do know how to listen. And what I heard was a new dimension, a new landscape, a new comet! Alec." Marian McPartland herself has often carried around with her as reassurance a faded letter from Wilder in which he cited and praised all her fine qualities and talents. Says McPartland today: "I wonder if he knew how much that letter would mean to me, how I'd look it over when I get depressed and insecure, and decide maybe I wasn't so bad after all!"

Over the years, musicians developed enormous respect for Wilder. They began to talk about him in the same reverent way the English used to talk about the royal family. Whitney Balliett defined his unique place as a standard-bearer in a note to his book *Alec Wilder and His Friends*. There he painted ten portraits of singers, musicians, composers, and comedians—all artists holding "a common vision of life that has lately fallen low. They are highly moral people who have guarded their souls, who have, no matter how bad the going, refused to compromise." He went on to say: "One more bond holds this small aristocracy together—Alec Wilder. He is their unofficial spokesman. The high standards he lives are theirs. The virtues he voices so eloquently they voice in their own timbres and tones. He is their symbolic ringleader, their touchstone." Balliett noted that until his appearance, "full-length and rampant," in the final chapter, Wilder was everywhere in the book—"evaluating, chastising, cheering, listening, talking. Mabel Mercer and Tony Bennett and Blossom Dearie sing his beautiful songs and Marian McPartland and Marie Marcus and Bobby Hackett and Ruby Braff honor them with embellishments and improvisations."

By the 1970s, even before that, Wilder's integrity was legendary. Accompanist and concert pianist Milton Kaye, and Kaye's wife, singer Shannon Bolin, were both attracted by the pure way he looked at music. Although they did not see him much—"he would come in bunches"—they had many long talk sessions. Says Kaye:

> One of the things I loved, because it's a reaction I had too, though not as
> positively as he did, is that when he sensed something shoddy or dishonest
> by way of a piece of writing, he was vehement. It was as if the Holy Grail
> had been defiled. That's a wonderful attitude. It was not that his was the only
> way to hear it, but to the degree he heard anything that seemed dishonest,
> he was quick to accuse.

Singer Barbara Lea remembers that Wilder "was quite fierce in a wonderful way. He loved the music that he loved fiercely, and he was fiercely against stuff that was not up to par, that was second or third rate and pretentious." Very properly to her mind, he took great umbrage that inferior music should be promoted and allowed to exist, and of course was deeply hurt that very inferior things would crowd out the good music that was around: "Not only his music. In fact, he seemed to make a point of not letting his ego get in the way. . . . He was pushing for quality in music, not just his, and in lyrics. He was the defender of the faith, not the only defender but one of the main ones."

That faith was clearly defined by Wilder in the course of telling Whitney Balliett that his list of "believers" was not very long, but that those who were on it were special people. Among them, certainly, he said, was singer Tony Bennett:

> But first I should say what I mean by a believer. He is one whose sights stay
> high, who makes as few concessions as he can, whose ideals will not permit
> him to follow false trails or fashions for notoriety's or security's sake, who
> takes chances, who seeks to convey, by whatever means, his affections and
> convictions, and who has faith in the power of beauty to survive, no matter
> how much squalor and ugliness seek to suppress it.

When a performer met his litmus test, Wilder would go to limitless trouble to further his cause. In 1972 he went to bat for pianist Ellis Larkins, telling the world in a page-long article in *Down Beat* that the artist was alive and well—living in New York and playing at Gregory's bar on First Avenue and East 63rd Street. Wilder had first heard Larkins some thirty years before: "I was at some gathering when a soft-spoken young man sat down at the piano—at the suggestion of John Hammond, the discoverer and champion of many talented musicians." Wilder liked the fact that Larkins played not only with taste and authority but without aggressiveness or bravura.

Larkins, he said, laid down a truth as old as art: "creating order, continuity, balance, euphony, reasoned dissonance, warmth, wit and profound love." In the intervening years, Larkins had apparently traveled a long and lonely road. Now he was back, and his special talent was casting "its lovely light over a small corner of the darkening world." Added Wilder: "His wit, manifested in interpolated phrases, is irresistible and his blues walk you right on down the aisle. His ballads are rich without being cloying and his up tunes are danced in felt slippers with an almost audible smile. Can you blame me for loving him?"

Wilder's idealism was beautifully expressed in his one-act opera *The Truth about Windmills,* which had its premiere performance in Avon, New York, in 1973. From beginning to end, this was an act of love, undertaken with no thought of financial return. Some time before, Arnold Sundgaard had written a tender libretto about two men and a woman who live in an old folks' home. They make toy windmills, wooden ducks, and mittens and sell them—more as an excuse to get together—to passersby and at a nearby bus stop. Then the bus begins stopping at a new location farther down the hill, and people no longer pass by. But the three old folk keep meeting anyway, and they are given new hope when the eight-year-old daughter of the home's new cook stops by to get acquainted and offers to take the windmills, the ducks, and mittens in her red wagon and sell them at the new bus stop.

Sundgaard, according to Wilder, had submitted the opera to Schirmer, which had already published those four short operas of theirs: "It was given short shrift on the grounds that no audience wants to see or hear an opera about old people." Wilder himself had found the libretto enormously loving and moving—the best Sundgaard had done, he felt—but realized it would probably have little hope in the "fat cat marketplace." Knowing the expense of copying the parts as well as the unlikelihood of its ever being given even a tryout, he kept putting off setting it to music. He was influenced, too, by all the other pieces he had written and never heard. Then early in 1973 he received word that Sundgaard had had a heart attack and was feeling down. What could he do? Send books, flowers, desperately cheerful letters? No, he concluded, the only thing he could do honorably as a friend, and the one thing that might cheer him up, was to write the music for *The Truth About Windmills.*

Wilder jumped into the task. Now it mattered not at all that the opera could never be a winner. From the start he did not want the first performance to take place in the city, for the opera's simplicity and gentleness, its absence of sophistication and "significance," made it unsuitable in his opinion for an urban audience. So why not Avon, a lovely rural spot, the site of *The Children's Plea for Peace,* and the domain of his beloved Father Henry Atwell of Saint Agnes Church? Wilder made a call to old friend Milford Fargo, Eastman School professor of music education, and told him about Sundgaard: "Some time ago he gave me this incredibly tender, gentle libretto. I want to set it for him to make him feel better." Wilder's enthusiasm drew a warm response. All who were asked climbed willingly on board: Fargo; the four talented singers (William Briggs, John Maloy, Virginia McConnell, Irene Stumberger); the scenic designer for the Eastman Opera Department, who agreed to make and install the set at cost; the director of Eastman Operas, who agreed to direct it for a token sum; and the instrumentalists, friends of Wilder who all were, or had been recently, first-chair players in the Rochester Philharmonic Orchestra.

That was the kind of rallying around that Wilder inspired. Father Atwell even agreed to rearrange the church bingo night so that room could be made for the opera in the school hall. Wilder was there for all the rehearsals, and, according to Fargo, good to have available. This labor of love showed the quintessential Wilder at work—breathing life into a gentle little opera whose premiere might also be its last performance, knowing it could never succeed in a larger arena, backing up Sundgaard's willingness to tackle such a subject, persuading everyone to do it for love, creating in the countryside a brief shining moment that would always be remembered by the few who were privileged to be a part of it. Wilder's standard-bearing was not an abstract thing. In music, his hand was always close to the plow, and the furrows ran true.

·‖16

The Final Years

In January 1974, just three months after the sweet savor of *The Truth About Windmills,* Wilder was chilled by the death at age sixty of John Barrows, his most cherished colleague and friend. That was the day he began measuring his own mortality. Although he would keep on composing right up to his own death in 1980— for the creative springs could never be long denied—the bouts of depression would occur more often and some of his more serious music would take on darker tones. More than anyone else, Barrows had opened to him the world of classical music and, more than anyone else, had persuaded him that he was indeed a composer worthy of the name.

Wilder made no premature surrender. He said defiantly at one point that he was damned if he would ever live in "one of those ghastly complexes for the euphemistic senior citizens." He had snorted mightily on the day he received a cheerful ("can you imagine it, cheerful!") form letter from the government telling him he would soon be eligible for Medicare: "I burned it in the scrap basket and caused consternation amongst the hotel maids who had smelled the smoke." Yet he knew the sun would not again shine as brightly as it had. The saddest element of old age, he said, "is the realization that the cement has hardened, that the party's over, that the age of miracles is past. Though there are compensations to old age, the end of magic makes creation that much more difficult." He would say to Marian McPartland's sister in England, Joyce Armitage, that it was not death that depressed him as a final macabre birthday party. "It's all the restricting, the slowing elements of old age, the ailments, the bad backs, the fading senses . . . ARGGH!!!"

Several things contributed to the gathering gloom: Wilder's drinking, his failing financial resources, and his declining health. For much of the sixties and for the early part of the seventies, he had, by most accounts, stayed sober. Indeed, he said in 1972 that he was quite sure his drinking days were over for good. In fact, they were not. The battle was never finally won. The testimony of his friends—and his enemies!—leaves no doubt that he was an alcoholic. Though painfully honest about his drinking, he was never able to use or accept the word *alcoholic*. He was never able to make that last leveling with himself. It's not clear what caused him to fall off the wagon in the 1970s. There seemed to be no one triggering event but rather a combination of things: age, health, the loss of close friends, the gathering conviction that his music was more than ever unfashionable, the squalor of the times as he saw them, loneliness, and the loss of affluence.

Wilder made plain his financial plight in several letters to Sibley Watson in July through September of 1974. He wanted to know at one point if Watson would mind if he kept his check uncashed in his pocket for a while, for that somehow made him feel less frightened: "I'm damn well going to try to avoid cashing it if only to show you that I'm stronger than water." And then a little sadly: "I *have* tried to do good work and I *have* tried to be a good man! Solemnly I swear it." He said in a following letter that he might try to live more frugally for a time by staying with a friend on Catalina Island. Wilder also told Watson that he would like to keep for a time a second check he had sent him, so that he could use it if necessary as partial repayment of a $5,000 grant toward an orchestral piece for the Rochester Philharmonic. He was afraid he might not be able to write it.

In spite of his despondency, Wilder was still capable of rising to a challenge. Old friend Harvey Phillips, now professor of tuba at Indiana University, had had a dream of massing four hundred tubas all in one place, all playing Christmas songs. In November of 1974 he started planning for a massed performance on December 22 on the ice rink of New York City's Rockefeller Center. "I called Alec in Rochester and told him I needed twenty Christmas carols and could he please arrange them." Wilder said he could not promise anything, for he was still feeling the pain of Barrows's death and was having trouble writing. Yet the very next day, he called Phillips, told him he had been up all night and had arranged twenty-two carols for massed tubas. That was the first of the massed-tuba concerts that have become a Christmas institution around the country.

Sometimes Wilder half believed in what he was composing; at other times he felt that little of it was worthy, for the world kept moving away from him and what he believed in. He found himself envying composers such as Warren Benson and Bernard Heiden, who, he said, could not write dishonestly if they tried and who yet moved into "marvelous waters which to me are uncharted and unswimmable." Being to a great extent, he maintained, "an untrained, untaught musician," he was sometimes unsure of his technical ground yet determined to live by his sense of what was honest and trustworthy. The act of creation was what counted, no matter how the pieces turned out: "Naturally I felt better if the piece was admired by someone I respected, but even the pieces which were duds were a great joy to write. Joy? Each piece was a sweaty, harrowing experience, and yet each one was as close to fulfillment as I'll ever get."

Creation was indeed the stuff of life, and just occasionally he confessed to feeling pleased with what he had written. "Damn it," he told Watson in August of 1975, "I *am* a better composer than I've always thought I wasn't. I've decided that much of what I've written *is music* and *worthy* of honestly listening ears." He listed some of the things he had composed that year: a five-movement orchestra piece, a five-movement brass quintet, a five-movement woodwind quintet, six pieces for unaccompanied flute, six pieces for unaccompanied French horn, six clarinet duets, one movement for flute, cello, and piano, a second tuba and piano sonata, and ten songs in the "popular" idiom.

Those popular songs ran like a thread through half a century, including the last decade of his life. In 1973 the three-act musical comedy *Nobody's Earnest* (book by Sundgaard) that premiered in Williamstown, Massachusetts, carried a score of Wilder songs. The lyrics for the songs were supplied by Ethan Ayer, the friend with whom Wilder often stayed. The ten songs he said he wrote in 1975 undoubtedly included several from *Western Star* (book and lyrics by Sundgaard), the revised version of the 1948 production *The Wind Blows Free*. Among the independent songs from 1975 were *My Kind of Blues* (with McGlohon writing the music in this case and Wilder the lyric).

The next year, 1976, produced at least a dozen freestanding songs. Four particularly are worth noting. McGlohon supplied the lyrics for two of them, *Where's the Child I Used to Hold?* and *Blackberry Winter,* and Johnny Mercer for two, *The Sounds Around the House* and *If Someday Comes Ever Again.* Mercer was a superb lyricist who collaborated often with Harold Arlen, another Wilder favorite. Wilder has noted that Mercer and Arlen wrote together for the first time in the 1941 movie *Blues in the Night:*

> This made for a very felicitous collaboration. They were not only two men
> who had been professional singers but they were profound lovers of jazz. Besides which, and most important, their love of the lonely and sentimental, the
> witty and the warm and the bittersweet, all part of the ethos of popular music, tended to make them work together like a single mind.

Wilder also said that in at least one of their songs, *One for My Baby,* the honors had to go to the lyric, marvelous though the musical setting was: "I've lived this story too many times, in too many towns, with too many long, long roads outside those doors, not to be hooked. Just imagine having the acuity and courage to start a song, as Mercer does, with 'It's quarter to three'!"

If Someday Comes Ever Again is an exquisite little song that deserves to be better known. In the TRO songbook *Songs by Alec Wilder Were Made to Sing,* Wilder says about the origin of it that in the course of interviewing lyric writers for his *American Popular Song,* he gathered the courage to ask Mercer if he would consider writing a lyric to a melody he had just finished. To his surprise, Mercer asked him to play the melody on tape. Wilder did so, and added a second melody: "The first one he sent me the lyric of shortly afterwards but there was no response to the second one. None, that is, for three years. Then without any warning appeared in the mail this dear, gentle, sad lyric. I love it but till now no one has sung or played it. I think it deserves a better fate." The song is included in the TRO songbook. "That's a healthy beginning," said Wilder at the time. "The Richmond Organization believed in it as I do." Mary Mayo sang it in one of the NPR *Popular Song* series; saxophonist David Demsey recorded it as an instrumental number; and soprano Eileen Farrell included it in her Wilder song album.

If Someday Comes Ever Again also caught the attention of Michael Lasser, the host since 1980 of the NPR program *Fascinatin' Rhythm,* winner of a George Foster Peabody Award in 1995. It explores the history and themes of American popular music through a series of radio essays illustrated by recordings. (Rochester's Public Television station, WXXI, originates the program.) Lasser, an independent-day-school teacher of English who has also taught the history of popular song at the university level, played the Farrell recording in his 1992 Wilder program. Mercer, he said, wrote with his typical sense of humor deepened with a sense of time passing: "In this song, the lapse of time makes it possible for dreams to come true. Wilder provides Mercer with a melody that matches the lyric in wit, buoyancy, and a darker tone beneath. The result is a tiny song that makes you wish they had collaborated often."

The other Wilder-Mercer collaboration was *The Sounds Around the House.* As with *If Someday Comes Ever Again,* it remains one of Wilder's lesser-known songs. It has been recorded by singers Dick Haymes and Helen Merrill (with pianist Roland Hanna), but by few others. However, in his informed analysis in 1987, Mark Tucker took the song to his heart, both for the melody and for the lyric. He identified what was best about Wilder's songwriting: "Vance Bourjaily has written about the power of old popular songs to 'stir memory, revive hope, promise beauty'; in *The Sounds Around the House,* a song neither old nor popular, Alec Wilder achieves these goals with composerly craft, and with a loving, gentle spirit all too rare in the music of our age."

Wilder had worked long distance with Mercer, and he had often collaborated via phone with Engvick, Sundgaard, and, in the later years, with McGlohon, who became quite skilled in telephone songwriting: "Alec wanted to write all the time. That was his life. He would ask me to send a lyric and he'd call and say he had a tune for it. He expected you to have a piece of manuscript right there by the phone to take it down—because he was by now very impatient to get your reaction to it." So they developed a shorthand style of songwriting. Wilder might say, "This tune is in the key of F and in $\frac{4}{4}$ time." He would call out the notes: "and the next are four eighth notes—they're D, F, B-flat, C, then 2 quarter notes and they're A, G." Wilder would dictate a whole song that way, and McGlohon would write it on the score he was working from, his own score, or a piece of paper or whatever he had at hand. "And some of them were really disreputable scraps of paper. Then he'd fill in the harmony and ask me to go to the piano and play it and call him back."

In the case of their 1976 collaborations, Wilder was more often than not in the McGlohon home. *Where's the Child I Used to Hold?* had an interesting genesis. On the day daughter Lauri went off to college, the McGlohons drove her to Greensboro, about a hundred miles away. Wilder stayed home to write music. When the McGlohons returned, they were feeling some pangs; for the first time in years, they had no child in the house. As soon as they entered the door, Wilder grabbed McGlohon and propelled him to the piano, saying "I've got a wonderful song." McGlohon would sooner have had a cup of coffee or a drink, but Wilder was in full flood. "No, no, I want you to hear this. It needs a really crazy lyric. It's a love song." What kind of love song? Wilder said he was not exactly sure but perhaps there would be a list of things "you're going to take to this girl you're in love with, like polka-dot giraffes, big balloons, purple elephants, crazy things like that." At first McGlohon listened out of politeness, but then found himself captured by the melody. "It's one of the great songs Alec ever wrote." But there was no way he was about to write a lyric about polka-dot giraffes. "Suddenly your home is empty, and I'm drained. If," he told Wilder, "you want me to write a lyric, I'm afraid it'll have to be as a catharsis."

Where's the Child I Used to Hold? has not been widely performed since Dick Haymes sang it, but that is certainly not true for *Blackberry Winter,* another 1976 Wilder-McGlohon collaboration, one set apart by its haunting sixteenth-note motive and its unexpected harmonic and rhythmic progressions. Eileen Farrell, Teddi King, Mabel Mercer, and Marlene VerPlanck, one of the best of the Wilder interpreters, have all recorded it; Mary Mayo and Barbara Lea have sung it in recital; and Joe Wilder and Robert Levy have played it beautifully on the trumpet. Wilder has recalled that he wrote the tune on a day when he was visiting McGlohon and fussing at the piano:

> Something I played pleased him so I worked out the idea into a full length melody. He expressed interest in putting a lyric to it. I was convinced that my rhythmically unconventional devices would seriously hinder any attempt to find adequate words. Not at all. Mr. McGlohon, in his usual impeccable taste, found all the right words even if the phrase "blackberry winter" is unfamiliar to Northerners.

The title, McGlohon has explained, refers to the sudden "cool spell" in the South that comes around the first of June, after the blackberry briars blossom. This unexpected and short "winter" lasts but a few days before warm weather returns to stay. When Wilder first played a fragment of the melody for him, McGlohon recalls, he, Wilder, depreciated it a little, saying, "I know it isn't significant, like one of those pieces you would write and dedicate to Lyndon Johnson's widow, but I do want to hear this phrase of 16th notes again and again." Adds McGlohon: "An hour later we had completed *Blackberry Winter,* and it was one of Alec's favorites." Ronald Prather has praised it as a lovely ballad.

One other song written by Wilder and McGlohon in 1976 should not escape notice. *Be a Child* was introduced by Cleo Laine and later recorded by Eileen Farrell, Teddi King, Mabel Mercer, and Marlene VerPlanck. It is a tender song that tells a child to paint his dreams and go find his special hill, and to do it today lest he grow up too soon. Only the chorus was sung in the first recordings, for the verse had been separated from the original manuscript. McGlohon found the verse later on a small scrap of manuscript.

As Wilder had so often shown with Engvick, notably in *Lullabies and Night Songs,* he seemed to have a passkey to the world of the child. In his radio review of Wilder songs, Lasser coupled Eileen Farrell's interpretation of *Be a Child* with Barbara Lea's singing of an earlier song that Wilder had written with Engvick, *Remember, My Child.* Lasser deemed these two songs to be among his most affecting songs about children: one "a testament from an adult who still feels the loss of his own remembered childhood," and the other "a sympathetic piece of advice to a child to hold onto childhood, itself." In the hands of singers of such sensitivity and lyricists to match, Wilder was able to work his magic. "His sad, almost brooding melodies," says Lasser, "suggestively underscore the intensity of the lyrics' conviction. The music's darker textures suggest an understanding of what children lose. Though deeply felt, the suggestions are gentle and unencumbered, reflecting a deeply felt longing for times gone by."

With such songs as these, Wilder, as he had so often done before, was showing again in 1976 his mastery of the small canvas. Yet he remained ambivalent about that kind of identification, both accepting and rejecting the appellation of miniaturist. Time and again he embraced the small gems of music, just as he preferred the single poppy to a scarlet field. "I have no reverence for mountain climbers or victorious armies," he once wrote, "for accounts of stupendous bravery, nor am I nourished by awesome sights. I'm a mouse writer, and mice seldom listen to me unless I write waltzes." Still, it bothered him that he seemed to be consigned and confined to a cameo role in music. "The public increasingly appalls and disgusts me," he said at one point. "But my sadness is that I'm convinced even my musical friends have, out of affection for me, encouraged my writing while all the while they have found the bulk of the work a child's finger painting. Perhaps I'm greedy to want any more than to have found a way to be less lonely."

James Maher is one musical friend who has never settled for the miniaturist, finger-painting label. The question, he believes, is one of form: Wilder did not have it in his creative nature to embrace the complex thematic developments of the music of the great classical composers. Nor would he have wanted to. But he could climb his own heights as a "pure-gold melodist" with a deeply rooted sense of song: "He did not think in miniature; he thought in song, and there's a difference." It was not a question of small scale, asserts Maher. "It's just that his native skill required a smaller compass for perfect realization." In part perhaps, it's the difference between a skylark ascending and a cloud of flamingoes. The one is soon lost from sight, but the song goes on.

Although Wilder may have disclaimed any ambition to write big orchestral works, he yet seemed to nurse the idea that he might one day break the miniaturist mold. It annoyed him intensely that he could not be taken as a serious composer unless he raised his sights to bigger structures. In 1977, the year after he had written those songs with Mercer and McGlohon, the Rochester Philharmonic Orchestra performed the premiere of what would be his last attempt at a reasonably substantial orchestral piece, *Entertainment No. 6*, commissioned by the New York State Arts Council and composed in 1975. There had been one other such premiere thirty years before, when the RPO in 1947, under conductor Erich Leinsdorf, played his *Piece for Orchestra* (1946). Wilder recalled that Leinsdorf was amused by his diffidence in calling the composition *Piece for Orchestra*. Wilder also said he was so terrified at the thought of having a piece performed by a symphony orchestra that he showed up each morning for rehearsals "totally hung over." The work did not make much of a splash.

Now in 1977, almost three decades later, he was about to hear a second Rochester Philharmonic premiere performance, this one *Entertainment No. 6*. Through all those in-between years, he had done very little in the way of large works: the brief *Suite for String Orchestra* in 1949, the sixteen-minute *Carl Sandburg Suite* in 1960, the thirteen-minute *Entertainment No. 2* in 1966 for the Madison (Wisconsin) Chamber Orchestra, and not much besides. Why did he not do more adventuring with larger forms? Why did this man who crossed so many boundaries not accept this as just one more challenge? He had to know, as Robert Freeman has said, that "if you want to make a go of it as a serious composer, you've got to write some symphonies, a piano concerto, some string quartets so that the critics can say, 'Well, compared with Bartok . . .'" One important reason is that he was intimidated and deterred by the musical establishment of those days. That establishment can be variously defined, but it included in one relationship or another those who make program decisions for the symphony orchestras, agents and arts presenters who book concert series, network radio and recording executives, the critics and the conductors, and the academic establishment that essentially controls the major awards made to composers. Sometimes separately, sometimes together, they constituted a formidable force in the 1940s, '50s, and '60s when Wilder was doing most of his writing.

Author Joseph Horowitz in his *Understanding Toscanini* brilliantly depicted the way in which the music world was cynically manipulated by promotional machines focused on celebrities, by the mass media, by individual powerbrokers such as RCA's

David Sarnoff and Arthur Judson, who managed the New York Philharmonic from 1922 to 1956. Horowitz deplored the rigid, exclusive professional caste of the modern orchestra, pointing out that the amateur musician, once so important in the age of Beethoven and Schubert, had been consigned to the role of spectator. He made this further point:

> Rather than naturally evolving according to their artistic utility, heroically scaled orchestras and opera companies, legacies of the late nineteenth century, evolved according to publicity and marketing strategies, a survival-of-the-fittest competition in which fitness was predicated on the conspicuous visibility and prestige of name-brand dinosaurs.

That kind of world was alien to Wilder. He could not find in it the purity of music-making he had sworn to uphold. Nor, with his wide streak of independence, was he prepared to pay his dues by courting the people who can often make or break a young composer's career. As Freeman has noted, one of Eastman School's concerns is teaching students not only how to write the music but how to get it played, how to get it published, and how to get it into the hands of the people who matter— essentially how a young composer must build his career: "If the young composer doesn't do that, then he's going to be willy-nilly in the situation of someone like Alec, looking in from the outside. Anyone from Rochester has that kind of problem. The power structure is not in Rochester, it's in New York City."

Making friends with the music establishment, knowing who are the people you must invite to your New York debut—that was not the kind of obeisance Wilder was prepared to make. "Alec," Freeman has shrewdly said, "will have felt he was above all that, and there were psychological reasons, too. I think he felt they wouldn't want to listen to what he was saying anyway, and if he steered a wide berth around them, then it would be their fault for not listening." Unlike Arnold Schoenberg, who also detested music's power structure, Wilder was not prepared to mix it up with the enemy. He avoided the battlefield rather than risk dying on it. As Warren Benson has put it, the establishment didn't really freeze him out. "His music eliminated him by choice. He didn't choose to fight the establishment and he wrote what he wanted to write for the people he wanted to write for and who needed his music."

It's Gunther Schuller's belief that Wilder simply gave up on the orchestra, feeling that no conductor or major orchestra would ever play his music: "Whereas it was easy for him to write something for a clarinetist, such as Glenn Bowen. He knew that Glenn would play the sonata, or whatever it was, the next time around. And so he kind of turned off on the orchestral establishment and wrote very little orchestral music." That did not help his stature as a composer. Adds Schuller: "It had the effect of his not being taken very seriously because, frankly, the way it is in this establishment, unless you make a few grand appearances in the orchestral world, you almost don't exist."

Intimacy was also a factor. Wilder was a man of close encounters, an intensely personal composer who liked to hang out with those he wrote his music for. Distrusting the big sweep, he found the truest expression in the chamber groups, the trios, the quartets, the quintets. Here, it was the individual performance that counted. His love of people, he always said, was of the individual person, never the larger group or the crowd. So it was with music. He agreed that every player in an orchestra might be superb, but he thought that the personal intensity got lost in the big sound. Besides, there were too many hiding places for poor composing. He could put his arm around a brass quintet but not an orchestra.

Even had he felt disposed to write for the big combinations, it's not certain that he had the ability to do so. David Demsey, who has played much of his saxophone music and has also studied him as a Wilder co-bio-bibliographer, feels that his natural compositional "voice," the sound that he heard in his head, was the small ensemble. Benson has observed that even Wilder's suites, sonatas, and operas often suffer, "as did Chopin's piano concertos," from being little pieces tied together. When Wilder wrote big pieces, they were made out of the smaller lengths that were the language of pop. "When you write big works," says Benson, "you have to be able to get seams that don't show and you have to use extensive phraseology." It was not, he adds, that Wilder was flawed as a composer. "He was genuine and generous and fearless. He knew the establishment looked down on him. He went ahead anyway. After all, he was writing music for friends, not to win a Guggenheim."

Writing for friends, however, did not adapt itself to orchestral work. Wilder's lack of formal musical training may also have closed him off to new influences as he grew older. In candid moments, he was willing to agree that he could have marketed himself without being corrupted, had he been willing to risk failure. With some of his large pieces for large groups, he once said, he had not even sought a reading because he assumed he had written a dud. But by putting the piece in the files, he could always assuage his spirits by thinking that "just maybe the piece was a winner."

Wilder kept going back and forth in his feelings about the big arena. He once wrote disgustedly to Sibley Watson about a review that had focused on the fugitive, delicate nature of his music: "I don't care for dynamic affirmations in music, but after this I'm certain that were I to write a piece containing only full fortissimo orchestration, the boys would still say, 'idyllic, delicate, nostalgic, winsome.'" He couldn't quite give up the notion that he might one day bring off a major work. Demsey believes that such orchestral pieces as he did write were composed for the same reason that many young composers feel the need to write a string quartet: "Wilder wanted to be considered a 'real composer' by the musical establishment." Freeman, too, has said: "I think of Alec as one who wrote in smaller forms and would have liked to have been thought of as a bigger boy, but didn't feel comfortable in the genre."

It was undoubtedly that unrealized dream that explained his reaction to the premiere performance in March of 1977 of *Entertainment No. 6*. The critics and the audience seemed to receive the piece well enough, finding it full of bold, nontraditional melodies. Wilder, however, was highly displeased with the circumstances of the performance, presented not in the handsome downtown Eastman Theater but in the suburban Dome Arena as part of one of the orchestra's pop concerts. That, he felt, was less than honorable treatment of a serious piece of music. "I'm not part of the club," he complained. "I've been labelled as a popular song composer on the basis of a song I wrote 40 years ago. The fact that Gunther Schuller has called me to ask for music doesn't interest them." He had never known, he said, of a first performance to be given at a pop concert. Good or bad, the piece should have been shown greater respect, particularly because it had been written on a state grant. Further, he said, the piece should have been played by the whole orchestra, not just the core orchestra with its reduced number of strings. He made no Olympian claim for the piece, he wound up, but it was not a "dog."

That was a revealing reaction. All his life Wilder had insisted that his music be treated as entertainment, never as big pretentious stuff, never as solemn program music. The Dome Arena was exactly the right venue for *Entertainment No. 6*. Here again Wilder was showing his ambivalence about his composer status. Even as he disdained it, he wanted to be given a place in the music world that he had never really claimed. He had hung around the edge of the crowds at the jousting tournaments but had never mounted up and entered the lists. Zola's comments to Cézanne might well be applied to Wilder's attitude toward big-time orchestral works: "You dread failure of any kind; your main principle is to let things take their course and leave yourself at the mercy of time and chance. . . . One thing or the other, really be a lawyer, or else really be an artist, but do not remain a creature without a name." For fear of failure, for lack of sympathy with the orchestral environment and the apparatus of the establishment, out of unwillingness to be an advocate for his music, and out of perennial self-doubt, Wilder never made a serious bid for the main prize.

But if Zola's remark was apposite in terms of Wilder's large-structure music, Einstein's estimate of Hindemith perfectly describes Wilder the chamber music composer: "There is nothing at all academic about Hindemith. He is simply a musician who produces music as a tree bears fruit, without further philosophic purpose." Here was a genre where Wilder was always completely comfortable, where he could be both creative and personal, where his music was eminently functional and suited to his talents. It was music he wanted to write and needed to write out of the sheer joy of creativity, and it allowed him to demonstrate what he felt music-making was all about.

Although his orchestral flirtation with *Entertainment No. 6* had turned out to be disappointing, he hardly broke stride with his instrumental writing. His compositions in 1977 and 1978 included *Brass Quintet No. 6, Concerto for Flute and Chamber Orchestra, Geiger Suite, Sextet for Marimba and Wind Quintet, Suite for Flute and Marimba, Suite No. 1 for Unaccompanied Trumpet, Woodwind Quintet No. 13, Brass Quintet No. 7, Little Detective Suite No. 1, Suite for Flute and Strings, Suite for Horn and Tuba, Suite for Trumpet and Marimba,* and *Suite No. 2 for Unaccompanied Trumpet.* He was walking a lonely road, for these were not the kind of pieces that would ever fill Carnegie Hall. But they made happy the musicians he was writing for and they helped to fulfill him.

This writing was done at a time when Wilder's health was continuing to deteriorate and when he turned often to drink. Alcohol, he told Sibley Watson, was "my wife, my sister, my Eros. Yet it will kill me." Tom Hampson and Lou Ouzer recall a drunken Wilder who had to be carried into the East Avenue inn he was staying at and put to bed. Wilder's body had apparently become rigid, as if rigor mortis had set in. So Hampson and Ouzer and two others took each an arm and a leg and carried him like a sack of potatoes, saying in embarrassed explanation to the desk clerk as they struggled by, "This is a distinguished American composer."

Yet there were still good things to be set against the bad, still happy interludes. Early in the winter of 1978, on a date close to Wilder's seventy-first birthday, Bob Levy and some of his band of Tidewater Festival players who had so buoyed Wilder a few years before, rallied around him for one last time. Wilder had been more than ever down in the dumps, drinking heavily and seemingly about ready to give up on himself and his music. Deeply concerned, Levy and Frances Miller talked about what they might do to restore some of his hope and faith.

They decided on a "Save Alec Night" at Miller's Manhattan apartment overlooking Central Park. They would surprise him with an evening of his music played by his young disciples. Wilder did apparently know that Levy would be there with his trumpet, but he didn't know that Virginia Nanzetta and Gordon Stout and Steve Harlos and Steve and Judy Hart and Linda Livingwood would also be on hand to serenade him. Wilder and his young friends had gone full circle. In the beginning, he had nourished them. Now they were nourishing him.

In the last half of 1978 Wilder seemed to become more and more out of sorts. In October, in the course of apologizing to Watson and his wife and to Ouzer for a long absence from Rochester, he said that he loved them no less but that he was suffering from "a dreadful form of self-centeredness and unease" that brought to his mind the expression "all the virtue is gone from me."

It was in 1978 also that the last rites were given to Wilder's much-troubled manuscript about the Algonquin Hotel, *The Elegant Refuge.* Wilder would always insist that he was badly treated by both the potential publisher and the hotel management, which gave him a room free of rent while he worked on the project. Almost from the time he entered into the contract in late 1975, he maintained he was being forced to fill the book with celebrities instead of being left alone to set out his own personal memoir of backstairs life.

When Wilder fell hopelessly behind the publisher's deadline, James Maher, his indispensable collaborator in *American Popular Song,* agreed to help. He quickly discovered that the manuscript was a mélange of anecdotes, unchecked backstairs gossip, endless accounts of drunken misadventures, and unedited interviews. Working furiously, Maher managed to get a manuscript of *The Elegant Refuge* (his title) to the publisher on time. It was rejected, and Maher became the reluctant co-owner of the manuscript. Still feeling that Wilder was being unfairly treated, and this time with the considerable assistance of Douglas Colby, grandson of the then owner of the hotel, Ben Bodne, Maher went to work again. But he was still dealing with a lightweight story, and only now did he find out to his dismay that Wilder had kept him in the dark all along about the true nature of the book. Andrew Anspach, the Algonquin's managing director, told Maher that the understanding always had been that Wilder would write a history of the Algonquin, seasoned by his own recollections; it was never to have been just a personal memoir.

Despite his bruised feelings, Maher finished his salvage work, wrote a foreword that sought to place the story in perspective, and, with the help of his own agent, sent it off to publisher after publisher to no avail. Maher still does not know if Wilder was engaging in a deliberate bit of duplicity about the true nature of the book or if he genuinely believed himself to be the aggrieved party. Ambiguity was always Wilder's patent and his shield.

More generously than deserved perhaps, Anspach spoke subsequently of the manuscript as a love letter to the people who worked there: "Alec was part of the family. The boys would help him upstairs when he had drunk too much. He was protected. He was not the only one, but he was treated with more love." It might be part of that same protection to note that Wilder in those last years was often broke and sick. That's the charitable view of his behavior. This man who made time for waifs and strays wore raking spurs that left personal scars long in the fading. In mid-1994, fourteen years after Wilder's death, Maher took a walk up to West 88th Street and stood in front of the brownstone where, thirty-eight years before, he had first met Alec Wilder: "At the corner I almost bought a flower to drop on the steps, then I remembered how Alec hated cut flowers (Or did he? Who really knew from one day to the next?). So, I snapped a small shiny pungent leaf from a shrub several houses away and dropped it on the stoop and walked away. I had finally bade Alec *adieu.*"

But Wilder's friends, Maher among them, never deserted him. The musician remained a cherished presence in spite of everything. "Alec," says Maher, "attacked all his advocates, all his collaborators, all his other selves—all those who were his creative mirror. And yet, there is the music." When all was said and done, this was a superb melody-maker whose creativity was at the center of it. Bill Engvick, who had his own wounds to nurse, has put it this way: "What really remains, after all the petards have been hoisted, is that Alec and his music nourished, comforted and encouraged me through some very bleak times. I am confident that my efforts did the same for him." Arnold Sundgaard mourns:

> I can only say that I feel a great sadness that we will never sit down to a piano again while he fleshes out the chords for a song. Actually I have never found another composer to work with, and my own work as a lyricist has been almost non-existent ever since. To say that I miss him is a massive understatement, and I'm sure all his other collaborators share this loss as well. The piques, the angers, the frustrations are all forgotten now.

On October 28, 1978, one of the principal underlying reasons for Wilder's erratic behavior was made clear when he wrote to the Watsons saying that although he would have been honored and pleased to attend their movie evening, he could not be with them "because I must go to Florida for an unsavory operation." He was grateful for their financial generosity: "It is a godsend, as I have no notion what the butchery will cost." His closing words were "I love you both very much, and hate to miss the occasion. Yet a creature has caught up with me. I trust, out of love for you both, that I shall survive." In November 1978 in Gainesville, Florida, under the direction of his physician, William Ploss, Wilder had a cancerous lung tumor removed. Dr. H. Rudolf Gertner removed the entire left lung, and was his chest surgeon from that time on. No biopsy had been taken of his chest lesion, for, according to Ploss, the X ray was proof enough of the nature of the lesion: "With my advice, he refused further diagnostic adventures by other specialists such as a bronchoscopy, and we opted for direct thoracotomy (opening of the chest) and removal of the tumor."

Wilder's lifestyle had caught up with him. Even his strong constitution could not stand up indefinitely to the siege laid by so much smoking and drinking. He seemed to have a late realization of what had caused his sickness to one degree or another. Recalls Ploss: "He handed the cigarettes to me while still on the X-ray table where his diagnostic film had been taken and, to my knowledge, never used them again (?)." For most of his life, Wilder had shaken his fist at fate and dared it to strike back. It was his life and his body, by God, to use or abuse as he chose, and full-speed ahead was the only way to go. He was not to be dissuaded. Music critic Richard Freed has said that, when he tried to discourage him from smoking by not providing ashtrays in the house, "he would simply deposit his ashes neatly in his trouser cuffs." Wilder told Lavinia Russ in *Letters I Never Mailed:* "It's MY music, MY extravagance, MY traveling, MY never unpacking a suitcase, MY sleeping in tomorrow's otherwise fresh shirt, MY shouting at poorly boiled eggs, MY sleeping pills, MY smoking and MY DEATH!"

All that unrestraint showed in his face even before it began to affect his health. "As he got older," Russ herself said, "he got that wonderful ravaged face that people get who have thought a lot and ached a lot and have been hurt a lot and loved a lot. He had a face that was a map of living, a topographical map of somebody who lived very intensely and deeply."

After the operation, Wilder spent some time recovering at the home of Frances Miller on Grand Cayman Island. He kept the Watsons informed. After regretting his inadequate earnings, he told them: "And now, cancer. Thank the Lord I have some form of Medicare and Medicaid." But the cost of the operation and X rays and "heaven knows what else" that were not covered would, he said, be relieved by Watson's check, and for that he was humbly grateful. He referred also to his "fearful depressions," and wondered if lithium carbonate would be helpful. He was finding it hard to put his life back together, telling the Watsons in a further letter: "Forgive my silence. I haven't been able to do much more than keep the boat from foundering. The mending, so-called, is slow. It's hard to concentrate on even the most superficial conversation, let alone a book. As for writing music, it's like a balloon escaped from a child's hand."

The bulletins continued gloomy. February 27, 1979: "Right now, I can't compose, construct puzzles, read books, see people." March 19: "It's of little consequence if I live, die, compose, stay silent. Yet I find, meaningless as it is, that I can do nothing else if I can't compose." July 23: "Until the popularity of 'rock' and 'country' music, I was able to make a fair living from song writing and from orchestrating others' songs for recordings. But no more, and ironically, the songs I've written in the past few years are the best I've ever written. . . . The checks you mail me are a godsend. I wish I were strong willed enough to move into a flea bag and send you back the checks. But I admit that they make life bearable."

Wilder kept on composing because it was the only thing he knew how to do. Although the creative impulse was burning lower, it still moved him to collaborate with McGlohon in the last year of his life on two final songs: *A Long Night* and *South to a Warmer Place*. Sinatra recorded them, although Wilder did not live to hear the album. Thus Sinatra was both one of the first singers to record Wilder and also the last in his lifetime. Though there were often long intervals of silence, the two men never became estranged. In an earlier period, Wilder had often visited with Sinatra in his home in Rancho Mirage in California. If he did not write about that, it was undoubtedly because he wanted to protect the friendship. Many people traded on their relationship with the singer, but Wilder wanted none of such trafficking. Although he let the friendship slide for some years, Sinatra never forgot Wilder, "the professor." Doubtless because he had heard about his illness, for Sinatra was always quick to go to the side of friends in trouble, he called Wilder in 1980 and asked him if he would write a song for his new saloon album *She Shot Me Down*. If Sinatra was indeed trying to raise Wilder's spirits, this was one way he could do it without being patronizing.

Despite his fast-failing health, Wilder kept on writing his letters as well as his music. In 1980 he wrote to his Cornish correspondent Arthur Jackson in these terms: "So I ask you, my friend of some thirty-odd years, is there any B & B place in your section of Cornwall that wouldn't charge $100 a night? I want to see you, your wife, bluebells, primroses and crocuses, after this New York life." Jackson and Wilder had met only once, in 1945 when an overseas posting led Jackson to New York:

> Mildred Bailey and the Delta Rhythm Boys were appearing at the Blue Angel way uptown. After a wonderful show, I headed back stage to pay my respects, and after saying hello to Mildred and the Deltas, I was introduced to a tall, gangling man shyly propping up the corner of the room. Alec Wilder was astonished that I knew his name and wanted his autograph.

A week later, on 52d Street, Jackson met Wilder again: "A familiar figure came striding down the street, hair flowing in the breeze and coat-tails flying." Jackson confided that he had wanted to get into the Hotel Astor Roof to see Harry James and his thirty-piece orchestra, but the Astor apparently frowned on unattached gentlemen. No problem, said Wilder, he would take care of it. He did, and Jackson had a musical evening he forever remembered.

During his last year, Wilder sent reports to Jackson of his various problems, but he still talked about catching the *Cornish Express:* "Just when I think I'm about to phone you to give you my arrival date, some other catastrophe occurs. I shan't bore you with all the ailments; they can't compete with Job's, but they're in the running! Perhaps I can arrange to have my funeral services take place at Land's End. My very best to you, dear friend. Alec." Jackson never heard from Wilder again.

In 1980, as in the year before, Wilder's behavior, long erratic, began to border on the bizarre. He often called Maher as many as five times a day, talking again and again about the "big pill" he had been saving to end his life. "Then one day he called seven times, and the following morning called again and merely said, 'goodbye,' then hung up. He once changed his mind about suicide and decided he wanted to be cremated, but on one condition—'they must promise not to sweep up the embers, just leave them there.'"

At intervals throughout 1980 friends rallied to Wilder in an effort to cheer him up and sustain him, though it was not easy to swim against the turning tide. Composer Benson, his wife, Pat, and their daughter, Sonja, had lunch with him at the Algonquin in the spring of the year. It was rather a sad occasion. "Alec was trying valiantly to pretend he was on the wagon," says Benson, "but he had two large goblets of red wine and poured another drink into some milk." Benson remembers that he looked like the wrath of God, sallow and thin and not well cared for. There was a note in his voice that seemed to say the future held nothing for him. "It was not a whine, more sadness, with a little edge of wit, and some self-pity was in it." When the Bensons left, they asked Wilder to be sure to visit his friends again. "Alec's mouth quivered, tears started up, and he said, 'I hope someone will have me.' That tore us up. He was often desperately lonely."

That magnificent independence was now seen to have its down side. Wilder had talked earlier to Lou Ouzer about getting older, about the changing world, and how it was harder to get around. Ouzer reminded him of his many friends. "But friends," said Wilder, "are like this," and he held up a hand with the fingers outstretched, "whereas family is like this," and he made his hand into a fist.

Later that year, Gunther Schuller apparently intervened in Wilder's behalf when a "con man musician in Rochester" (Wilder's words) asked him to compose a piece for a singer and a chamber group. Wilder told the man that Schuller determined the amount he should be paid for all new music. In a letter to Watson, Wilder said Schuller had written the man in these terms: "Alec has spent a lifetime writing music for nothing out of sheer love of the thing and love of his friends (for whom he has mostly written.) This is something that has got to stop. Alec is over 70 now and deserves better, and anyone who commits himself to 'inviting' a new work from Alec should commit himself to financing that 'invitation.'" In the same letter to Watson, Wilder wound up asking rhetorically, "Why have I been allowed to live so long? In order to be in better condition for hell? I know only that I'll never know."

The last few months were not all bleak. The collaboration with McGlohon on the songs for Sinatra had held back the waters for a time, and there were other invitations. Mitch Miller, there at the last like Sinatra, commissioned a piece for orchestra; *Four Sentiments and a Tune That Wouldn't Quit* is a work that was completed but has not yet been performed. Wilder was also to have written on commission a work for the Eastman Wind Ensemble. "But sadly," says Eastman School director Freeman, "he had neither the strength nor the time to do it. Nor was he able to see the completion of a recording of his music for Vox."

Wilder was not giving up without a fight, however. Joel E. Siegel would recall that just a month before his death Wilder had sent him a postcard thanking him for a review he had written of pianist Roland Hanna's album of Wilder songs. Siegel had explained in the review that he usually wrote about singers, and was uneasy when reviewing instrumentalists, particularly a player of Hanna's caliber. Wilder's card, "written in an unsettlingly shaky hand," said: "Just read your review of the Hanna record. I am deeply touched by your extremely articulate and considerate statement. Indeed, it'a model of how reviews should read, whether for or against. You're a very dear man and I'm in your debt. All my best! Alec." Siegel said he was not fooled by the postcard. "Alec surely knew that the Hanna piece was timid and uncertain. But his gesture of writing to me was so typical of his essential sweetness. You see, he could not resist taking a few moments out from the business of dying to encourage a friend."

Wilder also took time out from dying to make a final musical statement, one that could well have served as his memorial. That was the presentation in Rochester early in October 1980 of the church cantata *Mountain Boy*. Wilder had written earlier to Milford Fargo, telling him of a small musical piece that had come about from a conversation he had had with Father Atwell about the boy Jesus, what kind of child he might have been. McGlohon, he said, had written about two-thirds of the libretto, a parable of the Christ Child set in the Blue Ridge mountain country. If Atwell did not consider it a sacrilege, he said, he would like to set it to music. It would be accompanied by either piano or harmonium and guitar and flute, and it should all have a backwoods sound, no overt sophistication. Atwell, when approached, had found nothing sacrilegious about it, but he had wondered a little ruefully if he might again have to rearrange or cancel the church bingo if the cantata were presented in Avon.

The piece had been set aside for several years and was not again put on the front burner until 1980. Now, there was no possibility of presenting *Mountain Boy* in Avon, for Atwell, who had suffered for some time from an incurable heart disease, had died in March of that year. That was a heavy blow to Wilder, for his love of the gentle priest had run deep and true. His depression grew, but he was also more than ever determined that this simple parable be told. A performance was now urgent, for he knew he did not have much time left. He was also concerned to honor Atwell, and the Saturday and Sunday performances of *Mountain Boy* (presented in the sanctuary of the Downtown United Presbyterian Church) were dedicated to him.

Wilder told Fargo at one point that he did not think he would live to see the performances, but he drew on his last reserves and held on, superintending many details. The day of the first performance was raw, but the atmosphere in the sanctuary was warm, and the audience was quickly transported to the October hills of Appalachia. There, with the Winesap apples ripening in the sun and with the corn in the crib, they watched the brief unfolding and flowering of the life of a boy of unusual goodness who thought, "How big the Heaven is and how very small am I." The story and the performance ended with the chorus singing about a Mountain Boy who had but a tiny lamp, and how "the slender light it shines will grow and grow and grow."

In spite of the constraints caused by his illness—he was not well enough to attend the second night—Wilder was delighted by the whole *Mountain Boy* experience. After the first performance, he went up to Fargo, who had played the role of the father, and said to him: "You son of a bitch, you led that boy through the whole thing." Anyone overhearing him might have misunderstood, but Wilder was simply thanking Fargo for his good shepherding. Singer Virginia McConnell, who had played the mother, also went up to him afterward, noticing how thin he was. She gave him a hug and asked him when he would write another chamber opera. "I won't write any more," he said. McConnell said that perhaps when he felt better, he would do something; she wanted to sing more of his music. "No," he said again, "I shall never write again."

Mountain Boy had been a radiant moment, but several hard months lay ahead. Early in December Wilder was writing to Freeman in Rochester explaining that he was not able to compose because his health had taken a very bad change for the worse. He asked Freeman to hold that information in confidence. "Lou Ouzer, for example, would be desolated, as would a few other dear friends. I am immensely grateful to you for your countless kindnesses and concerns for my well-being." He said he wished he could compose the piece in question, but that it was now hard enough to get out of bed in the morning: "I shall be going down to an island very soon. What happens to me after that, the good Lord only knows."

Wilder was now in very bad shape, coughing heavily. He was also extremely short of breath. Frances Miller was on a trip to the British Isles, one that Wilder had planned to go on but had had to cancel because of his illness. When she learned that he was deteriorating, Miller cut short her journey and returned home to be with him. On December 9, she made all the necessary arrangements for him to go to Gainesville, Florida, where his physician was, and got him on board the plane by wheelchair at La Guardia. Miller and Dr. Ploss kept closely in touch by telephone over the next few days.

At first, it was hoped that Wilder might have another three to six months to live. He apparently had not been told everything at that point, and wanted to go to Grand Cayman Island. Ploss called again and told Miller that the entire picture had changed, that his patient had only until the end of the month, and that all island plans were pipe dreams. Wilder nevertheless asked Miller to stop by and pick up clothes for Cayman at the Algonquin. He was overjoyed when she said she would come to Gainesville; Miller was the one person above all that he wanted at his side. There at North Florida Regional Hospital, she did all she could to give comfort. When Wilder talked about being buried on Grand Cayman, she tried to discourage the idea, feeling that a tropical island was not a fitting final resting place. Wilder was now hallucinating badly, and was often difficult to handle. A touch of the old Wilder surfaced when he made his private nurses sit out in the hall at one point.

On December 20, Miller remembers, Wilder seemed a little better, although he was still hallucinating and still very short of breath. At times, he thought he was in California, looking at the mountains and the sea. He called often for Harry (Bouras of Chicago). He saw the faces of people and various shapes in the room and outside the window. At one point, he began to see his beloved steam trains going by beyond the window. "So at the very end," says James Maher, "there was that golden image, and I thought, my God, isn't that beautiful. At the end, that image of getting on a train and going somewhere. This is the man who was always on his way somewhere. And never found somewhere. It simply wasn't there."

As word spread that Wilder was sinking, messages flew back and forth among his friends. In Rochester, Ouzer told attorney Thomas Hampson that their Alec was in very tough shape. Hampson spoke with Ploss, who was cautioning people not to go down, for Wilder wanted no visitors. His will, however, was badly out of date (he used to carry the original around in his pocket) and urgently needed revising. Hampson recalls that Miller had apparently said to Wilder: "You're leaving things to four people and you're not even speaking to three of them." Wilder had roughed out a new will in the hospital on blank pages in a paperback book, but that would not have served. So Hampson flew to Gainesville in the morning of December 23, and got to see Wilder about three o'clock. When he walked in, Wilder's first words to him were "Tom, I'm sorry. I have nothing more to give." All his life he had been giving to others. Hampson told him not to worry, that he was not there to receive anything, just to help if he could. It was difficult to figure out what Wilder had for bequeathing, and difficult to write a will in the abstract. Hampson did determine that Wilder had a bank account of about $50,000 but that he was indebted to the Richmond Organization for $32,000 for advances. It was finally decided that 90 percent of the little that remained should go half and half to Ouzer and Lavinia Russ, with 10 percent for the "birds and bees."

Wilder seemed alert enough at the time, so Hampson told him he would need an executor, someone to handle his affairs. Did he have any thoughts? Wilder, propped up on pillows, oxygen tube in his nose, leaned forward with that Old Testament look and pointed to Hampson, "You." It was not a request Hampson could refuse, though attorneys prefer banks and others to perform that duty. Hampson went downstairs to the hospital business office, drafted and typed up the will, and went back with it some time after six o'clock. He was startled to see the deterioration that had taken place in those few hours. Wilder was hallucinating, still watching steam trains go by in the woods beyond the picture window of his room. Harvey Phillips had also arrived to do what he could, but Wilder continued to worsen. Though difficult in some of the demands he was making, Wilder, says Miller, "was very brave at the end." Nor did he at any time ask for the Big Pill that he always said he would use when the time came for the slide on The Big Toboggan to eternity. Says Ploss: "He never asked for the pills, and indeed, clung to life, fought until the end. There remains a deep gulf between how we'd like to behave, or appear to behave, and our deepest drives: survival is a strong one."

Wilder's hard fight against lung cancer ended early in the morning of December 24. It was just barely Christmas Eve, the season of the year he hated most, when he always made sure he was somewhere on a train far from joyous family celebrations. As Mike Miller has recalled, the idea at Christmas

> was to be in the middle of nowhere, really in the middle of nowhere, say Manitoba in Canada on Christmas Day. And that's an extraordinary thing to do because if it's a big train like the Canadian you're all alone on the train. You have the whole thing to yourself, the first and second calls to dinner, all for you, and you're nowhere near any sense of Christmas. He loathed Christmas, the quintessential family holiday.

Here at least was one Christmas he didn't have to worry about, but he would have been pleased to know that his body was being carried to Rochester by train.

He might have had more mixed feelings had he known that Sinatra had left word that he be given the very best of attention and that he, Sinatra, would take care of the cost. He had never, as far as Maher was aware, acquainted Sinatra with his declining fortunes. "Alec had played the role of prince at the Algonquin table year after year," says Maher, "and he just didn't want to let Frank Sinatra know he needed money." But Sinatra somehow learned of his final illness. As it happened, Ploss's expertise in handling Medicare and other matters meant that the offer did not have to be taken up. Although Wilder hated appearing threadbare to the world, he would have been pleased to know that Sinatra had cared enough to get in touch.

Wilder would have been struck, too, by the fact that on December 21 Gunther Schuller, not then knowing of the last illness, had started going through Wilder's music, the letters from him that he had in the house, the diary he had started, and *Letters I Never Mailed:*

> Suddenly I found myself totally mesmerized and immersed in this world of
> Alec Wilder, and though I didn't have the time to do this, I spent the next
> three and a half days reading everything we had of Alec's, and, on the third of
> those three days, he died. It was as if I was in communion with him and he
> with me, and some force from him compelled me to read his life as it were.

Wilder also would have approved the clues to his life to be found among the few possessions left by this man who traveled so unladen through life:

. . . Amtrak's National Train Timetables effective October 28, 1979.

. . . Some cards of blank bars of music, a Margun Music catalog, a letter from Dr. Max H. Presberg of Rochester saying that he often played the violin sonata Wilder had written for him.

. . . Books still in their original cartons sent to Wilder at his request by bookseller Howard Frisch: *Smallbone Deceased* and *Be Shot for Sixpence,* by Michael Gilbert; *An Improbable Fiction* and *Exit Murderer,* by Sara Woods; *The Elegant Auctioneers,* by Wesley Towner; *Uncle Dynamite,* by P. G. Wodehouse.

. . . A deed to his burial plot in Saint Agnes Cemetery in Avon.

. . . A copy of his will directing that there be no funeral or religious services.

. . . A request that in the event that his beneficiaries predeceased him, the remainder of the estate be paid to the Jersey Wild Life Preservation Trust in the Channel Islands; Save the Redwoods Society, California; the Sierra Club; the Audubon Society; Defenders of Wildlife.

. . . Affectionate letters from some of those closest to him: Frances Miller, Lavinia Russ, Bob Levy, and LB (Lorraine Bouras, as she then was). Lorraine spoke for all Wilder's friends when she said: "Oh, why can't you be here. I miss you something awful. Do you know how much you mean to me. I love you, Uncle Al."

. . . A letter from Arthur Jesson from Plymouth, England: "You have this God-given talent which has served you well over the years despite your own disregard of the marketplace. Financial considerations aside, the hell with the market. I'd rather have the respect of my peers than the fickle regard of that amorphous bunch, the public. This, you have in spades. I think you have always lived the life you wanted and made the friends you wanted."

Also testifying to the essential Wilder was a 1978 letter from Robert Ardrey from Cape Town saying in part:

> I don't want to bring tears to your eyes, but you and I have lived through a wonderful time when people like you and me were possible. We aren't any-more. We made it, just in time. . . . The glory of the individual and his can-tankerous movement through the stars is a story for future nostalgia, as to-day is the story of the thirties, but not for present or future deeds. We are dead heroes, buried in the lime of unlikelihood, and so be it. Yet we did things, pal.

The last word belongs to Wilder, and it can be found in the letter that fluttered to the floor from a novel by Sara Woods, one of his favorite mystery writers, as Frances Miller was taking the book from the shelf. McPartland told about the incident in the National Public Radio tribute broadcast in 1981. The letter, in Wilder's handwriting, was addressed "Dear Next Reader" and said in part:

> The person writing this is so far over on the seesaw of life or death that he finds his life's failure worse than he believed possible, yet better than the lives of most successful, even eminent people. The loathing of Wagner and the profound love of Poulenc, a moment as opposed to an hour, one tear rather than a tantrum. . . . These are what life was a couple of hours out of 73 years. The saddest of final breathing is not that the person died but that no one could ever know what his life had been. That, my next reader, is why art is profoundly godlike. It's the best of the lives of the dead who otherwise would have been silent or wholly unknown.

Epilogue

The life of Alec Wilder, the man and the musician, may never be wrapped up neatly. There are enough unanswered questions to keep the jury out for a long time. Was he, for example, a practicing homosexual? By his own account, and by the estimate of most of his friends, almost certainly not; and yet there remains a small shadow of doubt. One friend who feels Wilder was gay suggests that his denial flowed from the "Edwardian, not to say, Victorian, household he was born into. He never escaped the unforgiving hand of his heritage." Yet actual evidence of homosexual encounters does not seem to be there. There will always be conjecture.

Very little about Wilder follows a straight line. Did he trade on his eccentricities? Of course, and yet it seemed quite natural for him to sleep in his vest and stuff his pockets with bits and pieces of music manuscript along with his will and testament. No one reached out more generously to people, yet it was usually done on his terms. Even the telephone that was always in his hand was sometimes a moat, and it was he who lowered and raised the drawbridge. Instead of learning how better to conduct himself, he turned insult and apology almost into an art form, so that penance became performance. For example, after having been racially nasty in the Algonquin elevator to Ella Fitzgerald, whom he greatly admired—"What are *you* doing here?"—he sent her three dozen long-stemmed American Beauty roses the next day with one of his eloquent apologies. And later he told all within hearing about both his wicked gaucherie and his charming apology.

So much about him was confounding. He had no family responsibilities, no real responsibility toward anyone but himself, yet, like a celibate priest, he had all the answers to all the physical, emotional, and social problems of marital and family life. But did he in fact have a hidden responsibility? Did this man who spent so much of his life in a state of freefall, who rejected all possessions, leave behind him the most precious possession of all, a child from one of his affairs? Persistent rumor said that he had had a daughter by a woman he saw a good deal of in the earlier years in Rochester and elsewhere. He always denied it, but Arnold and Marge Sundgaard, for example, came to feel that the rumor may have had a strong basis in fact. They first heard it in Williamstown, Massachusetts, in 1973 when *Nobody's Earnest* was being played there. The headwaiter at a local restaurant told them he had met Wilder's daughter. The idea sounded so unlikely that the Sundgaards dismissed it then. However, they kept hearing the same story in Key West, where they wintered for many years. Finally, they met there the woman herself. She spoke quite openly to them, saying that she and Wilder had indeed been lovers and that a child had been born.

As related to the Sundgaards, some of the details of the affair have the ring of truth. Thus they met at a party in Rochester and Wilder told her he had train tickets for some distant destination and would be leaving early the next morning. That evening he took her down to the railroad yards and showed her the huge puffing locomotives that meant so much to him. She wore a collegiate cashmere sweater and walked with him among the panting beasts as he explained their power. (Consider the sexual symbolism there!) The next day he called to say he had canceled his trip. The affair was under way. Ultimately she became pregnant, and Wilder fled into the night.

Jump ahead now to the time when the child became a young woman. Sundgaard tells it this way: "When as a grown girl she walked up to Alec in the lobby of the Algonquin and introduced herself as his daughter he looked right through her and merely said, 'How's ——?' (the mother's name). He simply could not admit the fact of her existence. He had blocked her from his mind and in denying her existence he probably actually believed it."

The Sundgaards found the story of the woman herself believable. The woman, they said, was wealthy and was apparently not seeking any kind of recompense or publicity. They could find no reason that she would make up such a story. Wilder did not deny knowing the woman, but he totally rejected the idea that the affair had produced a child. Once, in the course of dismissing his eccentricities, he wrote: "Eccentric! I'm supposed to have had an illegitimate child, yet I've never made an attempt to see her, nor do I know her name. Monstrous!" The mystery remains.

Much else is unclear. Why did he detest so many women and yet hold two or three in such deep and genuine esteem? Did his mother's treatment of him warp his character and color his attitudes? Yes, undoubtedly. Did he also at times use that as a flimsy excuse for unacceptable behavior? Yes, that too. There may have been something more. Wilder said that as a young man he had contracted gonorrhea from an older nurse in New York. He told Sundgaard that that was the basis of his bitterness about women. As he saw it, he had been betrayed while still an innocent. The anomalies and contradictions can never be fully explained or reconciled. Perhaps the attempt should not be made. After all, uniquely, incorrigibly, and unrepentantly, he was simply Alec Wilder, take it or leave it.

More to the point than his personal makeup, how will his music be judged finally?

Composing was the generative force in his life. Here again, the verdict may be a long time coming. The critics will always have trouble coming to grips with a composer who would not stand still, whose output ranged over school chamber operas, film scores, orchestral pieces, keyboard music, popular songs, art songs, musical theater, lullabies for children, ballet music, chamber music, solo instrumental pieces with orchestra, band music, orchestrations, and arrangements. Often within the same tributary, his mixing of so many elements of music—popular, jazz, classical—also makes his trail hard to follow and to signpost. Many of his pieces, particularly in the earlier years, were written on an *ad hoc* basis without much thought of publication. Even later on, Wilder made no push for the appointment of scholars who might study his writing and put together a critical resume. Most of the time, until he sensed that time was running out, he wrote music just as something he did, not as something to blow his horn through. He gave the pieces to the people he dedicated them to—two sheets here, three sheets there, all over the place.

Thanks to the heroic efforts in the early years of Frances Miller and Bill Engvick, and to Schuller, Demsey, Phillips, and Levy in the later years, perhaps 80 to 90 percent of the music has been collected. That leaves a great deal still tucked away in closely guarded collections of friends, in piano benches, files, and other dusty hiding places. This kind of scattering was peculiar to Wilder, and it makes an overall assessment that much more difficult. Nor has any critical apparatus yet been established, no proper vocabulary developed for examining Wilder's style.

There is another problem. In a number of the instrumental areas he wrote in, there is not much that his work can be measured against. The literature is thin for some of the unusual, untraditional combinations he often composed for in an effort to oblige musician friends: sonatas for bassoon and piano, for euphonium and piano; trios for oboe, clarinet and bassoon; suites for marimba and trumpet; and many more such. Wilder's work is often so original and so different in focus that it is hard to know what to make of it. "Critics typically," notes Demsey, "react to a recording or performance almost entirely in terms of other similar or comparable performances they have experienced. Wilder's music is so unlike most other music that his songs appear to be over-ambitious when compared to the usual 32-bar jazz standard, and his classical music appears to be too 'light' and fluffy in comparison to the norm of 20th century works."

Wilder also wrote prolifically and unevenly. Cynics might say he was so eager to get his music into the hands of those he knew would perform it that he could not stop himself. More altruistically, he may have felt so strongly about creating art for those he respected and admired that he did not give full heed to the quality of the work. More time is needed. When all of Wilder's classical music is brought together in one place and scholarly studies are made, a clearer, fuller picture will emerge.

Even now, however, it can be said that lyrical melody seems destined to remain the single most distinctive quality of Wilder's music, all of his music. As James Maher has eloquently said,

> The melody was the key, even in the "outer movements" of his chamber music. . . . Alec was a far superior melodist to most 20th century composers, for whom "melody" was a succession of notes, which were then manipulated in the cleverest possible manner. Despite the fact that many composers wrote "lieder," few of them revealed a deeply rooted sense of song in their melodies. On the other hand, Alec could not help himself: melodies flowed from his pen to paper as automatically as breathing. The song was his genius.

That's true throughout his writing. It is the lyricism and the lush, altered jazz-related harmonies that endear the best of his classical work to many. Lyrical melody of course was in fullest flow in his songs, and this is likely to be seen as the strongest of his compositional fields. Wilder's pop-song language, as Benson points out, may not always be as catchy as someone else's hit tunes because many of his melodies were characterized by an idiosyncratic kind of harmony. "There was a little turn in the melody and harmony that was characteristic of him. His songs were not run of the mill. He didn't want to write 'smarmy' (a favorite word) kinds of tunes, not treacly, soft, sentimental stuff." So nearly always there was that little turn, that devious bit of harmony, that dark under edge. Adds Benson: "I think because of that his songs will be with us for a long time, and will become more and more like art songs. People are seeing them that way, almost like cabaret songs. His are not mainstream, dead-center hit tunes."

Benson speaks of Wilder's songs as touched with a kind of harmonic and melodic strangeness, at times a beguiling waywardness that took him more often down shaded side streets than sunny main streets. Songs were the continuous thread in his music. No matter what else he might be engaged in, Wilder could never resist the siren call of a good song and lyric. Levy remembers a week in 1977 when Wilder was working on a bassoon sonata at Levy's house: "Once when I came in to pick him up to go to dinner, I noticed a song he had written sitting on top of the piano. I asked him if he'd written it for anyone in particular and he said, 'No, I just found this absolutely lovely lyric and I simply had to set it.'" It's in our interest, Michael Lasser has said, to "know his songs, to sing them and to cherish them. They have enriched our music beyond our knowing and it's time to claim him as our own." That gift of song, Maher concludes, "may, in the end, have been his final refuge from the realities which he himself so richly (and self-destructively) jumbled."

In the years since Wilder's death in 1980, the man and his music have been celebrated in a number of ways. His admission to the Songwriters Hall of Fame, the Kool Jazz Festival in Carnegie Hall, concerts across the country, the opening of the Wilder Archive in the Sibley Music Library at the Eastman School of Music, and the dedication there of the Wilder Reading Room have helped remove a little of the neglect Wilder suffered in his lifetime. In the late 1980s and early 1990s, it has been left to singers such as Eileen Farrell, Barbara Lea, Jackie Cain and Roy Kral, and Marlene VerPlanck to proclaim their faith with new recordings. There have been other developments. Six years after Wilder's death, Schuller was pointing out that Wilder's chamber music, particularly his brass chamber music, "is played all over. There is no university or college or conservatory where the young people do not play his music, so I suppose that will be the sort of final legacy for Alec. And his popular songs. A few of them will live on forever." It may also be an omen that in 1993 some talented musicians who were never part of Wilder's family, the Manhattan Chamber Orchestra and a lineup of good soloists, recorded a new CD, *For the Friends of Alec Wilder.*

The path to Wilder's music, once overgrown, has been cleared and broadened significantly. In 1991, Margun Music, supported by Broadcast Music, Inc., the Richmond Organization (TRO), and the Harvey Phillips Foundation, published *Alec Wilder: An Introduction to the Man and His Music.* Almost three thousand copies have been distributed free by Margun. Included is a valuable list of works and discography compiled by Judy Bell of TRO. Bell also played a pivotal part in the preparation of the 1993 Greenwood Press Wilder bio-bibliography written by David Demsey and Ronald Prather. This extraordinarily comprehensive publication includes a short biography, a list of works and performances, a discography, a bibliography of writings by and about Wilder, and a summary of ancillary materials held by the Alec Wilder Archive at the Eastman School of Music and in the National Public Radio Library in Washington, D.C. The same Demsey also edits the *Newletter* of the Friends of Alec Wilder published annually at the William Paterson College of New Jersey and funded by the Wilder Estate in cooperation with the college. The Friends of Alec Wilder is an organization dedicated to perpetuating his memory and his work.

Perhaps the most notable tending of the flame has been done year after year at the annual birthday tribute in Manhattan, in Weill Recital Hall at Carnegie Hall and more recently at Saint Peter's Church. With the indefatigable, devoted Harvey Phillips doing virtually all the conceiving and orchestrating, many dozens of Wilder's artist friends have burnished his memory. For a decade (and still counting), this has remained a remarkable outpouring of love and affection, each celebration brought to a close with all present singing Manny Albam's lush arrangement of Wilder's standard *I'll Be Around.*

In one way or another, Wilder will always be around, but whether just for the faithful few or for a wider audience, only the decades will decide. Meanwhile, the composer in his many dimensions remains a vital presence in the Wilder Reading Room of the Sibley Music Library, where a memorial plaque says simply: "Composer, writer, sage, wit, standard-bearer, iconoclast, mentor, benefactor and friend—1907–80." To which might be added, "companion to the lonely." Even if

Wilder's music never attracts a crowd, the lost souls and the wounded birds will always be drawn to those bittersweet melodies that transcend time and place. Sheridan Morley, writing in *Playbill* for London theaters, once pictured Wilder as an "unhappy, lonely, generous man who wrote the kinds of songs that sound best when it's a quarter to three, and there's no one in the place but just you and me." Wilder would have liked that. He knew all about the quiet, secret moments when the rest of the world ebbed away. "I cannot forget," he once wrote, "sitting in the deserted lobby of the Algonquin with the only girl I ever liked enough to want to marry. While we engaged in the tender, bittersweet talk of young lovers, the only other sound to be heard was the chiming of the grandfather clock. The clock is still there, and still chimes late at night for those brave enough to sit there and dream. Or young enough." Or vulnerable enough.

Bibliography

American Popular Song: Six Decades of Songwriters and Singers. Smithsonian Collection of Recordings.

Balliett, Whitney. *Alec Wilder & His Friends.* Boston: Houghton Mifflin Co., 1968.

———. "Goodbye Oompah." *The New Yorker,* 15 December 1975, 46–62.

———. "Our Footloose Correspondents: American Song." *The New Yorker,* 28 June 1976, 19.

———. "The President of the Derriere-Garde." *The New Yorker,* 9 July 1973, 40–42.

———. "A Quality that Lets You In." *The New Yorker,* 7 January 1974, 34.

———. "A Queenly Aura." *The New Yorker,* 18 November 1972, 48–55 +.

Bergreen, Laurence. *As Thousands Cheer: the Life of Irving Berlin.* New York: Penguin Books, 1991.

Biographical Record of the City of Rochester, and Monroe County. Rochester: S. J. Clarke Publishing Co., 1902.

The Bird. Single-sheet anti-establishment paper written and distributed to Eastman School of Music Students and faculty in the early 1930s.

Bowen, Glenn H. The Clarinet in the Chamber Music of Alec Wilder. D.M.A. diss., Eastman School of Music, 1968.

Bradshaw, Jon. *Dreams That Money Can Buy: The Tragic Life of Libby Holman.* New York: William Morrow and Co., 1985.

Brzustowicz, John O. "A Tribute to Howard Hanson." *Democrat & Chronicle,* 16 July 1981.

Carpenter, Roger. Review of *The Lowland Sea. Opera* 14/75 (July 1963): 500–501.

Clune, Henry W. *The Rochester I Know.* New York: Doubleday and Co., 1972.

Demsey, David and Ronald Prather. *Alec Wilder: A Bio-Bibliography.* Westport, Conn.: Greenwood Press, 1993.

Engvick, William. Biographical introduction to *Songs by Alec Wilder Were Made to Sing* by Alec Wilder. New York: The Richmond Organization/Ludlow Music, 1976.

Freed, Richard. Liner notes to *Eileen Farrell Sings Alec Wilder.* Reference Recordings, RR36: San Francisco, 1990.

Hampson, Thomas M. "Alec Wider Revisited." Paper read at the Philosophers' Club, 26 January 1981, Rochester, N.Y.

Horowitz, Joseph. *Understanding Toscanini.* New York: Alfred Knopf, 1987.

Jackson, Arthur. *Alec Wilder: The Successful Failure.* Journal Into Melody, A Personal Memoir. Unpublished.

Kolodin, Irving. "For Barrows by Wilder." *Saturday Review of Literature,* 26 March 1960, 48.

Lee, Peggy. *Miss Peggy Lee.* New York: Donald I. Fine Inc., 1989.

Lees, Gene. "A Milestone for Alec Wilder." *High Fidelity Magazine,* August 1972, 20.

———. "Reading Alec Wilder's Mail." *High Fidelity Magazine,* May 1976, 19–20.

Lieberson, Goddard. Liner notes to *Frank Sinatra Conducts the Music of Alec Wilder.* Columbia Masterworks, Set M.637.

Maher, James T. Brassinity. Liner notes to *Wilder's Brass Quintet No. 7.* Tidewater Brass Quintet. Golden Crest, CRS 4179.

McGlohon, Loonis. "A Memory of Alec Wilder." *Collectors Record Club Newsletter.* Decatur, Georgia: 1981.

———. "The Music of Alec Wilder." *BMI: The Many Worlds of Music,* no. 1, 1983.

McPartland, Marian. "Alec Wilder: The Compleat Composer." *Down Beat,* 21 October 1976, 16–17.

Martinetti, Ronald. *The James Dean Story.* Revised and expanded. Secaucus, N. J.: Birch Lane Press, 1995.

Memorial Encyclopedia of the State of New York. Vol. 2. New York: The American Historical Society, 1916.

Mercer, Mabel. Foreword to *Songs by Alec Wilder Were Made to Sing* by Alec Wilder. New York: The Richmond Organization/Ludlow Music, 1976.

Prather, Ronald E. "Popular Songs of Alec Wilder." *Musical Quarterly* 74/4 (1990): 521–49.

Russ, Lavinia. *The April Age.* New York: Atheneum, 1975.

Schuller, Gunther. "Alec Wilder's Sonata for Bass Trombone and Piano (A response to Douglas Yeo and a defense of the new Margun Edition)." *International Trombone Association Journal* 13/3 (July 1985): 7–8.

Siegel, Joel E. "Remembering Alec Wilder." *Jazz Times,* March 1991.

Sinatra, Frank. Liner notes to *New Music of Alec Wilder Composed for Mundel Lowe and His Orchestra.* Riverside Records, RLP 12-219.

Sundgaard, Arnold. "Alec Wilder: Curt about Weill." *Kurt Weill Newsletter,* vol. 10, no. 2, Fall 1992.

Terkel, Studs. *Hard Times: An Oral History of the Great Depression.* New York: New York: Pantheon Books, 1970.

Tucker, Mark. "Behind the Beat with Mark Tucker: Songs by Alec Wilder (1907–1980)." *Newsletter of the Institute for Studies in American Music at Brooklyn College,* vol. 17, no. 1, November 1987.

Ulanov, Barry. "Smart Alec." *Metronome Magazine,* May 1947, 16.

Watson, Hildegarde. *The Edge of the Woods.* Privately published, 1979.

Watson, James Sibley, Jr. "The Films of J. S. Watson Jr. and Melville Webber: Some Retrospective Views." *The University of Rochester Library Bulletin* 28/2 (Winter 1975): 79–85.

Wilder, Alec. *American Popular Song: The Great Innovators 1900–1950*. Edited and with an introduction by James T. Maher. New York: Oxford University Press, 1972.

————. "Ellis Larkins: an Appreciation." *Down Beat,* 26 October 1972, 14.

————. "The Elegant Refuge: Memoir of a Life at the Algonquin Hotel." Unpublished manuscript, 1976.

————. *Letters I Never Mailed: Clues to a Life*. Boston: Little, Brown and Co., 1975.

————. "Life Story." Unpublished manuscript, c. 1970.

————. With William Engvick and Maurice Sendak. *Lullabies and Night Songs*. New York: Harper & Row, 1965.

————. "Nourishing the Arts." *Democrat & Chronicle,* 3 February 1974.

————. "Rock as Mass Hysteria." *New York Times,* 5 November 1972.

————. "The Search." Unpublished manuscript, 1970.

————. *Songs by Alec Wilder Were Made to Sing*. New York: The Richmond Organization/Ludlow Music, 1976.

Yeo, Douglas. "Bass Trombone Sonata: An Update." *International Trombone Association Journal* 19 (Fall 1990): 16–17.

Zinsser, William. *Writing to Learn*. New York: Harper & Row, 1988.

Index